THE

GOSPEL

AND

LETTERS

OF

JOHN

INTERPRETING
I·B·T
BIBLICAL TEXTS

THE
GOSPEL
AND
LETTERS
OF
JOHN

R. Alan Culpepper

ABINGDON PRESS
Nashville

THE GOSPEL AND LETTERS OF JOHN

Library of Congress Cataloging-in-Publication Data

Culpepper, R. Alan.
    The Gospel and letters of John / R. Alan Culpepper.
        p. cm.—(Interpreting Biblical texts)
    Includes bibliographical references and index.
    ISBN 0-687-00851-4 (pbk. : alk. paper)
    1. Bible. N.T. John–Criticism, interpretation, etc. 2. Bible.
N.T. Epistles of John—Criticism, interpretation, etc. I. Title.
II. Series.
BS2615.2.C855   1998
225.5'06–dc   98-18486
                                          CIP

02 03 04 05 06 07 — 10 9 8 7 6 5 4

MANUFACTURED IN THE UNITED STATES OF AMERICA

CONTENTS

CHAPTER 7
INTERPRETING THE FOURTH GOSPEL:
JOHN 5–12

CHAPTER 8
INTERPRETING THE FOURTH GOSPEL:
JOHN 13–21

CHAPTER 9
INTERPRETING THE LETTERS

PART THREE
RESPONDING TO THE JOHANNINE WRITINGS

CHAPTER 10
THE GOSPEL OF JOHN AS A DOCUMENT

FOREWORD

Biblical texts create worlds of meaning, and invite readers to enter them. When readers enter such textual worlds, which are often strange and complex, they are confronted with theological claims. With this in mind, the purpose of this series is to help serious readers in their experience of reading and interpreting, to provide guides for their journeys into textual worlds. The controlling perspective is expressed in the operative word of the title—*interpreting*. The primary focus of the series is not so much on the world *behind* the texts or out of which the texts have arisen (though these worlds are not irrelevant) as on the world *created by* the texts in their engagement with readers.

Each volume addresses two questions. First, what are the critical issues of interpretation that have emerged in the recent history of scholarship and to which serious readers of the texts need to be sensitive? Some of the concerns of scholars are interesting and significant but, frankly, peripheral to the interpretative task. Others are more central. How they are addressed influences decisions readers make in the process of interpretation. Thus the authors call attention to these basic issues and indicate their significance for interpretation.

Second, in struggling with particular passages or sections of material, how can readers be kept aware of the larger world created by the text as a whole? How can they both see the forest and examine individual trees? How can students encountering the story of David and Bathsheba in 2 Samuel 11 read it in light of its context in the larger story, the Deuteronomistic History that includes the books of Deuteronomy through 2 Kings? How can readers of Galatians fit what they learn into the theological coherence and polarities of the larger perspective drawn from all the letters of Paul? Thus each volume provides an overview of the literature as a whole.

The aim of the series is clearly pedagogical. The authors offer their own understanding of the issues and texts, but are more concerned about guiding the reader than engaging in debates with other scholars. The series is meant to serve as a resource, alongside other resources such as commentaries and specialized studies, to aid students in the exciting and often risky venture of interpreting biblical texts.

Gene M. Tucker
General Editor, *Old Testament*

Charles B. Cousar
General Editor, *New Testament*

PREFACE

This book is the by-product of having taught the Gospel of John for over twenty years. My former students from Southern Baptist Theological Seminary, Vanderbilt, Baylor, and the McAfee School of Theology will recognize phrases and emphases throughout the book—some of which we hammered out together. As such, this book also collects and remints material published in various projects along the way. Material from the following sources has been reproduced, abridged, or summarized with permission in this volume.

1 John, 2 John, 3 John, Knox Preaching Guides (Atlanta: John Knox, 1985).

"The Theology of the Gospel of John," *Review and Expositor* 85 (1988): 417-32.

"John." In *The Books of the Bible,* vol. 2, *The Apocrypha and the New Testament,* ed. Bernhard W. Anderson (New York: Charles Scribner's Sons, 1989), 203-28.

"The Johannine *Hypodeigma*: A Reading of John 13," *Semeia* 53 (1991): 133-52.

"A Literary Model." In *Hermeneutics for Preaching,* ed. Raymond Bailey (Nashville: Broadman Press, 1992), 77-104. Used by permission.

"The Plot of John's Story of Jesus," *Interpretation* 49, no. 4 (1995): 347-58.

"The Gospel of John as a Document of Faith in a Pluralistic Culture." In *"What Is John?" Readers and Readings of the Fourth Gospel,* ed. Fernando F. Segovia, Symposium Series (Atlanta: Scholars Press, 1996), 107-27.

"The Theology of the Johannine Passion Narrative (John 19:16*b*-30)," *Neotestamentica,* 31 (1997): 25-41.

PREFACE

I am grateful for the opportunity to test early drafts of sections of this book with the Johannine Seminar of the Society of New Testament Studies. Charles Cousar and Rex Matthews have defined this series and invited its authors to put into print what they teach, so that others can use it in the classroom also. I am grateful for their encouragement and guidance. I tell my classes that I hope the course on the Gospel of John will launch them on a lifelong love affair with this Gospel and that it will be for them a constant source of intellectual fascination and spiritual direction. I hope this book does the same.

CHAPTER 1

INTRODUCTION TO THE
JOHANNINE
LITERATURE

The Johannine literature is distinctive in several respects. John is the only Gospel in the New Testament that has letters related to it. The relationship is much closer than the Gospel of Luke and the Letters of Paul, or the Gospel of Mark and the Letters of Peter.

John differs from the other three canonical Gospels so dramatically that they are called Synoptic Gospels ("seeing alike"), whereas John is unique. John has its own language and idiom, its own chronology of the ministry of Jesus, its own view of Jesus' identity and works, and its own theology.

John is arguably the most influential book of the New Testament. It alone depicts Jesus as the Word (Greek, *Logos*), a fact which has made John the seedbed for much of the church's theology. One has only to think of the doctrine of the Trinity to see the importance of John for Christian thought. The relationship of Jesus to God as Son to Father breaks through only occasionally in the Synoptics, but it emerges full-blown in the Fourth Gospel. The double nature of Jesus as human and divine also confronts us more dramatically in

John than elsewhere, and John has more to say about the Holy Spirit than any other writing in the New Testament.

The engaging factor is that John is at once the simplest of the Gospels and the most difficult. It is the Gospel most frequently translated into other languages and the Gospel written in the easiest Greek. But it can also be difficult to understand. The Gospel always calls us to walk further with it and ponder it longer. In this respect, it is both a home and a horizon, a place of security and a place of challenge. (Because of this, you might wish to preface your study of John and your reading of this book by turning first to chapter 10 to gain an overview of some of the ethical, theological, and historical challenges these writings pose to communities of faith today.) I hope that you will find the study of this Gospel so engaging that it will never let you go. If this happens, you will gain a lifelong source of intellectual and spiritual stimulation that will never let you stop probing its mysteries.

WHAT IS JOHN?

Is John best understood as history, theology, or literature? John is a narrative that presents Jesus as the Christ, the Son of God who lived at a particular time in history. As a historical narrative it raises problems of the relation of history to faith, God to humanity, and time to the eternal. How could a writer convey the significance of the advent of the eternal Son of God in human history? Neither an unvarnished historical account nor a theological treatise would be adequate. The event was both history and revelation, so the events and content of that revelation interpret one another, and this in a narrative context.

As we wrestle to understand John and discern the extent to which it is history, we will learn that the evangelist is writing for a particular believing community facing a specific set of historical conditions. So, revelation both emerges out of history and is interpreted back into history. From your study I hope that you will also see ways in which the revelation imparted in the life of Jesus and interpreted for the Johannine community can reach into our own historical circumstances.

John as Literature

Suppose that you wanted to write a story about a divine being who had come to earth in human form—perhaps a script for a television series. What form might the story take? What plot lines would be open to you? There are two basic options that grow out of the premise of the story.[1] The first would be, How does anyone know that this human figure is a divine being if he looks, talks, and acts like a human being? How does his identity become known? That is the plot of the Gospel of Mark. According to Mark, no one knew at first who Jesus was, and even those closest to him only discover who he really is at or after his death and resurrection. The voice from heaven at Jesus' baptism is addressed to him alone. We readers know that Jesus is God's Son, but no one around Jesus knows until his death, and it is his death and resurrection, not his power or teachings, that make his identity known.

In John, by contrast, Jesus tells everyone who he is. From the very first chapter both he and others use the church's lofty titles to describe his identity. There is no question about how people discover who Jesus is—he tells them, and tells them repeatedly. Now the question becomes, How do people respond to his claim to be the Son of God? Why do some believe him and others do not? What different responses can we see in the Gospel, and what are the different levels or stages of faith?

While the Gospel tells the story of Jesus, it also draws us as readers into it and seeks to move us along the continuum of responses to a higher level of response to Jesus as the Revealer.

John as History

John is paradoxically both the most and the least historical of the four Gospels. Good arguments can be raised in favor of the accuracy of John's geographical references, its chronology of the ministry and death of Jesus, the nature of the debates or trials that led to Jesus' execution, and the relationship of Jesus to John the Baptist—to take only a few illustrative points. On the other hand, the style of Jesus' speech in John is thoroughly Johannine, resembling more nearly the way the author of the Johannine Epistles writes than the style and idiom of Jesus' teaching in the Synoptic Gospels. In John, Jesus usually speaks in long discourses rather than in the short sayings and parables characteristic of the Synoptics. In addition, Jesus speaks more explicitly of his identity and messianic role in John than in the Synoptics; this suggests that John reflects later Christian response to Jesus more explicitly while the Synoptics preserve the actual sayings of Jesus more accurately. Even where

15

the Synoptics may be more accurate historically, however, John perceptively highlights elements of truth about Jesus.

John as Theology

The Gospel and Letters of John were written in the midst of fierce theological debate. One's place within the community was defined by one's confession of Jesus as the Messiah. At first, believing Jews distinguished themselves from others in the synagogue by their confession that Jesus was the Messiah. Then, when the community of believers separated from the synagogue, their confession defined them over against the pagan, Greco-Roman world. When divisions developed within the community over the incarnation of Jesus and the meaning of his death, the elder who wrote the Johannine Epistles defined the community over against those who had gone out from it (1 John 2:19) by articulating once again the community's confession of Jesus Christ who has "come in the flesh" (1 John 4:2).

Whereas Mark begins with the baptism of Jesus, and Matthew and Luke with the birth of Jesus, John begins at "the beginning," before the creation. The first words of the Gospel tie the story of Jesus to the larger story of the God of Israel. The life of Jesus is interpreted in light of the Jewish Wisdom tradition. Originally wisdom was merely the knowledge or lore that enabled one to be a successful farmer, sailor, craftsman, or merchant. Kings had a particular wisdom: "By me kings reign, and rulers decree what is just" (Prov 8:15). Solomon in particular was noted for his wisdom. Israel's sages linked wisdom with the worship of God: "The fear of the LORD is the beginning of knowledge" (Prov 1:7). Gradually, wisdom was personified, wisdom was related to the commandments revealed at Mt.

The Role of Wisdom in Creation

The LORD created me at the beginning of his work,
   the first of his acts of long ago.
Ages ago I was set up, at the first,
   before the beginning of the earth.
When there were no depths I was brought forth,
   when there were no springs abounding with water....
When he marked out the foundations of the earth,
   then I was beside him, like a master worker. (PROVERBS 8:22-30)

16

Sinai, and wisdom was understood to be God's agent in the creation. The preexistent Wisdom, the divine Logos that was the agent of creation, John asserts, came in human form in the person of Jesus. The Logos came as the unique Son to reveal God as his Father, so that those who believed in him could know the only true God (John 1:18; 17:3).

As the Logos incarnate, Jesus exercises creative power over the natural elements. He is able to change water to wine, feed a multitude on five barley loaves, give sight to a man born blind, and raise the dead. He also knows what is in the hearts of others, and his nourishment comes from doing the will of the Father. Like a son working at his father's side, he does only what the Father gives him to do. He and the Father are one. Therefore, he has no need to ask the Father for anything (see Jesus' prayer at the raising of Lazarus in John 11), and the Johannine Jesus would never pray "not what I want, but what you want" (Mark 14:36). Even when he goes to his death, he knows who will betray him, and no one takes his life from him, but he lays down his life, and he has the power to take it up again (John 10:18). It is small wonder, then, that Ernst Käsemann said that the Johannine Jesus appears as "the God who walks on the face of the earth."[2] Nevertheless, this revealer sent from above is at the same time thoroughly human. He gets tired traveling; he weeps at the death of a friend; and he thirsts as he dies. The central focus of the Gospel of John is clearly on the figure of Jesus, and it leads the reader into a profound exploration of who Jesus was and the significance of his life.

Jesus is set in the context of the history of Israel and the Hebrew scriptures. Throughout the Gospel there are allusions to scripture, titles drawn from the scriptures, and scenes that confirm that Jesus is the fulfillment of the great festivals of the Jews. The Gospel also uses symbols of universal appeal—light and darkness, bread and water—to interpret Jesus. Yet, there is no account of the Lord's Supper in John. Some interpreters have therefore contended that John is antisacramental while others find in it a highly developed view of the sacraments. Similarly, the Gospel's attention is so focused on the fulfillment of Israel's hopes in the coming of Jesus that it says little about a "second coming" or resurrection and judgment in the future. Nevertheless, both present and future fulfillment are present side by side in the Gospel. In an endlessly fascinating way, therefore, the

Gospel of John poses challenges to its readers, who never doubt that this Gospel is the work of an early Christian theologian and writer without peer.

WHAT MAKES JOHN UNIQUE?
JOHN AND THE SYNOPTICS: A CLOSER LOOK

John's uniqueness is clearly evident when it is compared with the Synoptic Gospels. A skewed picture emerges, however, unless one considers both the similarities and the differences among the Gospels. We will first survey the similarities and differences between the two and then review briefly the shifts in scholarly opinion regarding the relationship between John and the Synoptics.

Similarities Between John and the Synoptics

For all their differences, the common ground between John and the Synoptics should not be overlooked. All interpreters, from the second century onward, have agreed that both John and the Synoptics are Gospels. That may seem to be an incredibly banal statement, but it is not insignificant—especially since the Gospel genre seems not to have any clear precedent or prototype. Both John and the Synoptics are written accounts of the ministry and teaching of Jesus from his baptism through his death and resurrection. The various canonical Gospels all combine accounts of Jesus' works and his words; all assess the significance of John the Baptist; all feature Jesus' relationship to his disciples and the religious authorities; and all contain accounts of the feeding of the multitude in Galilee, Jesus' demonstration in the Temple, the entry into Jerusalem, Jesus' last meal with his disciples, and the events leading up to his death on the cross and the discovery of the empty tomb. With such extensive similarities, one might wonder why the differences between John and the synoptics could be judged to be significant. Moreover, if all four are Gospels and there were no Gospels before these, then one can easily argue that if Mark was the first written Gospel, John as well as Matthew and Luke must have known Mark in order to be able to write a narrative so similar in form.

Differences Between John and the Synoptics

Although the similarities between John and the Synoptics must be accounted for in any interpretation of the origin of John or the Gospel genre, the differences between them are equally significant. Here we will treat the differences under five rubrics: journeys, chronology, signs, teachings, and Christology.

1. JOURNEYS

One of the more apparent differences among the Gospels is their account of Jesus' journeys. Only Matthew and Luke contain accounts of Jesus' birth in Bethlehem, and only Matthew records the holy family's flight to Egypt. According to the Synoptics, after Jesus was baptized he was tempted in the wilderness for forty days and then spent the duration of his ministry in Galilee, around the Sea of Galilee, with only an occasional excursion to the north or into the area of Caesarea Philippi. At the end of his ministry, he made one trip to Jerusalem, entering the city only the week before his death. Matthew and Mark then allude to or record resurrection appearances in Galilee while Luke records only appearances in and around Jerusalem.

According to John, however, Jesus moved back and forth between Jerusalem and Galilee repeatedly. John contains no account of temptations in the wilderness. In John 1, Jesus is with John at the Jordan and then goes to Galilee. After the wedding at Cana, Jesus returns to Jerusalem, "cleanses" the temple, and talks with Nicodemus before withdrawing to the Judean countryside (3:22). In chapter 4, Jesus journeys through Samaria on his way back to Galilee. In John 5, Jesus is again in Jerusalem, and in John 6 in Galilee. From John 7 on, Jesus is in Jerusalem and Judea or across the Jordan. He does not return to Galilee until the post-resurrection appearance in John 21.

This survey reveals that whereas in the synoptics all of Jesus' ministry up to the last week of his life occurs in or around Galilee, the only events of a Galilean ministry that are recorded in John are the wedding at Cana (2:1-11), the healing of the nobleman's son (4:46-54), and the feeding of the multitude and crossing of the sea in John 6. Whereas the synoptics feature Jesus' ministry in Galilee, John focuses almost entirely on his work in Jerusalem.

In the synoptics Jesus makes only one trip Jerusalem, but in

John he makes three trips, going up (one always "went up") to Jerusalem for the major festivals (Passover, 2:13; an unnamed festival, 5:1; and Tabernacles, 7:10). Correspondingly, Jesus returns from Jerusalem to Galilee in chapter 4 (going by way of Samaria) and at the beginning of John 6. After withdrawing from Jerusalem across the Jordan (10:40), Jesus returned to raise Lazarus and then withdrew once more (11:54) before returning for the Passover (12:1). The Jewish festivals in Jerusalem, therefore, are important both structurally and thematically in John.

2. CHRONOLOGY

John also differs from the Synoptics at significant points regarding the chronology of Jesus' ministry. On the basis of Matthew and Luke, the birth of Jesus is usually placed about 6 B.C., before the death of Herod the Great. John says nothing about the time of Jesus' birth, but it does provide references that help us calculate the time of his ministry. The references to the building of the Temple in John 2:20 can be correlated with Josephus's history to yield a date of A.D. 26 or 27 for John's account of the baptism and the cleansing of the Temple (20/19 B.C.—the beginning of work on the Temple according to Josephus—plus the 46 years from John 2:20 yields A.D. 26/27). The synoptics say nothing about the duration of Jesus' ministry. The events in their accounts could fit into as little as one year. According to John, however, Jesus' ministry spanned three Passovers (John 2, 6, and 12ff.). The traditional view of a three-year ministry, therefore, depends entirely on John's chronology.

John and the Synoptics also differ in regard to the date of Jesus' crucifixion. All four Gospels agree that Jesus was crucified on Friday, buried before the beginning of the Sabbath at sundown, and that the tomb was discovered empty on Sunday morning. All four accounts also agree that these events took place at the time of the Passover celebration. The point of difference concerns whether the last supper coincided with the Passover meal (as in the synoptics) or whether Jesus' death coincided with the slaughter of the Passover lambs (as in John).

The Passover meal was eaten on the evening which began Nisan 15. Like our celebration of Christmas, however, that day could fall on any day of the week. According to the Synoptics Jesus ate the Passover meal with his disciples (Mark 14:12, 16-17) and then died the next day (on Passover!). In contrast, according to John the Jews had not yet eaten the Passover meal when they brought Jesus before Pilate, and they refused to enter the Praetorium so that they might not be defiled and unable to eat the Passover meal that evening (John 18:28). Jesus died later that morning, on the day of preparation for the Passover (19:14, 31), at the time specified for the slaughter of the Passover lambs (compare also Exodus 12:1-8; John 1:29, 36).

All four Gospels, therefore, record the tradition that the crucifixion of Jesus took place at Passover, but they find different points of significance in the chronology. For the synoptics the last supper is the fulfillment of the Passover celebration, which focused on the Passover meal. For John, however, the Passover lamb prefigured the death of Jesus, and the time of Jesus' death pointed to its atoning significance.

3. SIGNS

The Synoptic Gospels record many miracles performed by Jesus: healing the sick, exorcising demons, stilling storms, feeding multitudes, and catching fish. The miracles emphasize his power, with which he attacked the power of evil by healing and restoring persons to wholeness. At times the miracles are also interpreted as lessons for Jesus' followers. In Acts, the apostles continue to perform the same kind of healing miracles Jesus had done, and Luke records these as proof of their apostolic authority as Jesus' successors.

In John, however, only a few miracles are recorded, and John distinctively refers to these as signs. Their significance is primarily to point to Jesus' identity, though in John they also serve to show the fulfillment of expectations associated with Moses and the prophets (Elijah and Elisha). Jesus was the Messiah who did signs like these figures from Israel's past, but since John the Baptist was not the Messiah he did no such signs (1:19-23; 10:41).

4. TEACHINGS

The Gospel records of the ministry of Jesus are composed of two types of material, Jesus' words and his works. One of the axioms of the form critics who traced the transmission of the Gospel material was that the words of Jesus were generally preserved in the tradition with less change than the stories that surround them. If anything, however, the words of Jesus in John are more different from the Synoptics than John's accounts of Jesus' signs. The differences are evident in both style and content.

Style. In the Synoptic Gospels Jesus speaks in short, pithy sayings. His words are terse. He tells parables that are drawn from everyday life. The parables are so familiar that most people immediately recognize the parables of the good Samaritan, the prodigal son, the lost sheep, and the sower who went out to sow.

In contrast, none of these parables appears in John. Indeed, although metaphorical language abounds, one is hard put to find a true parable in the Gospel of John. The closest examples might be the father and the son (John 5:19-20), the son and the servant (8:34-35), the sheep and the shepherd (10:1-5), and the true vine (15:1-8), but these are not stories. They are more nearly metaphors or images.

Moreover, instead of short pithy sayings, Jesus generally speaks in extended discourses in John. A quick glance at chapters 6, 8, 10, and 14–17 will give you some indication of the amount of monologue or discourse material in John. If the Synoptics give the impression of being collections of sayings, John gives the impression of being a treatise on theological themes. This difference has significant implications for the question of the historicity of John's account of Jesus' sayings. It is difficult to identify authentic sayings in John. That does not mean that there are none. Words of Jesus no doubt lie behind John's discourses and at times are buried or echoed in them, but they are more difficult to identify than the aphorisms and parables of the Synoptics. Indeed, as D. Moody Smith points out, the Johannine Jesus talks more like the elder of 1 John than the Jesus of the Synoptics.[4] The vocabulary and style of the discourses correspond more nearly to those of the elder than to the sayings of Jesus in the Synoptics.

Content. In the Synoptics the sayings of Jesus deal primarily with the Kingdom of God, the Son of Man, and the demands of discipleship. The Kingdom of God is the most prevalent theme of Jesus' sayings; the term "kingdom" (Greek, *basileia*) occurs 120 times in the Synoptics. Jesus announces that the expected kingdom is at hand (Mark 1:14-15). Both parables and aphorisms in the Synoptics deal with this theme, emphasizing alternatively that the Kingdom is imminent or that it is already present in the person of Jesus. In contrast, again, the Kingdom of God appears only in John 3:3 and 3:5, and the sayings of the Johannine Jesus concern his own identity and revelation of what he received from the Father rather than the coming of the Kingdom.

5. CHRISTOLOGY

Each Gospel interprets Jesus in a different light. The Gospels have often been compared to portraits painted by great artists. Each captures a different aspect of the subject. Gradually, interpreters have come to realize that the situation is not that John recorded one part of Jesus' ministry and the Synoptics another part, or that the Synoptics describe the public teaching of Jesus and John his private teaching to the disciples, or that the synoptics are historical and John is theological, but that all four gospel writers offer a portrait of Jesus that is both historically based and theologically developed. It is only because John is so distinctive that the other gospels were ever called "Synoptic Gospels." If we did not have John, the other three would not appear to be so similar.

Mark emphasizes the secrecy of Jesus' messiahship. Readers are told that Jesus is the Christ, the Son of God (Mark 1:1), but no one in the Gospel knows. John the Baptist does not bear witness to Jesus, and it is not clear that anyone but Jesus is aware of the events that accompanied his baptism. The unclean spirits know who Jesus is and seek to make him known, but Jesus silences them and tells those whom he heals to tell no one. Paradoxically, Jesus exercises great authority in his miracle working and in his confrontations with the religious authorities, but the Son of Man who has authority to forgive sins and who in the future will come with God's angels is also the one who came to give his life as a ransom for many (Mark 10:45). Mark gives great emphasis to the suffering death of Jesus. Peter confesses that Jesus is the Christ (Mark 8:27-30), but he does not understand that Jesus has to suffer and die in Jerusalem. Only when Jesus is hanging dead on the cross does anyone understand who he was, and then it is the Gentile centurion who confesses, "Truly, this man was God's Son" (Mark 15:39). In Mark it is not the miracles that Jesus does or his wise teachings that reveal his divinity. He was not primarily a wonder worker or a wisdom teacher, as some early Christians may have thought. Only his death on the cross reveals Jesus as the

Son of God. For Mark, therefore, to be a disciple of Jesus is to deny oneself, take up the cross, and follow him (Mark 8:34).

Matthew introduces Jesus by relating him to the lineage of Abraham and David. Following the genealogy, Matthew tells how Jesus was born in Bethlehem while the king sought to kill him. Matthew describes Jesus' birth with striking echoes of the story of Moses' early life, and reports that Jesus' father, like the patriarch Joseph, was instructed by God through dreams. Jesus was taken to Egypt and then brought back to Nazareth. Throughout the first two chapters, the evangelist reminds the reader that these things happened to fulfill what was written by the prophets, a claim supported by quotes from the Old Testament. Early in his ministry, Jesus goes up on a mountain in Galilee and gives his followers a new standard of righteousness while insisting that he had come to fulfill the Law and the Prophets and that not one jot or tittle should be lost from them. The teaching of Jesus continues throughout the Gospel, as does his demonstration of God's power in miracles like those performed by Moses and the prophets. By the end of the Gospel, Jesus' words have taken the place of scripture. He says that all power has been given to him and that his followers should go and make other disciples in all the nations, teaching them to observe all that Jesus had commanded. The Emmanuel theme is complete. God has come among the people of Israel, fulfilling the Law and the Prophets and providing a new standard of righteousness. Jesus' followers will therefore teach others to observe the commandments of the New Moses. For Matthew, being a disciple of Jesus means keeping his teachings.

Luke offers what is for many the most attractive portrait of Jesus. The Lukan Jesus has compassion on the poor, women, Samaritans, tax collectors, and outcasts of all sorts. He prays before each major event in his ministry and dies while praying, "Father, forgive them." His teachings frequently deal with the dangers of wealth, the need for social justice, and defense of the poor. The Lukan Jesus also models his teachings for others. His most characteristic action is eating with outcasts and sinners. He defends the woman who weeps on his feet. He allows Mary to listen to his teachings. He praises the Samaritan leper who turns back to give thanks. The Gospel of Luke is appropriate, therefore, as the first of a two-part work in which the gospel of Jesus is carried beyond Judaism to Samaritans and eventually to Gentiles.

The Lukan Jesus is a social reformer, and following him means doing as he did and challenging the social barriers that divide and alienate.

By contrast, the Johannine Jesus, as we have already seen, is the Son of God, the Revealer sent from above to reveal the Father. He is neither a part of this world nor welcome here, though he was with God at the creation. The world neither understands him nor receives him. Jesus spends his ministry attempting by means of both the signs that he does and the enigmatic words that he speaks to call others to see that he is the Revealer. John examines how various individuals and groups respond, and why some believe and some do not. Only those who are called and drawn by the Father can believe (John 6:44), only those who are born from above (3:3, 5). To those who believe in Jesus, he grants the status of being "children of God" (John 1:12). They have eternal life, drink living water, and eat the bread of life. For John, therefore, Jesus as the Son of God is the heavenly Revealer, and being a disciple means kinship, taking one's place among the children of God.

Each of the four Gospels presents a different portrait of Jesus, and consequently each has a different interpretation of what it means to be a follower of Jesus. Part of the challenge of studying the Gospel of John comes from learning to read it apart from the influence of the other Gospels and the amalgam of stories that typically condition the way we are accustomed to thinking about Jesus. John has its own understanding of Jesus, so to be a careful reader of the Gospel you will have to work to read it without interference from the other Gospels.

Interpreting the Relationship Between John and the Synoptics

The common view in antiquity was that John knew the Synoptics but wrote to supplement or complete them. Clement of Alexandria wrote that John was a "spiritual gospel." This view prevailed up to the beginning of this century. Hans Windisch challenged the prevailing consensus by arguing that John knew the Synoptics but wrote his Gospel to correct or replace the others. In 1938 Percival Gardner-Smith wrote a brief volume that changed many minds about the relationship of John to the Synoptics.[5] He argued that it is easier to explain the similarities between John and the Synoptics on the basis of common oral tradition than it is

25

to explain the differences between them on the assumption that John knew the Synoptics. His work convinced C. H. Dodd, and from 1938 to 1980 this view gradually became the dominant view. Since 1980 the issue has been reopened with sophisticated arguments regarding John's knowledge or use of Mark, the special relationship between John and Luke, and the origins of the passion tradition. One basic premise in the argument has been that if it can be shown that John knew or used not just Synoptic-like tradition but redactional material (that is, the work of one of the evangelists) from one of the Gospels, then John must have known that Gospel.

Opinion is now divided on these issues, so it is incumbent on scholars to defend whatever position they take. The view taken in this volume is that the arguments for the general independence of the Johannine tradition still stand. The differences are so great that John can hardly have drawn on the Synoptics as a major source for his material. John clearly relies on an independent source of tradition for his Gospel, one that he attributes to the Beloved Disciple. The similarities, such as they are, are more easily explained on the assumption that John used early Christian tradition that had developed its own peculiar turns of thought and expression in relative isolation from the Synoptic traditions. The composition of the Gospel, however, is an intriguing story in itself, and one to which we shall turn in the next chapter.

PART ONE

INTRODUCING THE JOHANNINE WRITINGS

CHAPTER 2

THE COMPOSITION OF THE JOHANNINE WRITINGS

AUTHORSHIP

The enigmatic beauty of the Fourth Gospel and its profound impact on the development of Christian theology have heightened interest in the question of authorship. By the time the Gospel was widely accepted, late in the second century, its attribution to the apostle John was also accepted. However, for reasons we shall examine, that tradition is viewed with considerable skepticism today. The evidence for and against apostolic authorship can easily be divided into two categories: internal evidence (drawn from the Gospel itself) and external evidence (the testimony of the early church fathers).

Internal Evidence

The Gospel itself is anonymous. It does not say who wrote it, and the superscription "According to John" was added sometime in the second century. The closest the Gospel comes to identifying its author is in John 21:24-25, verses which attribute the

Gospel to the Beloved Disciple. These verses also testify to an extended process of composition and shaping of the Gospel within an early Christian community, which for the sake of convenience we will call the "Johannine community." Read these verses closely and pick out the references that designate different individuals and groups: "This is the disciple who is testifying to these things ... we know ... I suppose..." Who is *the disciple*? Who is the *we*? And who is the *I* who wrote these verses?

The *I* is evidently an editor or redactor who worked on the Gospel after *this disciple,* whom we may identify as the evangelist. The question then is how much of the final form of the Gospel is to be assigned to each. At a minimum the redactor wrote the last two verses, but it may be that he wrote all of chapter 21 (note how the Gospel seems to reach a natural conclusion at the end of chapter 20 (vv. 30-31). The similarity between 21:24-25 and 19:35 suggests that the redactor may have added this verse, and perhaps the other references to the Beloved Disciple as well. After all, it is difficult to imagine anyone calling himself "the disciple whom Jesus loved." How much of the finished form of the Gospel, then, is due to the work of the redactor?

Various theories have been proffered regarding the identity of the *we* in John 21:24. Before settling on any one view, note the occurrences of the first person plural pronoun in John 1:14; 3:11 and 1 John 1:1-4. Do these all refer to the same group or do they represent different uses of the pronoun? Among the views that have been suggested are that *we* refers to the twelve apostles or a council of apostles or bishops, a group of eyewitnesses, or the Johannine school or community. Given the relative lack of attention to the Twelve in John and the absence of hierarchical authority in the Johannine Epistles, the latter view—that *we* refers to the community—is the most likely interpretation.

The most interesting and difficult question is still unanswered. Who is *this disciple* who wrote *these things*? The preceding verses link the disciple with the Beloved Disciple who was introduced at the last supper as the disciple closest to Jesus (13:23). The Beloved Disciple then appears at the cross (19:26-27, 35), at the empty tomb (20:3-10), and at the appearance in Galilee (21:7, 20-23). He is probably also the "other disciple" who was known to the high priest's family (18:15).[1]

Who then was this disciple? The closest the Gospel comes to

identifying him is the list of seven disciples in John 21:2. The two sons of Zebedee are included among the seven, but so are two unnamed disciples. There is no way, therefore, to determine which of these was the Beloved Disciple. He goes fishing with Peter, as would be natural if he were one of the fishermen from Galilee, but he is not introduced in John until the Last Supper, in Jerusalem. And, if he is the other disciple of John 18:15, it is difficult to understand how a Galilean fisherman would have been known to the family of the high priest, the ancient explanation that he delivered fish there notwithstanding. On the other hand, the Beloved Disciple and Peter are often paired together in the concluding chapters of John, just as Peter and John are in the opening chapters of Acts.

Arguments Against Identifying the Beloved Disciple with John

1. In Mark, John was among the group of three disciples who were present at the transfiguration, the raising of Jairus' daughter, and at the Garden of Gethsemane. In John, however, the inner three are not singled out as a group, and there is no record of these three momentous experiences. Jesus goes to a garden across the Kidron, but it is not named Gethsemane, Jesus does not take the three apart from the others, and there is no agony there.
2. James, his brother, is never mentioned (except in 21:2, and there not by name).
3. The Beloved Disciple hardly seems to have the character of a "son of thunder" (Mark 3:17).
4. John is a Galilean, but most of the Gospel of John deals with Jesus' ministry in Judea.
5. The Beloved Disciple is at the cross in John, but the synoptics say that the disciples all fled (Mark 14:50), and there is no record of any of them being at the cross.
6. It is unlikely that a Galilean fisherman would have been known to the household of the high priest in Jerusalem.
7. There are no exorcisms in John, but the only scene in which the apostle John appears alone in the synoptics involves the unauthorized exorcist (Mark 9:38). Moreover, in Luke 9:54 John and his brother want to call down fire on a Samaritan village, but the Gospel of John takes a positive attitude toward the Samaritans.

Not all of these arguments are of equal weight, but taken together they pose formidable internal difficulties for the view that the Beloved Disciple was John the son of Zebedee. On the other hand, an interesting case can be made on internal grounds for identifying the Beloved Disciple as Lazarus (see John 11).

Arguments in favor of Identifying the Beloved Disciple as Lazarus

1. Jesus is said to have loved Lazarus.
2. Lazarus does not appear until John 11, just before the Beloved Disciple is introduced in John 13.
3. The raising of Lazarus is the greatest of the signs.
4. Lazarus was a Judean, from Bethany.
5. Lazarus might have known the high priest.
6. The references to the grave clothes in John 20:6-7 take on an interesting significance if the disciple who witnessed them had himself been bound in such wrappings (11:44).
7. The belief that he would not die (21:23) might easily have arisen if the Beloved Disciple had already been raised from the dead.

Again, not all of the arguments are forceful, and even taken together they fail to overcome the fact that the Gospel stops short of identifying the Beloved Disciple with Lazarus. Many other theories have been advanced,[2] but on the whole it is best to conclude that the identity of the Beloved Disciple remains unknown. What is known is that he was an eyewitness, at least of the end of Jesus' ministry in Jerusalem, and that the Gospel attributes to him a place equal to that of Peter.

External Evidence

One of the surprises about John is that there is virtually no reference to the apostle or the Gospel during the first half of the second century. What evidence there is comes to us secondhand. Papias (A.D. 120–140) wrote five volumes on the "Exposition of the Lord's Oracles," but these survive only in quotations in later writers. Eusebius, who wrote an *Ecclesiastical History* in the fourth century, quotes the following passage.

This puzzling statement does not attribute the Gospel to the apostle John. It does not say that the apostle John lived in Ephesus. It does not say that Papias had ever seen the apostle John. It does mention both John the apostle and John the Elder, but it says that Papias heard not from the apostles or elders, but from those who had followed them.

The first attribution of the Gospel to the apostle John seems to

---

A Fragment from Papias, Quoted by Eusebius

But I shall not hesitate also to put down for you along with my interpretations whatsoever things I have at any time learned carefully from
the elders and carefully remembered, guaranteeing their truth. For I
did not, like the multitude, take pleasure in those that speak much,
but in those that teach the truth; not in those that relate strange commandments, but in those that deliver commandments given by the
Lord to faith, and springing from the truth itself. If, then, anyone came
who had been a follower of the elders, I inquired into the sayings of
the elders—what Andrew, or what Peter said, or what Philip, or
Thomas, or James, or John, or Matthew, or any other of the disciples
of the Lord said—and the things which Aristion and the Elder John,
the disciples of the Lord, were saying. For I did not think that what
was to be had from the books would profit me as much as what came
from the living and abiding voice. (Eusebius, *Eccl. Hist.* 3.39.3)

---

have come from the Gnostics, among whom the Gospel was popular in the middle of the second century. Heracleon, a Valentinian
Gnostic, wrote the first commentary on John, and it is quoted by
Ptolemy, another Valentinian Gnostic. John's popularity among
the Gnostics (along with its differences from the Synoptics) may
explain, in part at least, why it was slow in being accepted by the
church. From the last third of the second century, we begin to find
quotations from John in the church fathers. The leading advocate
of the Four-Gospel tradition was Irenaeus, bishop of Lugdunum
in Gaul. He accepted John and argued that it was apostolic.

Irenaeus, on the Apostolic Authorship of the Gospel

Afterwards, John the disciple of the Lord, who also had leaned on
his breast, did himself publish a gospel during his residence at Ephesus in Asia. (*Adversus Haereses* 3.1.1)

And all the elders associated with John the disciple of the Lord in
Asia bear witness that John delivered it [the Gospel] to them. For he
remained among them until the time of Trajan. (*Adv. Haer.* 2.22.5)

But the church in Ephesus also, which was founded by Paul, and
where John remained until the time of Trajan, is a faithful witness
of the apostolic tradition. (*Adv. Haer.* 3.3.4)

In another lengthy passage Irenaeus cites his source, saying that in his youth he had seen Polycarp, who used to tell them about John.

Irenaeus's Link with Polycarp

For what boys learn, growing with their mind, becomes joined with it; so that I am able to describe the very place in which the blessed Polycarp sat as he discoursed, and his goings out and his comings in, and the manner of his life, and his physical appearance, and his discourses to the people, and the accounts which he gave of his intercourse with John and with the others who had seen the Lord. And as he remembered their words, and what he heard from them concerning the Lord, and concerning his miracles and he teachings, having received them from eyewitnesses of the 'Word of Life,' Polycarp related all things in harmony with the Scriptures. These things being told me by the mercy of God, I listened attentively, noting them down, not on paper, but in my heart. And continually, through God's grace, I recall them faithfully. (Letter to Florinus, quoted by Eusebius in *Eccl. Hist.* 5.20.4-8)

The chain of testimony seems to be convincing, but questions remain concerning Irenaeus's credibility. Ignatius says nothing about John when he writes to the Ephesians (ca. 110). In a short letter to the Philippians, Polycarp himself says nothing about John. Papias mentions John but does not attribute the Gospel to him or say that he lived in Ephesus. And Justin Martyr (who lived in Ephesus and then Rome) says John wrote Revelation, but Justin did not use the Gospel of John or attribute it to John. So, those closest to John and to Ephesus during the early part of the second century are silent regarding John.

Irenaeus is the first writer to connect John with Ephesus. Irenaeus also said that Papias had heard John (*Adv. Haer.* 5.33.4, cited by Eusebius *Eccl. Hist.* 3.39.1), but Papias himself, as we have seen, made no claims to having heard the apostle. His information was secondhand at best. The claims of apostolic authorship surface at just the time the Gospel was beginning to be cited by orthodox Christians, and in all likelihood the argument that it was written by the apostle John was important in securing its acceptance by the church. Irenaeus was very young and Polycarp was very old when Irenaeus heard him, so while we may not doubt that Irenaeus believed what he reported, there is still reason to suspect confusion in the account.

The Authorship of John in Modern Scholarship

The traditional view has followed the testimony of the church fathers in attributing the Johannine writings to the apostle John. Since the rise of modern, critical scholarship, however, the question of authorship has been connected with the issue of the historicity of John and its relationship to the synoptics. In 1792, Edward Evanson, in a work entitled *The Dissonance of the Four Generally Received Evangelists,* noted the discrepancies among the four Gospels and concluded that John was not written by the apostle. Instead, he argued, it was written by a Platonist in the second century. The suggestion was rejected by most scholars at the time, but within a century it had become the dominant view. Karl Bretschneider (1820) and David Friedrich Strauss (1835) buttressed the attack on apostolic authorship.

During the nineteenth century, a mediating position began to develop: that John was written by a disciple or associate of the apostle. One suspects that many who supported this suggestion did so in an effort to maintain the Fourth Gospel's claim to authenticity and historicity while acknowledging some of the points scored by the opponents of apostolic authorship. David Friedrich Strauss (1835), Ernest Renan (1863), C. H. Weisse (1838), and J. B. Lightfoot (1875–76) were among the early proponents of this mediating position or "school" hypothesis. The Gospel was written by a member of the school of disciples the apostle had gathered around him.

Although the prevailing consensus rejected apostolic authorship, B. F. Westcott argued for apostolic authorship in his commentary (1882) with five famous arguments.

B. F. Westcott's Five Arguments for Apostolic Authorship

1. The author of the Fourth Gospel was a Jew.
2. The author of the Fourth Gospel was a Jew of Palestine.
3. The author of the Fourth Gospel was an eyewitness of what he describes.
4. The author of the Fourth Gospel was an apostle.
5. The author of the Fourth Gospel was the apostle John.[3]

In spite of Westcott's influence, the dominant view throughout the first part of the twentieth century continued to be that the Gospel was a later, Hellenistic, nonapostolic writing. J. A. T. Robinson summarized the position as follows.

The Critical Consensus of the Early 20th Century

1. The author depends on sources, including one or more of the Synoptic Gospels.
2. The background of the author is different from that of the events and teachings he is reporting.
3. The author is a witness for the Christ of faith, not to the Jesus of history.
4. The author represents Christianity at the level of theological development that is characteristic of the end of the first century (acute Hellenization).
5. The author is neither the apostle nor an eyewitness.[4]

The foremost advocate of nonapostolic authorship was Rudolf Bultmann, whose influential and groundbreaking work will be discussed in the next section.

Some conservative Protestant and Roman Catholic scholars have reaffirmed apostolic authorship while others have advocated the Johannine school theory. In one form or another, the latter view has been proposed by such leading commentators as Edwyn Hoskyns, C. K. Barrett, Raymond Brown, and Rudolf Schnackenburg. Others have reasserted the view that John the Elder, mentioned by Papias, was the author of the Johannine writings. The trend therefore has been generally away from the view that John is the work of the apostle, though the attribution of the Johannine writings to the apostle still calls for explanation. The precise role, if any, of the apostle's influence is still a matter of debate, but the question of the identity of the author has often been superseded by other issues, especially the sources, composition history, historical setting, and literary character of the Gospel.

Conclusion

What conclusions are we to draw from this mass of internal and external evidence? The Gospel itself claims that it was written or contains material written by an eyewitness, the Beloved Disciple. The identity of the Beloved Disciple is unknown, but by the end of the second century the tradition that this disciple was the apostle John had gained widespread acceptance, and the Gospel had a secure place in the canon of the New Testament. In all probability, the Gospel rests on early eyewitness testimony that was shaped by the worship and struggles of the Johannine community. The issue of authorship, therefore, should now be separated from that of the value or authority of the Gospel. The historical and theological importance of the Gospel can be maintained regardless of one's view concerning its authorship. Fascinating as it is, the question of authorship soon prompts us to ask about the sources behind the Gospel and the history of the Johannine community.

SOURCES

As we have seen, the question of authorship which dominated Johannine studies at least through the first quarter of this century led to interest in the sources which may lie behind the Gospel. If it could be shown that the author used sources, then it could be argued that he was not an eyewitness or an apostle. The traditional position, coupled with apostolic authorship, was that the apostle simply recorded his memories at an advanced age. The question of sources was also related to the issue of John and the synoptic Gospels. Both the traditional view that John, "the spiritual Gospel," was written to supplement the other Gospels, and the view of Hans Windisch that John was written to replace or correct the other Gospels assumed that John knew the synoptics. Scholars who identified sources in the Pentateuch developed methodological advances that allowed others to attempt to identify the sources used by the Evangelist by analyzing the theological tensions, literary difficulties, and stylistic differences evident in the text of the Gospel.

As early as the work of Julius Wellhausen (1907 and 1908), critics began to interpret literary breaks and inconsistencies *(aporia)* as evidence of the Evangelist's use of sources or as the work of an editor. Wellhausen pointed to the difficulty created by John 14:31, which seems to end the discourse, and John 18:1, where Jesus and the disciples finally do leave to go to the garden. Wellhausen concluded that "The whole is thus... a product of a literary process that went through several stages."[5] In a series of articles published in 1907 and 1908, Eduard Schwartz contended that the *aporia* show that sections of the Gospel have been displaced so that the original order cannot be recovered.[6] Emanuel Hirsch (1936) concluded that the author had used sources, which he supplemented with his own material, and that the Gospel was later revised by an "ecclesiastical redactor" to bring it more in line with the church's views.[7]

In 1941 Rudolf Bultmann published his epoch-making commentary on John. One of the contributions that he made to the debate was in the area of sources. Building on the work of Wellhausen, Schwartz, and Hirsch, Bultmann argued that the Evangelist drew together several diverse sources.

Sources Postulated by Rudolf Bultmann

1. The *Offenbarungsreden* or revelatory discourses. Most of the discourse material in John is assigned to this source. Bultmann finds it to be similar to the Odes of Solomon, the Hermetic and Mandaean materials, and the discourses found in second-century gnostic works.
2. The *Semeia Quelle* or signs source. The signs source contained an account of the signs or miracles contained in John. It is all narrative material.
3. The Passion Narrative, which was drawn from a source independent of the synoptic accounts.
4. Other sources and traditions. Bultmann assigns those passages which seem to echo the synoptics to these sources.

Bultmann contended that these sources were drawn together by the evangelist. The Evangelist himself was probably associated with the communities of John the Baptist, and some of these materials may have their origin in such communities also. After the Evangelist composed the Gospel, it suffered destruction, and an editor or redactor pieced it together and put it in the form in which we now have it. This "ecclesiastical redactor" also made minor changes to bring the theology of the Gospel closer to that of the emerging church in such areas as eschatology and the sacraments. In Bultmann's view, therefore, the sources come from different traditions, the Evangelist imposed his own theological perspectives, and the ecclesiastical redactor held a different perspective from the Evangelist.

Bultmann's work has exerted a formidable influence on Johannine scholarship. Even those who disagree with him, as nearly everyone does at some point, must deal with the issues on which he focused. His work was slow in reaching the United States, since it was not translated until 1971. The most thorough and lucid interpretation of Bultmann's theory may be found in the 1965 dissertation of D. Moody Smith, *The Composition and Order of the Fourth Gospel: Bultmann's Literary Theory*.[8]

Two different responses to Bultmann's source theory should be noted. The first involved detailed analyses of the style, grammar, and idiom of the Greek text of John. Eugen Ruckstuhl and Eduard Schweizer independently constructed lists of stylistic features one finds in John and then showed that statistically there is no difference in style among the sources Bultmann had proposed.[9] The signs, the discourses, and the work of the Evangelist all share the same stylistic features.

On the other hand, interest in the identification of a signs source has continued. The most significant and persuasive of the signs theories has been the work of Robert Fortna,[10] who argued that the Evangelist took up and revised a signs gospel composed of both accounts of the signs and a passion narrative. This signs gospel was used to present the gospel to Jews. A passion narrative was necessary to explain the death of this miracle worker. How and why did Jesus die such a death if he was a miracle worker? Fortna's work begins not with stylistic criteria or theological differences between the signs gospel and the rest of John but with the aporia, or breaks, gaps, repetitions, and incongruities in the text of John. Having completed his analysis and his identification of the source, Fortna then shows that there is a difference between its style and the rest of the Gospel.

The issue of sources is far from settled, however. Many, especially those who maintain apostolic authorship, reject any notion that the Evangelist used sources he did not compose. Others are reasserting the case for the influence of the Synoptics on John, so one can hardly speak of a consensus at this time.

CONSTRUCTING A THEORY OF COMPOSITION

The distinctive content, idiom, and thought of the Gospel and Letters are best explained on the basis of the relatively independent development of Johannine tradition. In the next chapter we will take up the question of the history of the Johannine community. Here it is sufficient to point out that an independent tradition implies a traditioning community in which the Gospel materials could develop in such a distinctive fashion.

Raymond E. Brown proposed a five-stage process for the composition of the Gospel.[11]

Raymond E. Brown's Composition Theory

Stage 1. "The existence of a body of traditional material pertaining to the words and works of Jesus." Brown concludes that this material was independent of the synoptic tradition.

Stage 2. "The development of this material in Johannine patterns." This development occurred over a period of perhaps several decades in a school with one principal preacher and resulted in written forms of material that had been taught and preached.

Stage 3. "The organization of this material from Stage 2 into a consecutive Gospel." Brown contended that this first edition of the Gospel contained both signs and discourses, in contrast to the theory that the first edition was a signs gospel and the discourses were added later (as Fortna suggested).

Stage 4. "Secondary edition by the evangelist." In Brown's view the principal preacher of stage 2 was probably the evangelist of stages 3 and 4. Others (for example, George Beasley-Murray) prefer to distinguish between the earlier witness (especially if he is identified with the Beloved Disciple) and the evangelist. New material from the Johannine tradition was introduced at this point.

Stage 5. "A final editing or redaction by someone other than the evangelist and whom we shall call the redactor." For Brown, the redactor was a disciple or close associate of the evangelist. Among the sections of the Gospel that Brown attributes to the redactor are John 6:51-58; 3:31-36; 12:44-50; John 15-17; and John 11-12. These were added at stage 4 or stage 5. The redactor also added material that had not come from the evangelist, such as John 1:1-18 and John 21.

The Gospel of John, therefore, may be understood as the result of a rather long process of composition, stretching over several decades, in which we may distinguish the tradition received from the Beloved Disciple, the work of the evangelist, and the revisions of the redactor. Tradition holds that the Beloved Disciple was John, the son of Zebedee, but most modern interpreters have concluded that the Beloved Disciple was instead an otherwise unknown teacher and theologian whose legacy has been passed on in the Fourth Gospel. The Gospel reflects not only his theological and literary genius but also the history of the community in which it was shaped, and to that fascinating story we turn in the next chapter.

CHAPTER 3

THE GOSPEL AND LETTERS AS THE LITERATURE OF A COMMUNITY

I n the course of exploring the composition of the Gospel in the previous chapter, we began to see evidence that it was shaped by the life of a particular early Christian community. We may speak of this community as the "Johannine community" in the sense that it is the community within which the Gospel and Letters were written. Naturally, communities do not write documents, so we should think of one or more individuals within the community as writing the Gospel and Letters, but the material is not just the work of one or two people in isolation. It grew out of and reflects the worship and instruction of an early Christian community and speaks to community concerns. Some of these concerns can still be seen in the Gospel and Letters.

COMMUNITY ISSUES AND CONCERNS IN THE GOSPEL

From various references in the Gospel we may begin to piece together some of the concerns of the Johannine community.

There is a danger of "mirror reading"—assuming that we can reconstruct the kind of situation that led to the expression of these concerns in the Gospel—but the following issues have been widely recognized.

Conflict with the Synagogue

In a trend-setting work in 1968, J. Louis Martyn proposed that the Gospel of John can be read as a drama on two levels.[1] On one level it tells of the ministry of Jesus, but on the other level it describes the setting within which it was written. Martyn drew fresh attention to the conflict between the Johannine community and the synagogue as it is reflected in the Gospel.

Three times the unusual word *aposynagogos,* which means to be put out of the synagogue, appears in the Gospel. During the farewell discourse, Jesus warns the disciples about conflict with the synagogue.

John 16:2

They will put you out of the synagogues. Indeed, an hour is coming when those who kill you will think that by doing so they are offering worship to God.

This warning has no exact parallel in the other Gospels, but conflict between Jews who believed Jesus was the Messiah and those who did not can be seen in Paul's letters (2 Cor 11) and in Acts. We may safely assume that this warning is included in the Farewell Discourse because the Johannine community had recently experienced conflict and persecution from the Jewish synagogue.

The hostility of that conflict is reflected not only in the reference to killing in John 16:2 but in the wording of John 9:22, the linchpin of Martyn's argument. During the investigation that takes place after Jesus gives sight to the man born blind, the Jews question the blind man's parents. The parents respond that the authorities should go and talk to their son because he was of age. What sort of persecution would lead parents to direct the authorities to their son in order to save themselves?

> **John 9:22**
>
> His parents said this because they were afraid of the Jews; for the Jews had already agreed that anyone who confessed Jesus to be the Messiah would be put out of the synagogue.

Martyn contends that the wording "had already agreed" suggests a formal action and that it is anachronistic since the Jewish authorities took no such formal action during the ministry of Jesus. As we see in Paul's letters and in Acts, the early Christians continued to have access to the Jewish synagogues. Martyn concluded that John 9:22 is a reference to the twelfth of the Eighteen Benedictions—the prayers pious Jews recited daily. The twelfth Benediction, or the *Birkath ha-Minim* as it is called, was composed at Jamnia late in the first century or early in the second century. Rather than seeing in John 9:22 a reference to the *Birkath ha-Minim,* it may be better to view the sequence in the opposite direction and understand the persecution echoed in John 9 as the kind of practice that was formalized by the *Birkath ha-Minim.*

> **The *Birkath ha-Minim***
>
> And for apostates let there be no hope;
> and may the insolent kingdom be quickly uprooted, in our days.
> And may the Nazarenes and the heretics perish quickly;
> and may they be erased from the Book of Life;
> and may they not be inscribed with the righteous.
> *Blessed art thou, Lord, who humblest the insolent.*[2]

The reason for the exclusion from the synagogue is not known. The preaching of the Johannine Christians, the emergence of a high Christology, their acceptance of non-Jewish converts, and differing attitudes regarding the Jewish revolt of A.D. 66–70 may each have contributed to the exclusion. Regardless of the precise cause, it appears that originally the Johannine Christians were part of the Jewish synagogue but that at some point they were excluded from the synagogue and formed a separate community. If we assume that the Beloved Disciple was the source of the Johannine tradition, he may well have been a leader of this emerging Christian community.

The Johannine community's conflict with the synagogue may also help to explain the hostile references to "the Jews" in the Gospel of John. Jesus and his disciples were all Jews, so at first Christianity was a movement within Judaism. The Gospel of John seems to look back on Jesus from the perspective of a time after the split between Jews and Christianity had become irreversible. Within the Gospel story, as we shall see, it is clear, however, that not all Jews opposed Jesus. Even the common translation "the Jews," may not give an accurate picture. In various contexts in John those referred to as *hoi Ioudaioi* seem to be the religious authorities in Jerusalem, or the Judeans, but not all the Jews (see John 7:11, 13).[3]

Secret Believers, Samaritans, and Greeks

References to particular groups in the Gospel may signal something of the role of such groups in the experience of the Johannine community.[4] The third reference to being put out of the synagogue suggests that in the midst of such hostility not only were parents and children set against one another, as seems to be the case in John 9, but also there were those who believed in Jesus but kept that belief secret.

John 12:42

Nevertheless many, even of the authorities, believed in him. But because of the Pharisees they did not confess it, for fear that they would be put out of the synagogue.

Joseph of Arimathea is explicitly identified as a secret believer when he is introduced in John 19:38, and Nicodemus, who came to Jesus at night, may have been a secret believer also (3:1-10; 7:50-52; 19:39).

Because the secret believers sought to remain within the synagogue, they would not confess their faith publicly. Here we may take note of the Gospel's insistence that John the Baptist confessed and did not deny that he was not the Messiah (1:20), and the role of Peter, a disciple who denied his faith (18:25-27). One of the reasons for writing the Gospel may have been not only to strengthen the community but to appeal to the secret believers to confess their faith and join with the community of believers.

John also tells of Jesus' ministry in the Samaritan village and the conversion of Samaritans (John 4). At a later point there is talk of Jesus' going to the Greeks (7:33-36), and some Greeks come asking to see Jesus (12:20-22). If John reflects not only the events in Jesus' ministry but the experience and concerns of the community also, it may well be that these references point to the inclusion of Samaritans and Greeks among the believers at some point in the history of the Johannine community. We can only guess what effect such an influx of non-Jewish believers had on the community.

Followers of John the Baptist

Actually, John is not called "the Baptist" in the Gospel of John. Instead, he is given the role of a witness to Jesus, and that is his only role. John is introduced in the prologue as a man sent from God to bear witness to the light (1:6-8). Because the Word was from the beginning, John says that Jesus ranks ahead of him (1:15). When he is introduced again a few verses later, John is fulfilling his role, testifying to Jesus before the authorities and before his own disciples. Indeed, the first disciples (and some think the Beloved Disciple himself) came from the followers of John.

Unlike the Gospel of Mark or the Gospel of Matthew, the Gospel of John does not actually narrate Jesus' baptism. Instead, John recalls the event and testifies concerning it (1:29-34). The effect is to disarm any who would respond that Jesus was baptized by John, not the other way around, and therefore that John was the greater of the two. In fact, in each appearance hereafter John continues to bear witness concerning Jesus and to elevate Jesus over himself (3:23-30; 10:41).

From the book of Acts we learn that the movement that John started did not dissolve with his death. Some thirty years later there was a group of followers of John the Baptist in Ephesus (Acts 18:25; 19:1-7). If, as early tradition records, the Gospel of John was written in Ephesus, the Johannine community may have had a special interest in declaring that those who followed John ought now to recognize the one to whom John had borne witness.

Petrine Christianity

Our survey (in chapter 2) of the passages in which the Beloved Disciple is mentioned revealed that the Beloved Disciple nearly always appears alongside Peter. At the last supper the Beloved Disciple is closest to Jesus, and Peter motions for him to find out who the betrayer is (13:23-24). If the "other disciple" mentioned in John 18:15 is the Beloved Disciple, then the Beloved Disciple may have been in the courtyard when Peter denied Jesus. The Beloved Disciple was at the cross, but Peter is not mentioned (19:26-27). Later, however, the Beloved Disciple and Peter are the first disciples to reach the empty tomb. The Beloved Disciple got there first, and he was the first to recognize the significance of what they saw there—he believed (20:3-10). Finally, it is the Beloved Disciple who recognizes the risen Lord and tells Peter (21:7). The Beloved Disciple is following Jesus when Peter is told to do just that (21:20-22). Peter would be a shepherd, a good shepherd. He would lay down his life for Jesus, but the Beloved Disciple would bear a true witness (21:15-19, 24).

In the Synoptics, Peter is remembered for the confession, "Thou art the Christ" (KJV, Mark 8:29; Matt 16:16; and Luke 9:20), but in John, Andrew tells him right at the beginning that they have found the Christ (1:41). The effect of the characterization of Peter in the Gospel of John is to recognize his role as an apostle, but to insist that the Beloved Disciple had equal authority by virtue of his special relationship to Jesus. Given the importance of Peter for the apostolic church as described in Acts and reflected in the Synoptic Gospels (especially Matthew) and in the Petrine Epistles, we may well suspect that in the figures of Peter and the Beloved Disciple we see something of the concern of the Johannine community to reply to those who represented churches that looked to Peter as the leading apostle. The role of Peter was recognized, but the Beloved Disciple had given them a tradition they knew to be true.

The Death of the Beloved Disciple

The closing verses of the Gospel note the misunderstanding that had spread among the Johannine Christians. Apparently many believed that the Beloved Disciple would not die until the Lord returned. The redactor is concerned to set the record straight. The Lord had not said that the Beloved Disciple would not die. The implication many have drawn from this odd conclusion to the Gospel is that the Beloved Disciple had in fact died or was near death. If that is the case, the death of their apostolic authority would have precipitated, if not a crisis, at least a new stage in the life of the community. John's affirmations regarding the continuing role of the Paraclete in teaching the community, Jesus' promise not to leave the disciples orphans (14:18), and Jesus' prayer for those who would come after the disciples (17:20-26) all take on new meaning when read in light of the evidence that the Gospel, at least in its finished form, addressed a second or third generation of Christians.

From these various references we may begin to fill in aspects of the life of the Johannine community. The evidence of concerns at issue in the letters offers another glimpse into the history of the community.

COMMUNITY ISSUES AND CONCERNS IN THE LETTERS

The letters reflect a mixture of concerns, some of which are similar to issues dealt with in the Gospel and others on which the Gospel is either silent or offers a different perspective. Johannine scholarship is divided over the question of whether the letters reflect an earlier or later period in the life of the community.[5] For reasons that will be given later, we will treat the letters as a reflection of a period late in the composition history of the Gospel. The elder seems to share many of the concerns and perspectives of the Redactor, but it is uncertain whether they are the same person or two different writers. The similarities between the Gospel and the letters are such that there has been considerable debate as to whether they are the work of the same author or not. At the least, they are related to the same community and written about the same time.

Evidence of an Intra-Johannine Schism

First and Second John reflect a community torn apart by theological differences.[6] By the time 1 John was written the differences had precipitated a schism.

---

1 John 2:19

They went out from us, but they did not belong to us; for if they had belonged to us, they would have remained with us. But by going out they made it plain that none of them belongs to us.

Several interesting issues arise from this reference: Who were those who went out from the community? What issues divided them from the elder and those who remained loyal to him? How many left the community, and can these be identified with any known groups in the second century?

Sinlessness and Perfectionism

In the first two chapters of 1 John there are pronouncements that look like they are allusions to the teachings of the elder's opponents, those who have left the community. In 1 John 1:6, 8, and 10, we find the phrase, "If we say . . . " followed by some statement regarding sinlessness. The elder rejects each of these, citing increasingly severe consequences.

The Dangers of Slogans Regarding Sinlessness

1:6 If we say that we have fellowship with him while we are walking in darkness, we lie and do not do what is true.

1:8 If we say that we have no sin, we deceive ourselves, and the truth is not in us.

1:10 If we say that we have not sinned, we make him a liar, and his word is not in us.

Similar quotations and warnings appear in 1 John 2:4, 6, and 9. If the elder is here quoting slogans or teachings that he deemed dangerous to the community, it may be that these slogans represent the teachings of those who had left the community, and the warnings represent the elder's response to such teachings. We may infer, then, that this group believed that they had no sin and perhaps even that they had never sinned.

Such beliefs represent a form of perfectionism, the view that it is possible to be perfect or blameless (cf. Matt 5:48; Phil 3:12-16). Certainly the pervasive dualism of the Gospel of John, with its sharp division between light and darkness, truth and falsehood, leaves little middle ground for sin among those in the Christian community. Neither does the Gospel speak of individual sins or vices. Instead, sin in the Gospel of John is primarily willful blindness (9:41) or the refusal to believe (16:8). It is plausible, therefore, that some who had once been part of the Johannine community maintained that because they believed in Jesus and

49

were in the light, they had no sin. As we will see when we deal with 1 John 3:3-9 and 5:16-17, the elder shares the conviction that there is no room for sin in the Christian life, but he also acknowledges the reality of sin and the possibility of forgiveness.

Christology

Because Christology is so central in the Gospel it is not surprising that differences over the nature and work of Christ also divided the Johannine community. References in both 1 and 2 John point to differing interpretations of the Incarnation and the significance of the death of Jesus.

Incarnation. Following the admonition to test the spirits and the warning about false prophets at the beginning of 1 John 4, the elder offers a test for distinguishing the Spirit of God:

> Every spirit that confesses that Jesus Christ has come *in the flesh* is from God. (4:2)

The emphasis on Jesus' having come in the flesh appears also in 2 John 7:

> Many deceivers have gone out into the world, those who do not confess that Jesus Christ has come *in the flesh;* any such person is the deceiver and the antichrist!

The statement of purpose at the end of John 20 lacks this qualifier. The emphasis in the Gospel is simply believing that Jesus is the Messiah:

> But these are written so that you may come to believe that Jesus is the Messiah, the Son of God, and that through believing you may have life in his name. (John 20:31)

Why is the phrase "in the flesh" added in 1 and 2 John, when it is not present in the Gospel? To put the matter baldly, it appears that at the time the epistles were written it was not enough to believe that Jesus is the Christ, now one had to believe that he had come *in the flesh.* Evidently some Johannine Christians confessed that Jesus was the Messiah but did not believe that he had come in flesh. Such a belief probably drew from the Greek view of the dualism of body and spirit and the judgment that the flesh was inherently evil. The Christ, therefore, could not have actually come in flesh.

The Gospel of John is marked by a high Christology in which Jesus hardly seems to be human at times. He sees Nathanael before he comes to him (1:48), he knows what is in the hearts of others (2:24), and knows that Judas will betray him (6:70-71). Jesus' food is to do the will of the Father (4:32-34). He is from above and returns to the Father (16:28). It is not difficult, therefore, to see how the view of the opponents could have arisen among the Johannine Christians. This heresy tends in the direction of Docetism, the belief that Jesus only seemed to be human. Indeed, this Johannine aberration may have led to the emergence of Docetism in the second century. It is not impossible that the group that went out from the Johannine community were the direct predecessors of those whose traditions appear in the Acts of John by Leucius and those who carried the Gospel of John into the Valentinian Gnostic communities.

The elder's opponents probably believed that they held not a lower but a higher Christology, one that recognized the full divinity of Christ uncompromised by the flesh. The elder and those who remained with him asserted the fundamental significance of the Incarnation. Christianity is not a religion of those who believe that the Son of God appeared to be human but was not; it is the faith of those who recognized that the Son of God had lived among them as a human being. The prologue to the Gospel makes the same assertion:

And the Word became flesh and lived among us, and we have seen his glory. (1:14)

The parallel between this verse and the emphasis on Jesus' having come in flesh in the epistles is one of the reasons that many interpreters think that the prologue was added rather late in the composition of the Gospel.

The Death of Jesus. The opponents' denial of the Incarnation was probably also coupled with a view of the death of Jesus that the elder found inadequate and dangerous. He insists that Jesus Christ came "not with the water only but with the water and the blood" (1 John 5:6). The allusion to water may refer either to

Jesus' human birth or more likely to his baptism, and the reference to blood is almost certainly an allusion to his death. The elder also insists that Jesus is "the atoning sacrifice for our sins" (1 John 2:2; 4:10).

The death of Jesus, it is often noted, is treated distinctively in the Gospel of John. It is the first step in Jesus' exaltation and his return to the Father. Jesus speaks of his being "lifted up" (3:14; 8:28; 12:32). It is his "hour" and the time of his glorification. It can also be seen as his coronation as "the king of the Jews." The opponents, therefore, may have seized the Johannine tradition's interpretation of Jesus' work as revealer. For them Jesus' saving work was not his death but his revelation of the Father. The elder opposes that distortion by returning to a more traditional, or earlier, emphasis on Jesus' death as atoning sacrifice, thereby also bringing Johannine teachings more in line with the doctrine of other orthodox Christian communities for which the Synoptic Gospels and the letters of Paul were normative.

Obedience to the Love Command

The elder also charges that the opponents did not observe Jesus' command to love one another, the "new commandment" of John 13:34 (see 1 John 2:7-11; 3:11-17, 23; 4:7-12, 20-21). We do not know how this lack of love was manifested, but it may have resulted in some refusing to share with other Johannine Christians who were in need (1 John 3:17). Neither do we know what the opponents were saying about the elder and his followers, but clearly the differences on other issues had resulted in a lack of love within the community. Indeed, the terms of hostility that are directed against "the Jews" in the Gospel are turned against the opponents—those who had once been part of the Johannine community—in the letters. They are children of the devil (1 John 3:10-11; cf. John 8:44), who walk in darkness (1 John 2:9-11; cf. John 8:12; 12:46); and in whom the prophecy of Isaiah is fulfilled (1 John 2:11; cf. John 12:38-40).

Eschatology

The elder does not condemn any specific eschatological statements in 1 John, but we may suspect that there were clear differences between him and the opponents on this subject also. If the opponents held that they were without sin, they may have also denied that there would be a final judgment or resurrection. According to Johannine teaching (that the elder also shared), they had already crossed from death into life (John 11:25-27; 1 John 3:14). They were abiding in Christ (1 John 2:6), and they were in the light (1 John 2:9). For the elder, however, these conditions were tied to an ethical responsibility, loving one another and keeping Jesus' commandments.

Perhaps in the face of such an emphasis on realized eschatology (the teaching that our hopes about the future are already realized in Christ), the elder reasserted the traditional hope for the future fulfillment. What we will be has not yet been revealed, but we will be like him at his coming (1 John 2:28; 3:2-3). The Gospel of John develops a distinctive realized eschatology, which may again have provided the basis for the development of the opponent's view, but the Gospel also preserves a strain of the more traditional, future eschatology (John 6:39-40, 44, 54).

Pneumatology

The elder condemns "false prophets" who have gone out from them (1 John 4:1). These false prophets no doubt claimed to teach by the authority of the Spirit, so the elder reminds the community that they all have the Spirit (1 John 2:20, 27) and that they are to test the spirits (1 John 4:1). The Johannine teachings on the Paraclete promise the conferring of the Spirit of truth to the community, but these statements are neatly balanced. The Spirit will teach them all things, but it will also remind them of what Jesus had taught (John 14:26). Any new teaching, therefore, would be consistent with the tradition they had received from the beginning (1 John 2:24). Consequently, the elder reasserts the authority of tradition as a control on prophetic enthusiasm in a manner not unlike what we find in the Pastoral Epistles in the Pauline tradition.

The Authority of the Elder

The belief that all Christians were anointed by the Spirit led to a very egalitarian community in which all were the sheep who heard the shepherd's voice (John 10:4, 27) and all were branches of the same vine (John 15:1-8). The Johannine Christians should therefore not be misled by the false prophets.

On the other hand, the common anointing of the Spirit also meant that there could be little hierarchical authority. The elder never appeals to his authority by virtue of office. He can only call the community back to its tradition and reason with them. In 3 John we will see evidence that the elder's authority was not acknowledged by some in communities that the elder felt should be receptive to his leadership. Along with the struggle to define correct doctrine, therefore, we also see in the Letters a struggle to define authority and positions of leadership in the Johannine community and its satellite communities.

CONSTRUCTING A THEORY OF THE HISTORY OF THE JOHANNINE COMMUNITY

We have now looked at the major indications of the life setting of the Gospel and Letters of John. Most theories of the history of the community are efforts to explain how these facets of the life setting can be connected in a pattern that makes sense of the development of the Johannine tradition.

Two elements in particular suggest that the situation in the Letters reflects a period later than the Gospel or during the latter stages of the composition of the Gospel. First, the Letters reflect a division in the community over theological issues. "The Jews" and the conflict with the synagogue are not mentioned. One must suppose either that this struggle now lies in the past or that it has not yet occurred. If it had not yet occurred, one would have to suppose a period of intense Christological debate prior to the time the Johannine believers were associated with the synagogue, but such a reconstruction hardly makes sense. The sequence of events is far more likely to be the reverse. The period of debate and schism within the Christian community followed its separation from the synagogue. Second, this sequence also seems to be reflected in the added emphasis on the necessity of confessing Christ having come 'in flesh' that we find in the Letters (compare 1 John 4:2 and 2 John 7 with John 20:31).

While acknowledging that much of what follows is conjecture or historical imagination, the reflections of the life setting of the Gospel and Letters that we have examined above can be explained on the basis of a history of the Johannine community that is divided into five periods.[7] Although little can be known about the first two periods, events in the latter three can be reconstructed with more confidence. The description of the first four periods is based solely on inferences from the Gospel itself. The final period is reconstructed from evidence provided by the Johannine Epistles.

1. ORIGINS

The story of the Johannine tradition seems to begin with an eyewitness of the ministry of Jesus, one known from the Gospel as the Beloved Disciple. This disciple was undoubtedly attached to a group of the early disciples, and he may originally have been a disciple of John the Baptist (see John 1:35-40). The tradition itself reflects a detailed knowledge of Jerusalem, Judea, and the Jewish festivals. Parallels to the language and dualistic thought of the Qumran scrolls may also point to a Judean origin or to a person or group that had connections with the Essenes at one time. The simple, Semitic style of the Gospel may also derive from Aramaic influence. Oscar Cullmann proposed that the Johannine Christians were associated with the Hellenists in the early church in Jerusalem.[8] Such a connection is more problematic, but it is not impossible that the Beloved Disciple and his associates were forced to leave Judea at the time that other Christians moved to Antioch and surrounding areas (Acts 8:1; 11:19-21).

2. EARLY PERIOD WITHIN THE SYNAGOGUE

Following J. Louis Martyn's thesis, the history of the Johannine community from its earliest days as an identifiable group can be divided into an early, middle, and late periods, though I will define the contours of each period in ways that extend Martyn's work.

The specific data of locations and dates are the most tentative and problematic parts of this history. Once the earliest Johannine Christians were forced to leave Judea, they may have gone to Antioch, or directly to Ephesus. Those who see a close connection between the Gospel of John and early Gnostic thought champion Syria as a probable location.[9] If one is disposed to use the book of Acts in the absence of other data, the hypothesis that the community spent a period of time in the area of Antioch receives a measure of support. We know that early Christians from Judea settled there, and later, when Acts describes Paul's ministry in Ephesus, there is no mention of a group of Johannine Christians. Linguistic and conceptual parallels between the Gospel of John, the Odes of Solomon, and the letters of Ignatius can also be explained more easily if Johannine Christians spent some time in this area.[10]

At this point one may also raise the troubling question of the role of Samaritans among the Johannine Christians. The Gospel of John clearly devotes unusual attention to the Samaritans. Interestingly enough, the last reference to the apostle John in the book of Acts leaves him in Samaria (Acts 8:14, 25). Were Johannine Christians engaged in mission work among the Samaritans? Did Samaritan converts join them in such numbers that they influenced the development of Johannine Christology? Perhaps, but it is difficult to define the specific nature of the contact with Samaritans.

During this early period, Johannine Christians functioned more or less comfortably within the Jewish synagogue. They lived as Jews and thought of themselves as Jews who had found the Messiah. As John 1:35-49 suggests, they regarded Jesus as the fulfillment of messianic expectations drawn from the Hebrew scriptures. For them, Jesus was the prophet like Moses (but one greater than Moses), the returning Elijah (the fulfillment of the prophets), the king of Israel, and the coming Son of man. Because of the heavy influence of the Elijah-Elisha materials on their Christology, the proclamation of signs was an appropriate way to proclaim Jesus to fellow Jews.

The passion narrative in John makes extensive use of references and allusions to the Hebrew scriptures. Moreover, it is difficult to see how the proclamation of signs could have continued long without some interpretation of Jesus' death. The passion narrative, therefore, may have been shaped during this period also. The signs were collected in a written "signs source" and eventually the passion narrative was attached to the collection of signs, forming a "gospel of signs" (Robert T. Fortna).

3. MIDDLE PERIOD: FORMATION OF THE JOHANNINE COMMUNITY

The middle period begins with the exclusion of the Johannine Christians from the synagogue. The factors that precipitated this break in relations with the Jewish community are probably multiple. Raymond E. Brown suggested that the exclusion of Christians came as the result of the development of a new, higher Christology that was not based on the Davidic pattern.[11] On the other hand, the development of a higher Christology—which was based on the wisdom tradition of the Old Testament and Apocrypha, resulted in John's distinctive Logos Christology, and characterized Jesus as the Incarnation of the divine Word of God—could just as well have occurred after the exodus from the synagogue. It is difficult to establish a causal relationship between a theological development and a social crisis. Either may have provoked the other, but theological developments are often precipitated by social crises.

The relaxation of the Law in ritual and cultic matters by Johannine Christians may have eventually led to their exclusion from the synagogue. Differences between Christian Jews and non-Christian Jews over the war of 66–70 may also have hardened relations between the two groups. The action in view in John may not have been the enforcement of the *Birkath ha-Minim* as argued by J. Louis Martyn,[12] but it probably reflects the kind of situation that led to the adoption of this blessing.

Caught in this traumatic development, some Johannine Christians elected to stay within the synagogue rather than confess openly their faith in Jesus as the Christ. The Gospel brands such persons as "secret believers" (12:42; 19:38). Others confessed their faith openly and were separated from the Jewish community. Undoubtedly, some families were divided, with various members responding to the crisis differently.

Those who were excluded from the synagogue gathered around the Beloved Disciple as the center of their new community, their living link with Jesus. He was the source of their teaching. The middle period, therefore, marks the emergence of the Johannine community. Under the leadership of their founder, the Beloved Disciple, members of the community began to establish their identity as the true children of God who had responded faithfully to the revelation received through Jesus. By observing the role of the Beloved Disciple within the community, they also began to formulate their understanding of the work of the Paraclete or Holy Spirit among them. The teachings of the Beloved Disciple became the normative guide to the interpretation of Scripture and the words of Jesus. Those closest to the Beloved

Disciple gathered his sermons and discourses. The Beloved Disciple and his own disciples shaped the emerging Gospel tradition in light of the liturgical, polemical, apologetic, and catechetical needs of the community. Baptism, the sacramental meal, and foot washing were probably practiced by the community.

The discourses now contained in the Gospel were developed in the context of these diverse aspects of the community's life. Some of the discourse material evolved from reflection on various aphorisms and *logia* ("sayings") received from Jesus (e.g., John 3:3, 5; 5:19, 24, 25; 6:26, 32, 53; 8:34-35; 10:1-5; 12:24; 13:16; 16:20, 23).[13] Other discourses developed through preaching and teaching the "signs source" (as in John 5, 6, 9, and 11 especially). Yet other parts of the discourse material may reflect the activity of Christian prophets among the Johannine Christians, who declared words they had received from the risen Lord. Eventually the community found it necessary to test prophetic utterances against the norm of the tradition received from the Beloved Disciple. Throughout this process, the Beloved Disciple and the school that was developing around him reflected on their situation in light of Jesus' conflict with the religious authorities of his day. Once formulated, some of this discourse material was inserted into the early "signs gospel." The new gospel gave more attention to the radical demand for obedience and confession of one's faith, the conflict between Jesus and "the Jews," and examples of individuals caught between Jesus' demands for faith and "the Jews'" rejections of his claims.

The community now used more dualistic language to describe its faith and its relationship to the world around it. From a "greater than Moses" Christology, the community heightened the authority of its Lord by Christianizing the high claims that were made for Wisdom, which had been personified as the divine agent of creation (for example, Prov 8:22ff.). They had a higher revelation than that given to Moses. Jesus was the preexistent Logos who had become flesh and whose revelation gave them "grace and truth" (1:17), a revelation that supplanted the authority of the Law of Moses.

The community was persecuted by the Pharisaic authorities from the synagogue (15:18–16:2). The writing of the Gospel (on the basis of the earlier signs gospel) was in part a response to this persecution. If the community had been located in Antioch or

Syria during this period, it may have been forced by the persecution to move to Ephesus at this time. The Revelation to John, which is somehow related to the Gospel and the Johannine Epistles, came from this area, and the early patristic evidence locates the writing of John in Ephesus. When, why, and how the community came to Ephesus remain matters of conjecture.

4. MIDDLE PERIOD: THE SECOND GENERATION

Sometime during the middle period the community was shaken by the death of the Beloved Disciple. Evidence for his recent or imminent death is furnished by John 21:23. Many in the community believed that the Beloved Disciple would not die until the Lord returned. The need to correct that misunderstanding is most easily explained on the assumption that the Beloved Disciple had in fact died or was about to die.

The death of the Beloved Disciple provoked further reflection on the role of the Spirit in the community. This reflection resulted in an affirmation of the role of the Paraclete (or Counselor), who would be with them always (14:16).[14] Because of this reaffirmation of the role of the Spirit within the community, no hierarchy or structure of authority developed. The community retained its egalitarian character since all possessed the Spirit. The chief concern for the emerging second generation, referred to in John 17:20, was that it preserve the unity of the community—with one another and with the risen Lord (17:21-23). It was crucial to the survival of the community that they love one another (13:34) and that they "abide" in the risen Lord and his words as they had received them through the tradition coming from the Beloved Disciple. These emphases are reflected in discourse material that was added to the Gospel during this period, especially chapters 15–17.

The relationship between the Johannine community and other Christian groups was becoming an issue. The expulsion of Christians from the synagogues created several groups of Jewish Christians. The other groups were "other sheep that do not belong to this fold" (10:16), and the Johannine Christians sought unity with these other groups of Jewish Christians in their area. Evidence of the relationship between these communities can be gleaned from 2 and 3 John. The elder—the author of the Epistles—sought to maintain a position of leadership with these communities by sending emissaries like Demetrius (3 John 5-6, 12) and by sending letters like 2 and 3 John. This network of churches may also be related in some way to the seven churches addressed in Revelation, chapters 2–3.

At this point we may identify an inner group that had been closely related to the Beloved Disciple and that participated in the leadership of the community, led in worship, and produced the community's written materials. This group can be called the "Johannine school." The "Johannine community" was the center of the network of churches that can be called "Johannine Christianity."

Johannine Christianity also faced rival claims that came from churches that regarded Peter as their apostolic authority. The Johannine Christians recognized Peter's pastoral role in the church but defended the authority of their tradition by telling stories that maintained the superiority of the Beloved Disciple (John 13:23-26; 18:15-16; 19:26-27; 20:3-10; 21:2-14, 20-23). Eventually, however, internal schism so destroyed the community that its members were absorbed by other Christian groups.

5. LATE PERIOD: SCHISM

This period is characterized by the emergence of a group advocating a "higher" Christology that emphasized the divinity of Christ while minimizing the humanity of Jesus (1 John 2:19; 4:2). This group also taught that believers had been delivered from sin and had already crossed from death into life (1 John 1:8, 10; 3:14). Such a heavy emphasis on realized eschatology led in turn to a disregard for the necessity to continue to resist sin. Dissension resulted in schism, and the elder charged that those who had left the community were false prophets and teachers who had gone out into the world, thereby violating the community ethic of love for one another (1 John 2:19; 3:10; 4:1-6). In response to this crisis, the elder wrote 1 John to warn the community of the dangers of this false teaching and to encourage those who remained to continue in their faithfulness. Second John was written to warn a sister community of the dangers that were posed by this group.

The relationship between the final redaction of the Gospel and the composition of the Epistles is still open to debate. The prologue to the Gospel, John 6:51-58, the references to the Beloved Disciple, and chapter 21 were probably among the passages added to the Gospel during this period. These passages are the work of one who, like the elder, was a member of the Johannine school.

The last we see of the Johannine community, it is wrecked by dissension and struggling for survival. The elder's group was probably absorbed by the dominant Christian groups of the early second century. The elder's opponents, on the other hand, probably found their way into the Gnostic communities of the mid-second century. The community's legacy was its story—the Gospel that tells the story of Jesus in such a way that it had become their story also. In the next chapter we will see how the Gospel functions as narrative.

CHAPTER 4

THE GOSPEL AS LITERATURE

T o this point we have been considering the Gospel as history. It is time to take up the second lens through which we will view the Gospel and explore it as literature. Whatever else it is, the Gospel is a narrative. It tells a story. Jesus and those around him are the characters. A narrator tells the story, and in the process introduces the characters, settings, and conflicts that follow. The story has a beginning and an ending, which conveys a sense of closure. In this chapter, we will be interested in what kind of story the Gospel is and how the story is told.

GENRE

What are the Gospels? The answer to such an apparently simple question has proved surprisingly elusive. Our understanding of the Gospels is shaped by our assumptions regarding whether they are history, biography, drama, preaching, or theology. Once the Gospels were thought to be *sui generis*, a distinctive creation of the early church, resembling one another but distinctively different from any other form of literature. More recently, scholars have pointed to the flexibility of ancient genres and similarities between the Gospels and various forms of literature, renewing efforts to identify the genre of the Gospels. Literary genres have evolved, however, so that modern expectations regarding history or biography differ from the ways these genres were understood in antiquity. Would an ancient reader have understood that John fit into one of the conventional literary genres, and if so how does the genre of the Gospel affect our understanding of its plot?

The Gospel of John has been interpreted alternately as biography and as drama in recent discussions of its plot. A brief review of the development of these two lines of interpretation may serve to clarify both the issue of the genre of the Gospel and the bearing its genre has on its plot. F. R. M. Hitchcock observed that the Fourth Gospel "appears to be cast in dramatic form."[1] Like a Greek drama, Hitchcock contended, the Gospel has five divisions with a prologue and an epilogue: prologue (1:1-18); Act 1 (1:19–2:12); Act 2 (2:13–6:71); Act 3 (7:1–11:57), in which the raising of Lazarus is the center of the plot; Act 4 (12:1–19:42), in which the dénouement *(lusis)* begins with the scene in the garden, and the discovery *(anagnorisis)* is attempted by the soldiers and Pilate, but will not be achieved until Act 5 (20:1-31) with Mary and Thomas; and the epilogue (21:1-25). The reversal of fortunes *(peripeteia)* occurs with the crowd's rejection of Jesus in favor of Barabbas, and the *pathos* characteristic of drama fills the crucifixion scene.

Following Hitchcock's lead, Mark W. G. Stibbe adapted Hitchcock's analysis of the structure of the Gospel as having five acts or stages with prologue and epilogue.

Mark Stibbe's Analysis of the Structure of the Gospel	
Prologue	John 1
Act I	John 2–4
Act II	John 5–10
Act III	John 11–12
Act IV	John 13–19
Act V	John 20
Epilogue	John 21[2]

Drawing parallels to Euripedes' story of Dionysus in the *Bacchae,* Stibbe argues that the basic story-type or *mythos* of the Fourth

Gospel is tragedy. As in the *Bacchae,* the essential elements of a tragedy are evident in John: purpose (commission), passion *(pathos),* and perception *(anagnorisis).* In the end, however, by virtue of the fact that "Jesus suffers the nemesis he ought to have reaped on others" John subverts the *mythos,* and the passion narrative "signals the death of tragedy."[3] The analysis of the Gospel that follows will show that John has developed and extended the *anagnorisis* into a major plot element.

In recent scholarship, the earlier judgment that the Gospels are *sui generis,* conforming to no established genre, has yielded to evidence that the Gospels fit within the general category of ancient biography.[4] Charles H. Talbert identified as "constitutive of ancient biography that the subject be a distinguished or notorious figure" and that the aim be "to expose the essence of the person."[5] Accordingly, biography may be distinguished from history in that "whereas history focuses on the distinguished and significant acts of great men in the political and social spheres, biography is concerned with the essence of the individual."[6] The issue has often been confused, Talbert contends, because the variability of the genre has not been recognized, and elements accidental to it have been regarded as essential. This confusion has resulted in failure to recognize the Gospels as *bioi* (biographies). Given this variability, we are dealing with biographical

---

Seven Elements "Accidental" to Ancient Biography

(Charles Talbert)

1. It is incorrect to describe ancient biography as an account of the life of a man from birth to death.
2. The hero's character was assumed to appear not only in his deeds but also in insignificant gestures or passing utterance.
3. There is virtually no interest in tracing development.
4. Some biographies have as their aim to affect the behavior or opinions of their readers either positively or negatively.
5. The "life" of a subject may be described in mythical terms or may be devoid of myth.
6. The literary form in which "lives" are presented varies. The dominant form is a prose narrative similar to history except that it is anecdotal and unconcerned about cause and effect.
7. Ancient biographies perform a multiplicity of social functions.[7]

---

traditions in antiquity any time we meet "the concern to depict the essence of a significant person."[8] This characteristic of ancient biography is particularly important for John, in which other characters serve as foils for the reader's success or failure to discern and affirm Jesus' true identity.

Richard A. Burridge has compared the Gospels with Graeco-Roman biographies, noting especially the similarities in opening features, subject, external features, and internal features. As a genre, *bios* moves between the extremes of history on one side and encomium on the other.[9] The genre was flexible and developed over time, making it critical that the Gospels be compared with Graeco-Roman biographies of their period.

Richard Burridge's Conclusions from the Study of Ancient Biographies

1. "Biography is a type of writing which occurs naturally among groups of people who have formed around a certain charismatic teacher or leader, seeking to follow after him."
2. "A major purpose and function of *bioi* is in a context of didactic or philosophical polemic and conflict."
3. "*Bios* is a genre capable of flexibility, adaptation and growth."
4. "Therefore it is eminently sensible to begin a search for the genre of the Gospels within the sphere of *bios*, but such an attempt to consider the Gospels as *bioi* must always take account of this wider picture of its flexible and developing nature."[10]

After establishing detailed observations regarding the external and internal features of the Graeco-Roman *bioi*, Burridge draws the following conclusions regarding the Fourth Gospel's membership in this class. The superscription *kata Ioannēn* shows that the Fourth Gospel was perceived as belonging to the same genre as the Synoptics. The focus on Jesus' activity in the narrative and the attention to his teaching fit the pattern of the *bioi*. In size the Gospel also fits the genre of *bioi*. Robert Morgenthaler calculated that John has 15,416 words,[11] which places it midway between Mark on the one hand and Matthew and Luke on the other. It fits the length of a medium-range *bios*. John's structure of discourse and dialogue material inserted in a chronological outline and arranged topically is "typical of the structure found in many *bioi*."[12] "The narrow scale [that is, focus on Jesus] is another link with both the Synoptic Gospels and Graeco-Roman *bioi*."[13] "The Fourth Gospel is composed mainly of stories, dialogues, and speeches or discourses, which are the typical material of *bioi*, especially those of philosophers and teachers."[14] The use, adaptation, and revision of oral and written sources is typical of the writers of *bioi*, "particularly those writing about philosophers and teachers within the context of their particular schools and followers."[15]

Typical methods of characterization in the *bioi* include "deeds and words, sayings and imputed motives."[16] Burridge identifies the following as characteristic topics of the *bioi*: ancestry; birth, childhood, and education; great deeds; virtues; and death and consequences. Although there are differences, John shares "a similar range of topics to that found in the Graeco-Roman *bioi*."[17] The flat, repetitive, unified style of the Gospel accords well with the style in which popular *bioi* were written. John's steady, "serious and even worshipful approach may be slightly less varied than that found in the Synoptic Gospels, but it still remains similar to their atmosphere and to that of other *bioi*."[18] John's presentation of Jesus as the Christ falls short of a realistic human portrait, but "such an ambivalent quality is not dissimilar from the mix of stereotype and reality found in both the Synoptic Gospels and Graeco-Roman *bioi*."[19] Burridge argues that John reveals nothing "definite about its setting and occasion" other than "the need to relate Jesus and his teaching to both the Johannine community and those around it," a setting and occasion "well within the scope of *bioi*."[20] The Fourth Gospel has several purposes: evangelistic, didactic, apologetic, and polemical—and these are "some of the most common purposes of Graeco-Roman *bioi*, particularly those originating within philosophical schools."[21]

On the basis of these common features, Burridge concludes that the Fourth Gospel is best understood as a *bios Iesou* (biography of Jesus). Not to be missed is his repeated observation that the Gospel fits particularly well among the *bioi* produced within philosophical schools, honoring the school's founder and offering a definitive interpretation of his teachings.

PLOT

Although the term *plot* has been defined in various ways—ranging from a summary of the story line to analysis of the causal factors that move the story along, and from its structure to its effects on the reader—all four factors must be considered: sequence, causality, unity, and affective power. Sequence has to do with the order and progression of events. Causality describes the relationships which lead the story from one event to another. Unity is the result of a plot that coheres and conveys a sense of wholeness and completion. Good plots also have the power to move readers to various responses; they have affective power.

The story of the Gospel can be viewed from various perspectives. Most outlines of the Gospel focus alternately on the progression of geographical settings, the signs, the journeys, or the Jewish festivals. Any analysis will elevate certain elements of the narrative over others. The question to be raised, then, is what does each analysis bring to light.

The conclusion that John is biography has fueled several significant analyses of its plot. Here we will note the interpretations of John's plot by Fernando Segovia and Mark W. G. Stibbe.

Fernando Segovia finds particularly significant the Gospel's use of the motif of journey and the technique of patterns of repetition and recurrence. Following the generic conventions of biographical literature, Segovia identifies "an overall threefold division of the plot in terms of the Gospel as a biography of Jesus, the Word of God: a narrative of origins (1:1-18), a narrative of the public life or career of Jesus (1:19–17:26), and a narrative of death and lasting significance (18:1–21:25)."[22] Moreover, among ancient biographies, John may be classified as belonging to the chronological rather than the topical type. It relates the life of a holy man, in particular the holy man as a son of god.[23] The cosmic journey of the Word of God provides the framework for the plot of the Gospel, which unfolds in a series of geographical journeys marked by repetitive patterns.[24] Guided by these considerations, Segovia proposes that the narrative of the public life or career of Jesus (1:19–17:26) is structured around four journeys to Jerusalem and three return trips to Galilee.

Journey Cycles in the Gospel of John

(Fernando Segovia)

A. First Galilee/Jerusalem Cycle (1:19–3:36)

B. Second Galilee/Jerusalem Cycle (4:1–5:47)

C. Third Galilee/Jerusalem Cycle (6:1–10:42)

D. Fourth and Final Journey to Jerusalem (11:1–17:26)

The subunits of each of these sections need not concern us here. John 18:1–21:25 concludes the Gospel with an account of the preparatory events (18:1–19:16) and a narrative of death and lasting significance (19:17–21:25).

The strengths of Segovia's analysis are clear. It makes constructive use of external criteria and abandons redactional concerns in favor of literary ones. Its focus on the career (that is, "journey") of the Word of God lends coherence to the whole. The focus on the geographical journeys of Jesus is also an advance over analyses of the structure of the Gospel that are based on repetitive or chiastic features, since the journeys are related to the genre of the Gospel (a *bios*), its mode (narrative), and its *mythos* (the journey of the Word of God who descends and then returns to the Father).[25] Moreover, it relates the plot of the Gospel to its structure without losing sight of either generic or plot considerations. Its weakness is that it fails to develop either the underlying conflict in the Gospel (the conflict between belief and unbelief as responses to the revelation of the Word) or John's distinctive use of the *anagorisis* as a motif drawn from Greek drama.

Mark W. G. Stibbe's recent work moves beyond his earlier concentration on John as tragedy without abandoning it. First, Stibbe refutes the "common-sense theory of John's history-writing," namely that John merely reproduced his sources and therefore represents "an entirely objective account of historical realities."[26] Stibbe produces a revealing structural analysis of John's plot. The Father is the *sender*, who sends Jesus (the *subject*) to complete the work of bringing eternal life to the children of God (the *object*). It appears that Jesus has no *helpers* and numerous *opponents* (the Jews, chief priests, Caiaphas, Judas, Annas, the world, and the devil), but paradoxically, the forces of evil overreach their purposes and "contribute towards God's eternal plan."[27] John actually has both a main plot, "Jesus' quest to do the work of the Father," and a counter plot, "the quest of the Jews to destroy Jesus."[28] The counter plot, moreover, is a satirical parody of the main plot: the sender is the devil, who sends the Jews to kill Jesus. Jesus is the devil's opponent, and Judas is the devil's helper.[29]

The strength of Stibbe's analysis of John's plot is that he is eclectic in his analysis and recognizes that the Gospel is a plotted narrative. He recognizes further the presence of elements drawn from drama, biography, and theodicy, while agreeing with those who have shown that in genre the Gospels are biographies.

If our interest is in discerning the plot of the Gospel of John, the most obvious approach may be through the role of conflict in propelling the action toward the death of Jesus. The first chapter of John characterizes Jesus' mission in three ways: he will give authority to the "children of God" (v. 12), he will reveal the Father (v. 18), and he will "take away the sin of the world" (v. 29). Jesus will constitute a community, for whom he will be both Revealer and Redeemer. As the story unfolds, the Gospel relates the threats to the fulfillment of this mission and how Jesus fulfills his mission in spite of opposition (see John 19:30, "It is finished").

The primary conflict between characters is between "the Jews" (who appear to be the religious authorities) and Jesus. The conflict is introduced in the prologue (see John 1:10-12) and hinted at when John the Baptist is questioned (1:19-28) and again at the interrogation of Jesus in the temple (John 2). Nevertheless, there is little overt conflict in the first four chapters. In John 5, however, "the Jews" are introduced as a group seeking to kill Jesus because he violates the law.

**The Charges Against Jesus:
Sabbath Violation and Blasphemy**

Therefore the Jews started persecuting Jesus, because he was doing such things on the sabbath. But Jesus answered them, "My Father is still working, and I also am working." For this reason the Jews were seeking all the more to kill him, because he was not only breaking the sabbath, but was also calling God his own Father, thereby making himself equal to God. (John 5:16-18)

In chapters 5–12, the level of hostility against Jesus rises, leading ultimately to the plot to arrest him. Ironically, Jesus' enemies succeed in putting him to death, but his death is also "the hour" of his exaltation. In fact, his death is the means by which he fulfills his mission. From the cross he constitutes the nucleus of a new community in his mother and the Beloved Disciple, he reveals the Father (and hands over the Spirit), and dies as the Passover Lamb, delivering "his own" from sin.

The Gospel, therefore, tells a story that on one level ranges from "the beginning" to "the last day." It is focused, however, on the ministry of Jesus from the time of John's witness to him through his death and resurrection. The Gospel tells of the coming of Jesus as the Logos who reveals the Father, thereby evoking both belief and unbelief. The hostility toward Jesus is an expression of unbelief, so the contest throughout is between belief and unbelief. Each has its champion. The Father draws some to faith, while the devil is the father of those who oppose Jesus (8:44) and leads Judas to betray him (6:70-71; 13:2, 27).

The plot of the Gospel is also played out in each major episode. Every time Jesus encounters a new character he reveals something of his identity and calls the person to believe in him as the Revealer. The characters react variously; some believe while others do not. The conflict between belief and unbelief thus dominates the whole of the Gospel and infuses each of its parts. Each episode repeats the story of Jesus as the Revealer calling others to faith, while the varying responses allow us as the readers to consider the responses to Jesus that we might make. The disciples follow. Many in Jerusalem believe because of the signs, but Jesus does not trust himself to them (2:23-24). The Samaritan woman comes step by step to believe that Jesus is the Christ (4:1-42). The man at the pool of Bethesda is healed but seems not to be moved to believe (5:1-18), in contrast to the man born blind, who believes and is cast out of the synagogue (ch. 9). Progressively, the Gospel reveals the nature of faith and the causes and consequences of unbelief. The conclusion of the Gospel reports that "these things are written so that you may believe" (20:31, author's translation) and by that point the rhetorical design of the narrative has prepared the reader to respond with faith.

John's plot is related to its genre and structure. As the foregoing discussion has shown, John's plot derives from both internal

70

factors (causality; conflict between belief and unbelief as responses to Jesus) and external factors (which are conditioned by its genre). The Gospel contains elements of drama (especially its use of recognition scenes) and biography (a depiction of "the essence" of the hero through a narrative of his origins, public work, and death). Also, John structures the ministry of Jesus around his journeys. As a biography, John reflects both the form of Greek drama and the content of the Moses stories and the Elijah-Elisha cycle. One of John's distinguishing features is its depiction of Jesus as the Revealer and the various responses to him in a narrative that draws the reader to affirm the narrator's perception of Jesus' identity through a series of episodes that describe attempted, failed, and occasionally successful *anagnoriseis* (recognition scenes).

It is scarcely possible to take up the question of plot without recalling Bultmann's influence on the way in which we understand the Gospel and its leading themes. "The theme of the whole Gospel of John," Bultmann asserted, "is the statement: 'The word became flesh.' "[30] Each person who encounters the Revealer is then faced with "the decisive question whether he will accept or reject him."[31] The difficulty is that "the divinity of the figure of Jesus in John is completely lacking in visibility,"[32] and "the Revealer appears as a man whose claim to be the Son of God is one which he cannot, indeed, must not, prove to the world."[33] The plot of the Gospel, therefore, revolves around the question of how the world, the religious authorities, and the disciples respond to Jesus' claims.[34] Who will recognize that Jesus is the Word become flesh, and how do they come to perceive his true identity?

Bultmann's interpretation of the distinctive way in which John portrays Jesus as the Revealer, with its correlative question regarding how each of the persons he encounters will respond to him, is instructive for understanding the plot of the Gospel because the Gospel is constructed around a series of recognition (or nonrecognition) scenes. Belief and unbelief, recognition or nonrecognition of Jesus as the Revealer, is the fundamental opposition on which the plot is developed. The Gospel has taken the element of the recognition scene in drama and used it as a recurring type-scene in the Gospel. It occurs not merely as the climactic scene near the end of the story, but throughout the Gospel.

71

Anagnorisis as a Type Scene

A favorite device of ancient drama was to give the audience information that the characters on stage did not have. Drama and irony were heightened by allowing the audience to watch one or more of the characters act in ignorance of the true identity of the hero or another of the characters. Aristotle described this device and suggested some of its varieties in his *Poetics*.

Aristotle's Definition of Recognition

Recognition is, as its name indicates, a change from ignorance to knowledge, tending either to affection or to enmity; it determines in the direction of good or ill fortune the fates of the people involved. (*Poetics* 1452a)[35]

The three parts of Aristotle's definition lead us further into the functions of recognition. In its simplest form, a recognition scene narrates a character's discovery of the true identity of another principal figure in the narrative. The discovery typically occurs in the denouement and resolves the dramatic irony that has built as the reader or audience watched the character act in ignorance of the other figure's true identity. Aristotle observed, second, that the recognition typically changed the relationship between the two characters, "tending either to affection or enmity." Third, the recognition and the change in relationship determined "the fates of the people involved." These characteristics of recognition scenes in ancient literature have obvious relevance to the Gospel of John.

Artistotle also commented on the artistry of various types of recognition. The least artistic species of recognition is "recognition by visible signs," while the best kind is "that which arises from the actions alone" (*Poetics* 1454b-1455a). As Aristotle noted, recognition scenes take a variety of forms, and it will be helpful to analyze the varieties of *anagnorisis* or recognition in ancient literature further before proceeding to discuss their function in the Gospel of John.

For convenience, we may call the two characters the *recognizer* and the *recognized*. Common elements include the recognizer's ignorance or false assumptions, which may be reported by the narrator, depicted by actions or speech, or left implicit. At some point, the recognizer learns the true identity of the recognized.

The recognizer typically declares, announces, or confesses the recognized's identity. The recognized may then confirm the recognition or offer a proof. As Artistotle observed, the recognition changes the relationship between the two and the fate of the recognizer or of both characters.

Recognition scenes also fall somewhere on a spectrum based on whether the recognized's identity is disclosed or discovered. Does the recognized actively reveal or disclose his or her identity? Or does the recognizer discover the other's identity? If the recognized reveals his identity, the recognizer is likely to be less astute or assertive. Initiative lies with the "revealer," who may issue a claim or self-disclosure ("I am ... "), perform a characteristic action, or offer a proof of identity.

If the recognized's true identity is discovered rather than revealed, the initiative shifts. The discoverer, by definition, is more astute and assertive. The discovery may occur through looking closely, observing a pattern of actions, finding an article of clothing or personal effects, rational deduction, or catching the recognized in a revealing moment or action.

We may also distinguish three levels of subtlety or complexity in recognition scenes. On the first level the recognizer learns the identity of the recognized. In order to be significant the recognition requires some narrative context in which action turns on the recognition. For example, the recognition may resolve a mystery, confirm some wondrous occurrence, or lead to other discoveries or reassessments.

At this point we move to a second level: when the recognizer also recognizes the implication of the recognition. For example, in Luke's account of the miraculous catch of fish, Peter not only implicitly recognizes Jesus' divine power, but pleads, "Go away from me, Lord, for I am a sinful man" (Luke 5:8).

The recognition may also function on a third level, in which the reader or audience recognizes the implied author's implicit purpose, aim, or intent in the recognition scene. The recognition scene then changes not only the recognizer (character in the narrative) but also the reader, who has become a metanarratival recognizer, and who may or may not then also recognize the implication of his or her recognition. Some examples will clarify this taxonomy of recognition scenes before we turn to the function of *anagnorisis* in the Fourth Gospel.

In Aristophanes' *Plutus,* Cario and Chremylus do not recognize the god Wealth until he finally says, "Then listen, both: for I, it seems, must needs reveal the secret I proposed to keep. Know then, I'm Wealth!" Chremylus persists, "Are you really he?" and Wealth declares, "I am." Later, Cario says they had thought he was "a disgusting old fellow, all bent and wrinkled, with a most pitiful appearance, bald and toothless; upon my word, I even believe he is circumcised like some vile barbarian" (lines 265-267).[36] The classic case of nonrecognition in Greek tragedy is Sophocles' Oedipus, who step by step discovers that he has killed Laius, his real father, and taken his real mother as his queen.

The full dramatic power of the motif of nonrecognition followed by an *anagnorisis* is exploited in Euripides' *Bacchae.* In the opening scene Dionysus, the son of Zeus and a human woman, returns to the land of Thebes, the land where he was born; he is a god incognito, disguised as a man. Pentheus, the new king of Thebes, has neglected the worship of Dionysus. Neglecting prophetic warnings, Pentheus commands his servants to arrest the effeminate Dionysus. Dionysus, however, persuades Pentheus to dress in a woman's robe so that he can go out and observe the Bacchic rites occurring outside the city. Pentheus goes and is eventually torn to pieces lest he divulge the secrets of the religion of the women's god. Pentheus pulls aside his disguise, but Agave, his own mother, seized by the power of the god, dismembers him and takes his head back to Thebes thinking it is a lion's head. Soon enough she discovers what she has done.

The Recognition Scene in Euripides' *Bacchae*

Cadmus: What head is that thou barest in thy arms?
Agave: A lion's; at least they said so, who hunted it.
Cadmus: Consider it aright; 'tis no great task to look at it.
Agave: Ah! What do I see? What is this I am carrying in my hands?
Cadmus: Look closely at it; make thy knowledge more certain.
Agave: Ah, woe is me! O sight of awful sorrow!
Cadmus: Dost think it like a lion's head?
Agave: Ah no! 'tis Pentheus' head which I his unhappy mother hold.
Cadmus: Bemoaned by me, or ever thou didst recognize him.
Agave: Who slew him? How came he into my hands?
Cadmus: O piteous truth! how ill-timed thy presence here!
Agave: Speak; my bosom throbs at this suspense.

Cadmus: 'Twas thou didst slay him, thou and thy sisters.

. . . .

Cadmus: Ye were distraught; the whole city had the Bacchic frenzy.
Agave: 'Twas Dionysus proved our ruin; now I see it all.
Cadmus: Yes, for the slight he suffered; ye would not believe in his godhead.[37]

When Agave pleads for mercy from Dionysus, he replies "Too late have ye learnt to know me; ye knew me not at the proper time" (line 1347). Euripides' pointed critique of the Bacchic rites turns therefore on the failure to recognize Dionysus and the tragic recognition, too late, of the identity of both Pentheus and Dionysus.

Agave recognizes the head of Pentheus only when Cadmus prompts her to examine it closely. Then, even having recognized it, she fails to grasp the implication (that she herself had killed him) until Cadmus tells her what happened. Nevertheless, Agave grasps the deeper implication, no doubt the one that the implied author hopes the audience will also grasp: "'Twas Dionysus proved our ruin; *now I see it all.*"

The first level of this recognition scene is Agave's recognition that the head she is carrying is that of Pentheus and that she herself had killed him. The second level is the recognition that this tragedy occurred because they failed to recognize Dionysus and were carried away by the Bacchic rites. This second level mirrors in the story Euripedes' critique of the cult of Bacchus, the recognition of which is the intended third (and meta) level of the *anagnorisis*. It is too late for Agave to recognize Dionysus, but it is not too late for the audience.

The motif of nonrecognition and subsequent *anagnorisis* can be found in the Old Testament and the apocryphal narratives as well. Abraham extended hospitality to the Lord when he was visited by three strangers near the oaks of Mamre (Gen 18). Years later, the Lord appeared to Gideon under the oak at Ophrah, but Gideon did not recognize the one who challenged him to deliver his people from the hand of Midian (Judg 6:11-24). An angel of the Lord also appeared to the wife of Manoah, but she thought he was "a man of God" until the angel ascended in the flame of a fire on an altar (Judg 13:3-20): "Then Manoah realized that it was the angel of the LORD" (Judg 13:21; cf. Heb 13:2).

An *anagnorisis* of a different kind functions dramatically in Nathan's parable of the man who took his poor neighbor's lamb. When he heard the story, David responded, "As the Lord lives, the man who has done this deserves to die" (2 Sam 12:5). Nathan then unmasked both the parable and the king: "You are the man!" Recognizing his treachery, David responds by pleading, "I have sinned against the Lord" (2 Sam 12:13)—a second level *anagnorisis*. The function of the *anagnorisis* here is not unlike that of the unmasking of the patriarch's abuse of Tamar in Genesis 38. When Judah declared that Tamar was to be burned, she sent a signet, cord, and staff to Judah, saying that the owner of these personal items was the father of her child: "Then Judah acknowledged them and said, 'She is more righteous than I'" (Gen 38:26 RSV).

In Tobit, Raphael, the angel, accompanies Tobias on his travels, but Tobias does not recognize Raphael (Tobit 5:4-5). Ironically, Tobit sends them off saying to Tobias, "Go with this man; God who dwells in heaven will prosper your way, and may his angel attend you" (Tobit 5:16 RSV). After Tobias has completed his mission, Raphael reveals his identity to Tobit and Tobias, saying that God had sent him because of Tobit's good deeds. He continues:

> "All these days I merely appeared to you and did not eat or drink, but you were seeing a vision. And now give thanks to God, for I am ascending to him who sent me. Write in a book everything that has happened." Then he stood up; but they saw him no more. (Tobit 12:19-21 RSV)

The classic examples of nonrecognition in the Gospels are found in Luke and John (the Johannine examples will be treated below).[38] In Luke 24, the risen Lord walks with two of his disciples on the road to Emmaus, but they do not recognize him until he breaks bread. In this instance the *anagnorisis* underscores the point that Jesus' followers continue to meet him in the context of the breaking of bread and the opening of scripture.

Although these are only a selection of recognition scenes from ancient Greco-Roman, biblical, and apocryphal literature, they are sufficient to establish that recognition scenes can be found in drama, patriarchal narratives, parables, and folktales. In both the Greek tragedies and in the Old Testament and apocryphal writings, the recognition scenes often occur at the unveiling of a divine or angelic being. They resolve the plot that revolves around the question of when and how the characters will recognize the divine or angelic being that has appeared to them in human form.

Recognition Scenes in John

The Gospel of John has taken the *anagnorisis* and developed it as a recurring type scene, not just at the end of the Gospel, but throughout. The narrative is composed of a succession of recognition scenes, partial recognitions, and failed efforts to recognize Jesus, as the following synopsis of the Gospel makes clear.[39]

JESUS' ORIGINS, JOHN 1

The prologue provides the reader with initial, reliable exposition of the identity of Jesus.[40] We are told that Jesus is the Word, the true light, the Word that became flesh, and the only Son from the Father. Verses 9-13 (and verses 6-18 more broadly) serve as an initial plot summary. The true light comes into the world, but the world does not recognize him. He comes to his own people, but his own do not receive him. Nevertheless, those who believe in his name are empowered to become "children of God." As the Gospel story unfolds, Jesus' identity will be confirmed for the reader by reports of both what Jesus does and what Jesus says: his works and his words. There should be no question about who Jesus is as one reads the rest of the Gospel. Rather, the reader watches, much like the audience of an ancient tragedy, as others in the Gospel story act in ignorance of Jesus' true identity and strive to discern who he is. All the while the Gospel challenges the reader to respond in faith to the disclosure that Jesus is the Revealer.

The narrative of Jesus' work as the Word incarnate systematically confirms the information given to the reader in the prologue. The first chapter contains three recognition scenes: John the Baptist, Andrew, and Nathanael. The story opens with the question posed to John by those sent by the priests and Levites: "Who are you?" (1:19). In the verses that follow, John declares, "Here is the Lamb of God who takes away the sin of the world!" (1:29). His recognition of Jesus is possible because the One who sent him to baptize had told him that the one on whom the Spirit descended and remained would be the one who would baptize with the Holy Spirit. John baptized as he had been sent to do, he saw, and he bore witness (1:31-34).

The second recognition scene begins with John's pointing to Jesus and again announcing, "Look, here is the Lamb of God!" (1:36), and culminates with one of his two disciples, Andrew, finding his brother and saying, "We have found the Messiah" (1:41). In this instance Jesus does no sign, nor is there a visible manifestation of the Spirit. Instead, Jesus challenges the disciples and invites them to believe by means of language that is rich with double meanings, and they "remained with him that day" (1:39).

In the third recognition scene Philip substitutes for Andrew and reports to Nathanael, "We have found him about whom Moses in the law and also the prophets wrote" (1:45). Nathanael at first doubts the report, thinking that nothing good could come from Nazareth. When he comes to see Jesus for himself, Jesus calls him an Israelite in whom there is no guile and says he saw him before Philip called him. Nathanael confesses, "Rabbi, you are the Son of God! You are the King of Israel!" (1:49).

JESUS' PUBLIC MINISTRY, JOHN 2–12

The first journey cycle begins in John 1:43, when Jesus goes to Galilee. John 2 narrates the first of Jesus' signs, at the wedding at Cana. The narrator reports that the sign "revealed his glory," and then reports that "his disciples believed in him" (2:11). By changing water to wine, Jesus had done what only the Word through whom "all things came into being" (1:3) could do. The sign, therefore, serves to confirm for the reader the truth of what the narrator said about Jesus in the prologue. The disciples do not speak their confession, however, because their confessions are reserved for later in the story and because while they believe, the rest of the story will show that there is still much they do not understand about who Jesus is. Much of the Gospel story is therefore devoted to the disciples' struggle to understand more about the one in whom they believed as a result of the signs that Jesus did.

The first journey to Jerusalem is reported in John 2:13, at the time of the first Passover mentioned in the Gospel. The skepticism of Nathanael grows to the first challenge to Jesus' activity. When Jesus confronts the money changers in the Temple, the authorities fail to recognize who he is. Many others "believed in his name because they saw the signs that he was doing," but their lack of understanding is underscored by the narrator's report that in spite of their belief Jesus "would not entrust himself to them" (2:23-24). The narrator's summaries at the end of the wedding at Cana and the confrontation of the money changers serve to open questions about the nature of belief, the basis for belief, and relation of belief to the recognition of Jesus as the Word made flesh.

Nicodemus represents those who believe because of the signs but still do not recognize Jesus as the Revealer. He says, "Rabbi, we know that you are a teacher who has come from God" (3:2), but he cannot grasp the revelation in Jesus because he is from below. To recognize Jesus, he must be born from above. The conversation with Nicodemus is therefore a failed *anagnorisis*. It has become evident, however, that the sequence of scenes—each of which focuses on the question of Jesus' identity and how the character in the scene will respond to Jesus—leads the reader ever deeper into the mysteries of revelation, Christology, and faith. If believing in Jesus' name (cf. 1:12) because of the signs is not adequate, and if recognizing that Jesus is "a teacher who has come from God" is not acceptable, what constitutes an acceptable response? The rest of chapter 3 completes John's testimony to Jesus and reinforces themes introduced in the prologue. It develops the characterization of Jesus as the only Son (3:16), the light (3:19), the bridegroom (3:29), and the one from above (3:31).

The second journey to Galilee serves as the occasion for Jesus' conversation with the Samaritan woman (4:1-42) and the second sign—the healing of the royal official's son (4:46-54). The conversation with the woman at the well is set up as a recognition scene by Jesus' challenge: "If you knew ... who it is that is saying to you, 'Give me a drink,' you would have asked him, and he would have given you living water" (4:10). In the course of the conversation that follows, the woman comes step by step to see who Jesus is and to share her recognition with the rest of the town: "you, a Jew" (4:9); "Sir" (4:11); "Sir, I see that you are a prophet" (4:19). Then, after Jesus says, "I am he" (that is, the Messiah who will proclaim all things), the woman returns to the city, saying, "Come and see a man who told me everything I have ever done! He cannot be the Messiah, can he?" (4:29), and many believe in Jesus because of her and say, "We know that this is truly the Savior of the world" (4:42).

Similarly, a recognition of a kind takes place in the healing of the nobleman's son at the end of John 4: "The father realized that this was the hour when Jesus had said to him, 'Your son will live.' So he himself believed, along with his whole household" (4:53). The second sign underscores the link between believing and having life. The royal official believes Jesus, and his son lives.

Jesus' second journey to Jerusalem (John 5) is the setting for the first real opposition to Jesus. The healing of the man at the pool of Bethesda fails to produce an *anagnorisis*.[41] In this instance, the man does not ask to be healed or affirm that he wants to be made well when Jesus persists. The man is made well, and then he gets up. When the healing is confirmed by the interrogation of the *Ioudaioi* ("the Jews"), the man does not know who healed him. Later, when Jesus finds him again, the man reports Jesus to the *Ioudaioi,* and they begin to persecute Jesus. This sign fails to produce an *anagnorisis* and instead mobilizes the opposition against Jesus. In a sense, the trial of Jesus occurs throughout his ministry. In John 5, Jesus calls as witnesses John, the works he does, the Father, the scriptures, and even Moses.

The third and final journey to Galilee occurs during the second Passover in the Gospel. At the beginning of John 6, the crowds are following Jesus because of the signs that he has been doing. At Passover, when many were going to Jerusalem to commemorate the Exodus and Moses' feeding of the people in the wilderness, Jesus feeds the multitude. When the people witness the multiplication of the loaves, they respond, "This is indeed the prophet who is to come into the world" (6:14). John shows that this is only a partial *anagnorisis* because immediately thereafter the people come to force Jesus to be their king, and he withdraws to the mountain.

In the epiphany on the sea, Jesus again makes himself known to the disciples: "It is I; do not be afraid" (6:20). The dialogue that follows further clarifies Jesus' identity as the prophet like Moses and the Bread of Life, but the people turn away from him. Just as their ancestors murmured against Moses in the wilderness, the people "murmur" against Jesus and fail to recognize who he is: "Is not this Jesus, the son of Joseph, whose father and mother we know?" (6:42). They cannot recognize who Jesus is because they have not been drawn by the Father (6:44). At the end of the chapter Jesus is left with only the Twelve, and one of them will betray him. It is another failed *anagnorisis,* except that Peter, speaking for the Twelve, says, "You have the words of eternal life. We have come to believe and know that you are the Holy One of God" (6:68-69). Peter is at least moving toward a full *anagnorisis,* but later scenes in the Gospel show that he still has a long way to go. Jesus knows, also, that Judas will betray him.

Although "the Jews" in Jerusalem are seeking to kill Jesus, he goes up again to Jerusalem in chapter 7 for the festival of Booths (the third journey to Jerusalem; 7:10, 14). Jesus' brothers challenge Jesus to go up to Jerusalem to show himself to the world, "for no one who wants to be widely known acts in secret" (7:4). When Jesus does go to Jerusalem, the people debate among themselves about his identity: "While some were saying, 'He is a good man,' others were saying, 'No, he is deceiving the crowd'" (7:12). They ask if Jesus is not the man whom the authorities were seeking to kill (7:25), and ask whether perhaps they know that Jesus is the Christ after all (7:26). They claim to know where Jesus comes from and therefore conclude that he cannot be the Christ (7:27). Jesus challenges their mistaken *anagnorisis:* "You know me, and you know where I come from?" (7:28 RSV). Again the people are divided, some claiming that he was really the prophet or the Christ, but others objecting that he came from Galilee (7:40-44).

The debate in the Temple treasury opens with Jesus' declaration that the people have failed to recognize him: "You know neither me nor my Father. If you knew me, you would know my Father also" (8:19). When Jesus challenges the people further, they ask, "Who are you?" (8:25). But they will not know who he is until he has been lifted up (8:28). The debate that follows reveals that the people do not recognize either their own father or Jesus' father. They claim that Abraham is their father, but Jesus responds that because they seek to kill him their real father is the devil. The *Ioudaioi* respond that Jesus is a Samaritan (8:48) and has a demon (8:48, 52)—again they fail to recognize who he is. Jesus knows his Father, however, while the *Ioudaioi* do not. At the end of the debate Jesus' opponents take up stones against him (8:59), which constitutes another failed *anagnorisis* that further clarifies for the reader both Jesus' identity and the opposition against him.

81

In John 9, Jesus, the light of the world (9:5), gives sight to a man born blind. First the neighbors must establish the identity of the blind man (9:8-9, 18-20). The questions then are who healed him and how the granting of sight occurred. The interrogators assume Jesus is a sinner (9:16, 24); the man says he is a prophet (9:17). They do not know where Jesus comes from (9:29); the man only knows that Jesus opened his eyes. When Jesus finds him again, challenges him to believe in "the Son of Man," and then announces, "You have seen him" (9:37), the man accepts Jesus' self-identification: "Lord, I believe" (9:38). The man sees, while the Pharisees have their blindness exposed. The story of the blind man and the Pharisees, therefore, interprets what is involved in an *anagnorisis* and why some fail to recognize Jesus.

In chapter 10, by means of the allegory of the shepherd and the sheep, Jesus further images his role and characterizes his opponents as hirelings, robbers, and wolves. In contrast, Jesus is the good shepherd who calls his sheep by name and lays down his life for his sheep. "The Jews" are divided further; some oppose him, while others say that his works are not the works of one possessed by a demon. They challenge him to tell them who he is: "If you are the Messiah, tell us plainly" (10:24). But Jesus has told them, and they have not believed. Only those who are his sheep will hear his voice. Again, therefore, there is no *anagnorisis*, and they seek to arrest him.

By now it is winter, the time of the festival of the Dedication (Hanukkah; 10:22), and Jesus is still in Jerusalem. As at other festivals, Jesus does a sign or says something that demonstrates that he is the fulfillment of that to which the festival pointed. In this case, he is the fulfillment of the presence of the glory of God (the Shekinah) with God's people. He and the Father are one (10:30). For this presumed blasphemy the people again take up stones against Jesus, and he withdraws across the Jordan.

John 11 and 12 are pivotal chapters that bring to a climax the mighty works of Jesus and set the stage for his death. At the request of Mary and Martha, Jesus returns to Judea, to Bethany, to raise Lazarus from the grave. Just as the Word came into the world to give life to those who would receive him, so Jesus returns to Jerusalem to give life to his friend, knowing that it will cost him his own life. The scene turns once again into an *anagnorisis* when Jesus claims, "I am the resurrection and the life"

(11:25), and Martha responds, "Yes, Lord, I believe that you are the Messiah, the Son of God, the one coming into the world" (11:27). As a result of the raising of Lazarus, many of the *Ioudaioi* believe in Jesus, but some go and tell the Pharisees what Jesus has done. The giving of life, paradoxically and poignantly, becomes the impetus for Jesus' death. Some of the Jews believe; others go to the authorities. Caiaphas judges that it is better for Jesus to die than for the whole nation to perish (11:50), and the narrator comments that as high priest Caiaphas prophesies that Jesus must die, but he does so not knowing Jesus' true identity (11:51).

Jesus withdraws to Ephraim (11:54), and the authorities begin to search for him in order to arrest him. At Jesus' entry into Jerusalem, the crowd hails him as "the King of Israel" (12:13), but even his disciples do not understand what he is doing until after Jesus is exalted (12:16). No declaration of Jesus' identity prior to his being lifted up, his death and resurrection, could be a full *anagnorisis*. After Mary anoints Jesus, who says that it is "for the day of my burial" (12:7), Jesus speaks of his being "lifted up" (12:32; cf. 3:14; 8:28)—an allusion to his death. When the Greeks come seeking to see Jesus, it is a sign to him that his hour has come. The public ministry of Jesus ends at the conclusion of John 12, therefore, with the lament that the light has come, but the people have been blind to it.

JESUS' FAREWELL DISCOURSE, JOHN 13-17

John 13–17 contains Jesus' farewell address to his followers, a type-scene found in both Jewish and Graeco-Roman literature.[42] The foot washing scene in John 13 begins with the narrator's report of Jesus' knowledge that his hour had come to depart to his Father and that the devil had already decided that Judas should betray Jesus. Because the disciples do not have this knowledge, the story that follows revolves around Jesus' act of foreshadowing the meaning of his death by washing their feet.[43] None of the disciples grasps the meaning of Jesus' act at that time. Peter, who is not prepared to die with Jesus, resists having his feet washed, and Judas goes out to betray Jesus. The failure to recognize Jesus has become tragic.

The farewell discourse takes up related motifs at various points. Thomas confesses that they do not know where Jesus is going (14:5), and Philip pleads, "Lord, show us the Father, and we will be satisfied" (14:8). Jesus' answer, "Have I been with you all this time, Philip, and you still do not know me?" (14:9). Both Jesus' words and his works reveal his true identity (14:10-11). By the end of the discourse, the disciples think they know that Jesus came from God (16:30), but when his hour comes they will be scattered (16:32).

JESUS' DEATH AND RESURRECTION, JOHN 18-21

The revelatory motif continues in John's account of the arrest, trial, and death of Jesus. The soldiers who come to arrest Jesus do not know him either. Jesus asks them, "Whom are you looking for?" They answer, "Jesus of Nazareth," but when Jesus says *ego eimi* ("I am" or "I am he") they all fall back on the ground (18:4-6). The scene is repeated a second time for emphasis (18 :7-8). Then, because he has failed to recognize the necessity of Jesus' death, Peter denies Jesus three times, saying *ouk eimi* ("I am not [his disciple]"; 18:17, 25, 27). All the while, Jesus is asserting that he has done nothing in secret (18:20).

The trial before Pilate in John is a report of Pilate's effort to ascertain who Jesus is. Jesus is brought to Pilate as "an evildoer" (18:30). The interrogation opens with Pilate asking Jesus, "Are you the King of the Jews?" (18:33). In the seven scenes of the Johannine trial narrative, Pilate pronounces Jesus innocent three times, calls Jesus "the King of the Jews" in mockery (18:39), and presents him to the crowd wearing a crown of thorns and a purple robe. Pilate is "more afraid than ever" when the *Ioudaioi* say that Jesus has made himself "the Son of God" (19:7-8). At the end, Pilate says, "Here is your King!" (19:14), and then writes the inscription which may not be changed, "The King of the Jews" (19:19-22). Pilate knew more of Jesus' identity than he was able to confess. The trial and the inscription, therefore, represent yet another failed *anagnorisis* that once again depicts the true identity of Jesus for the reader.

The events that surround the death of Jesus continue to unfold and underscore his identity as the Word incarnate. Jesus provides care for his mother and the Beloved Disciple, and scripture is fulfilled in the casting of lots for his garments and in the piercing of his side. His dying words are "It is finished" (19:30); his mission is completed.

Four recognition scenes occur in the last two chapters of the Gospel: The Beloved Disciple (20:3-10); Mary Magdalene (20:1-2, 11-18), Thomas (20:24-29), and the Beloved Disciple (21:1-14). The narrator's report that the Beloved Disciple "saw and believed" (20:8) is peculiar in that it is the only confession or report of recognition in the Gospel at which Jesus is not present. The story opens with Mary Magdalene's repeated lament that she does not know where they have taken Jesus (20:2; cf. 20:13, 15).[44] It may be argued that this scene should not be listed among the Johannine *anagnoriseis,* if one is convinced that John 20:8 reports only the confirmation that the tomb was empty or that the body had been removed. On the other hand, if the narrator is reporting that seeing the grave wrappings led the Beloved Disciple to believe that Jesus had been raised from the dead, then that report implies recognition of something that for John is vital to Jesus' identity: "I came from the Father and have come into the world; again, I am leaving the world and am going to the Father" (16:28; cf. 13:1). Recognizing where Jesus had gone is as important in John as recognizing where he had come from.

Mary Magdalene's recognition of Jesus develops dramatically. The reader is told that Jesus, now risen, has appeared to Mary but that she did not recognize him (20:14). Jesus spoke to her, but again, the narrator tells us, Mary supposed that he was the gardener (20:15). Only when he calls her by name (cf. 10:3) does she turn and exclaim "Rabbouni!" (20:16).[45]

Thomas's confession "My Lord and my God!" (20:28) stands in a climactic position. The resurrection of Jesus has already been reported, as has his commissioning of the disciples. Thomas, who was not present, declares that he will not believe unless he too sees the risen Lord and touches him (20:25). When Jesus appears again a week later, he invites Thomas to do just what Thomas had said he would have to do in order to believe: "Put your finger here and see my hands. Reach out your hand and put it in my side. Do not doubt but believe" (20:27). The confession that follows affirms Jesus' Lordship and divinity. Jesus' response returns the emphasis to seeing rather than touching, and he pronounces a beatitude on those who, unlike Thomas, would believe without having seen.

The story of the great catch of fish in John 21 is also constructed as an *anagnorisis.* The disciples have returned to fishing, but they catch nothing. At daybreak Jesus stands on the beach, but again we are told that the disciples do not recognize him (21:4). As in the previous recognition scenes, the story turns on whether, when, and how the disciples will recognize Jesus. When they follow Jesus' directions and enclose a great catch, the Beloved Disciple tells Peter, "It is the Lord!" (21:7). Peter is appointed as a shepherd, who like his master will lay down his life (21:15-19), and the Beloved Disciple bears witness to the things written in the Gospel: "We know that his testimony is true" (21:24).

The Gospel of John, therefore, is an ancient biography in dramatic form. Based on the pattern of Wisdom's descent and return, it tells the story of Jesus as the Word incarnate who fulfills the Father's commission to reveal the Father, take away the sin of the world, and empower the "children of God." The authorities put Jesus to death, but paradoxically Jesus' death is the hour of his fulfillment of his mission. The repetition of recognition scenes throughout the Gospel and the role that they play in the larger theme of Jesus as the unrecognized Revealer suggest that the Evangelist has taken the *anagnorisis*, a plot motif that was common in Jewish literature and Greek drama, and used it as one of the central elements in the plot of the Gospel. Jesus, the Revealer from above, has entered human experience as a man. Those who recognize him are the children of God and share in his eternal life (17:3; 20:30-31).

CHAPTER 5

THE THEOLOGY OF THE JOHANNINE WRITINGS

T he influence of the Gospel of John on Christian theology—both orthodox and heretical—can hardly be measured. Evidence of its popularity among the second-century Valentinian Gnostics is provided by Heracleon's commentary on the Gospel, the first commentary ever written on a Gospel.[1] Even before Irenaeus's spirited defense of the Gospel against its appropriation by the Gnostics, however, John was esteemed by the church. There are echoes or allusions to John in several second-century church fathers, and the Montanists based their doctrine on John's words about the Paraclete.

The Gospel of John continued to influence the development of Christian theology during the Arian controversy and the debates over the nature of Christ. Clement of Alexandria tagged John with a description that still rings true; he called it "a spiritual gospel."[2] It is no exaggeration to say that the Gospel of John exerted a greater influence on the church's Christology, and its theology in general, than any other Gospel.

The Influence of John's Theology

Jaroslav Pelikan: "By the fourth century it had become evident that of all the various 'titles of majesty for Christ' adapted and adopted during the first generations after Jesus, none was to have more momentous consequences than the title Logos, consequences as momentous for the history of thought as were those of the title King for the history of politics."[3]

The Gospel of John is not a systematic theology, however. It is a Gospel narrative, recounting and interpreting the ministry of Jesus. One who is interested in understanding the theology of this Gospel must, therefore, confront the issue of method: How can we extract a system of thought from a narrative? Where do we find its theology?

Rather than coming to the Gospel and finding a set of theological propositions, we participate in a revelatory process as we read it.[4] Our interpretation of the theology of the Gospel then arises from our effort to make sense of what we have experienced while reading it. Theology is our effort to bring sense and order to the affirmations and responses to which the Gospel leads us. Sensitivity to the narrative form of the Gospel is therefore essential. Individual passages must be considered in context, in sequence, and as facets of a narrative rhetoric. The Gospel leads readers to a response of faith that is shaped by the way the story is told.

In the process, theological affirmations are made. Some of these affirmations are implicit, and others are quite contradictory, so the task of sorting them out is thrust on the reader. Consider, for example, the challenge of the following pair of verses on the relationship of Jesus to the Father:

"The Father and I are one." (10:30)
"The Father is greater than I." (14:28)

Similar, though less sharply stated, tensions appear in John regarding the value of Baptism and the Lord's Supper and regarding present and future fulfillment of eschatological hopes. John affirms traditional theological formulations, yet leads the reader to consider new and distinctively Johannine insights.

Jesus, the Christ, the Word, the Son of God, dominates the Gospel of John. The Gospel is thoroughly Christological. It is structured so as to bring the reader into an intimate confrontation with Jesus, to which the reader will respond with faith. The Gospel, therefore, interprets who Jesus is, in scene after scene, by means of the plot and the narration. All other aspects of the theology it presents are secondary to its Christology. The reader's response to John's eschatology, its sacramentalism, or its ecclesiology is not essential. Distinctive perspectives on each of these are conveyed by the Gospel, but in the end all that really matters is that the reader "believe that Jesus is the Messiah, the Son of God" (20:31).

The bumper sticker that declares "Jesus is the answer" is not wrong. It just does not tell us what Jesus is an answer to. The role of Jesus is bound up with the human condition apart from God. Jesus provides a solution to that human condition; therefore, how one understands that condition determines in large measure how Jesus' role will be understood. We will begin with John's depiction of the human condition apart from God, then consider in sequence the revelation in Christ, the experience of salvation, the model of the church, and the eschatology of the Gospel.

HUMANITY APART FROM GOD

One of the most distinctive characteristics of Johannine thought is its sharply defined dualism. Every category is accentuated by its opposite: good—evil, Christ—the devil, light—darkness, love—hate, and above—below. This is not an absolute dualism such as one finds in some ancient Near Eastern and oriental religious thought.[5] God is supreme and has no rival. The world, however, is under the power of "the ruler of this world" (12:31; 14:30; 16:11), who must be identified with the devil (8:44; 13:2; cf. 6:70) and Satan (13:27).

In John *the world* (Greek, *kosmos*) is used in both a neutral and a hostile sense. The Gospel refers to the world as the whole of the created order (1:9-10*a*). God loves the world (3:16). On the other hand, the world can represent all that has fallen under the power of evil and is opposed to God (1:10*b*; 7:7; 8:23; 1 John 2:15).[6] The natural condition of the world is darkness (1:5; 3:19) and sin. Jesus therefore comes as the light of the world (8:12; 9:5) and the "Lamb of God who takes away the sin of the world" (1:29, 36).

At this point we must ask about the nature of sin according to the Gospel of John.[7] The New Testament writings give different answers: Sin is disobedience and transgression of the Law, so for-giveness is required; sin is bondage to the power of evil that leads to death, so deliverance is needed; sin is a defilement that requires cleansing; sin is violation of a relationship, so the sinner needs to be reconciled; and sin incurs a debt, so restitution is required. How we understand the condition of the sinner deter-mines in large measure our understanding of Christ's saving work.

John speaks of both "sin" and "sins," but the former is more common. There is nothing like the Sermon on the Mount or a Pauline list of vices in John to specify what actions are sinful. The most revealing statement on sin in the Gospel describes one of the functions of the Paraclete:

> And when he comes, he will convince the world concerning sin and righteousness and judgment: concerning sin, because they do not believe in me ... (16:8-9 RSV)

Sin for John, therefore, is primarily unbelief. Sins result from unbelief and lead to judgment and death (8:21, 24). Sin enslaves a person (8:34). Sin is so closely tied to rejection of the revelation of God that Jesus can also say:

> If I had not come and spoken to them, they would not have sin; but now they have no excuse for their sin.... If I had not done among them the works that no one else did, they would not have sin. But now they have seen and hated both me and my Father. (15:22, 24)

These words are spoken as Jesus explains the world's persecution of the disciples (see 15:18-19). They force the question, how can Jesus be announced as the one who has come to take way "the sin of the world" (1:29, 36), if the world would have no sin if he had not come? It would be perverse, though, to say that sin is a conse-quence of revelation. The "Lamb of God who takes away the sin of the world" was probably a traditional formulation. The more distinctively Johannine interpretation is found in John 15:22, 24, and related passages. From this we see the conservatism of the Johannine tradition. It carried along traditional understandings while formulating new interpretations.

John's understanding of sin is further defined in the dialogue following the healing of the man born blind. The disciples asked,

"Rabbi, who sinned, this man or his parents, that he was born blind?" (9:2). The Greek particle *hina* ("so that") must introduce a result clause here. Obviously, no one sinned "in order that" he might be born blind. Jesus rejects the connection that was often drawn between sin and suffering (see 9:3-4, but see also 5:14). The ultimate result of the man's blindness is "that God's works might be revealed in him." The theological significance of this event is drawn out in the concluding verse of chapter 9, where Jesus responds to the Pharisees:

> If you were blind, you would not have sin *(hamartian)*. But now that you say, "We see," your sin *(hamartia)* remains. (9:41)

The Pharisees assumed that the man was a sinner because he was born blind. They also assumed they were righteous. The dramatic reversal of both of these assumptions illustrates that the blind man is an "every person" character; we are all born blind. We all need to receive our sight and see the light of the world, but only those who know they are blind can receive their sight. The world lies under the power of the evil one (1 John 5:19). John's distinctive emphasis, however, is that sin is, above all, willful unbelief. Sin does not consist in being born blind but in denying that we are blind and rejecting the revelation in Jesus Christ.[8]

Closely related to the analogy of blindness is the Gospel's use of darkness as a symbol for the human condition apart from God. Apart from God the world lies in darkness (1:5). Sin, however, involves love of the darkness. The light has shined, but some loved the darkness instead; their works were evil (3:19). Why do some reject the revelation? Their love is false: they love the darkness.[9] Yet, those who walk in darkness do not know where they are going. They stumble (12:35). Deliverance from the darkness comes by believing in Jesus: "I have come as light into the world, so that everyone who believes in me should not remain in the darkness" (12:46).

The second false love that characterizes sin is love of the glory of others rather than the glory of God (5:41). Believing requires seeking the glory of God, but belief is blocked when we seek glory from one another (5:44). This condition is illustrated by the leaders who believed but would not confess Jesus for fear that they would be put out of the synagogue (12:42-43). Those who seek glory from others, finally, are seeking to glorify themselves (see 7:18) not God (12:28). They cannot believe because belief is not intellectual assent to certain theological principles but an opening of oneself to the knowledge and glory of God revealed in Jesus.

The third false love that characterizes sin is loving one's own life rather than seeking eternal life: "Those who love their life lose it, and those who hate their life in this world will keep it for eternal life" (12:25). The person whose primary concern is amassing material goods and enjoying the pleasures of life cannot simultaneously lead a life of faith, a life centered in glorifying God. Sin and belief are therefore mutually exclusive. Each person must choose one or the other.

Sin also leads to death: "You will die in your sins unless you believe that I am he" (8:24). Those who ate bread in the wilderness died, but those who feast on Jesus will never die (6:58). John interprets the real meanings of death and life in the account of the raising of Lazarus. Death is like sleep (11:4, 11-14). One who believes is delivered from sin and death: "Those who believe in me, even though they die, will live, and everyone who lives and believes in me will never die" (11:25-26). Those who believe, therefore, have crossed from death into life (5:24; 1 John 3:14). Just as the man born blind is an every-person character, so the raising of Lazarus is a sign that points to the reality of the life that all believers share.

Sin, therefore, is defined by John primarily as the response of unbelief to the revelation of God in Christ. Sin is associated with darkness and characterized by false love and death. Jesus came to bring life to all who would respond to his revelation with belief. To these he gave authority to become children of God (1:12), and the Gospel itself serves the same redemptive purpose as the Incarnation: "But these are written so that you may come to believe that Jesus is the Messiah, the Son of God, and that through believing you may have life in his name" (20:31).

THE REVELATION IN CHRIST

The Christology of the Gospel of John is so multifaceted that only its four primary elements can be explored here: Jesus as Word, Revealer, Redeemer, and Son.[10]

92

Word

The Logos concept has rich associations in ancient thought, and its presence in both Greek and Jewish traditions needs to be recognized. The Stoics identified the Logos as the rational principle that gave order to the universe. In Jewish thought the Logos was closely associated with Wisdom. Both Greek and Jewish readers could therefore find meaning in the opening words of the Gospel.

The primary source of John's confession that Jesus was the Logos was probably reflection on the Wisdom tradition of Israel.[11] Over the centuries, Wisdom had been personified. She existed with God even before the world was created, and she was God's agent in creation (Prov 8:22-23; Sir 24:9; Wis 6:22). Wisdom was associated with light (Wisd 7:10, 26, 29) and descended from heaven to dwell on earth and reveal heavenly things (Prov 8:31; Sir 24:8; Wisd 9:10, 16-18). God's people are invited to eat and drink of Wisdom's bread and wine (Prov 9:5). By the first century, Wisdom was also associated with Torah, so when Jesus as the Word incarnate fulfills the Torah, his words and deeds confirm the confession that Jesus was the preexistent Logos. Jewish speculations regarding the nature of Wisdom seem, therefore, to have had a formative influence on John's Christology.

Logos is used as a title only in the prologue to the Gospel, but Jesus acts and speaks as the Logos throughout the Gospel. All things were created through the Logos, and Jesus continues to have power over the creation. For example, as the creative Logos incarnate he is able to change water to wine. An ancient poet commented with wit and perception: "the water recognized its creator, and blushed."[12] Jesus also multiplies bread and fish and walks on water (cf. Job 9:8; Ps 77:16, 19). Evoking the creation account in Genesis 2, John describes how Jesus makes clay and fashions eyes that see for a man born blind (9:6). Later he breathes the Holy Spirit into the disciples (20:22). He even brings to life a man who had been dead four days (11:38-44). In the Gospel of John, therefore, Jesus both acts and speaks as the Logos who has descended from above. He fulfills the Law, and he continues the creative, revelatory, and redemptive work of the Logos.

Revealer

The prologue ends with the assertion: "No one has ever seen God. It is God the only Son, who is close to the Father's heart, who has made him known" (1:18; cf. 5:37). Jesus' role is defined from the outset as that of revealing the Father. Throughout the prologue the emphasis falls on revelation rather than atonement. Jesus' mission as the revealer is itself redemptive. In him was life and light (1:4). He was the true light coming into the world (1:9). To those who received him he gave authority to become children of God (1:12). The community confesses: "We have seen his glory, the glory as of a father's only son" (1:14). Grace and truth have come through him (1:17). Jesus' mission was redemptive because he revealed the Father. Salvation, or eternal life, consists in coming to know God through this revelation and living in response to this knowledge of God (cf. 17:3). That, ultimately, is what it means to believe.

One of the anomalies in the study of Johannine theology is that so much is written about the Christology of the Gospel and so little about its *theo*logy. In part this anomaly reflects the paradox that

> Jesus' words never convey anything specific or concrete that he has seen with the Father. Not once does he communicate matters or events to which he had been a witness by either eye or ear. Never is the heavenly world the theme of his words.... His theme is always just this one thing: that the Father sent him, that he came as the light, the bread of life, witness for the truth, etc.; that he will go again, and that one must believe in him.[13]

Nils Dahl called God "the neglected factor" in New Testament theology.[14] What does the Gospel of John reveal about the nature of God? Whatever we say in response to this question must be inferred from what Jesus says and does.

As the revealer, Jesus does what he sees the Father doing (5:19, 30), and he says what the Father has taught him (8:28). As one sent by the Father—his emissary and his Son—he acts and speaks with the authority of the One who sent him. Both his signs and his words point beyond themselves, beyond Jesus, to the Father. They are the words and works of the One who sent Jesus. Whoever has seen Jesus, therefore, has seen the Father (12:45; 14:9).

Redeemer

Jesus' role as the Logos, the Revealer, is clearly redemptive in the sense that he brings life to those who believe and delivers them from bondage to sin. The children of Abraham thought they

94

were already free, but Jesus promised they would find real free-dom if they would abide in his word (8:31-32). Jesus freed persons from the "ruler of this world" (12:31; 14:30; 16:11). John retains the traditional language of sacrifice (1:29, 36) and neither omits nor denies the value of Jesus' redemptive death. Nevertheless, this Gospel translates the sacrificial imagery into an idiom more compatible with a Christology that features Jesus as the Logos, Wisdom incarnate, Jesus as the revealer. Disciples are cleansed by Jesus' word (15:3). Redemption takes place primarily through the response of faith in Jesus as the revealer. To those who come to the light, Jesus gives life; they are the real children of God.

Son

John uses "Son" (18 times), "Son of God" (9 times), and "Son of Man" (13 times) to describe Jesus. The occurrence of the title in 1:18 is uncertain because some of the best ancient manuscripts read "God" there rather than "Son." The title first appears, there-fore, either at the end of the prologue or in the testimony of John the Baptist: "I myself have seen and have testified that this is the Son of God" (1:34). Jesus is the only, the unique son (*mongenēs*; 1:14, 18; 3:16, 18).[15]

C. H. Dodd suggested that behind John 5:19-20 lies a parable.[16] Jesus, the son of a carpenter, had learned the secrets of his father's craft in the carpenter's shop. Later he claimed that what he was doing and teaching he had learned from his heavenly Father. Jesus maintains his absolute dependence on the Father. His food is to do the will of the Father (4:34). All who come to him have been given by the Father (6:37, 44, 65), and Jesus does noth-ing on his own authority. He says only what the Father has taught him (8:28). The Son, therefore, is glorified by the Father so that he may glorify the Father in return (17:1).

As the Son, Jesus shares in the character and nature of the Father. Indeed, he can say, "The Father and I are one" (10:30), though the Father is still greater (14:28). Because Jesus is one with the Father, it would be entirely inappropriate for him to pray, "not what I want, but what you want" (Mark 14:36), as he does in the Synoptics. Those who have seen Jesus—at least in the distinc-tive Johannine sense of seeing—have seen the Father (14:9).

The outstanding feature of the thirteen references to the Son of Man in John is that they consistently deal with his descent to earth and his ascent to heaven (3:13; 6:62), his exaltation (3:14; 8:28; 12:34), and his glorification (12:23; 13:31). These are not unrelated. In contrast to the Synoptic scheme in which Jesus will be raised, ascend, and then return in glory, John reverses the sequence. John emphasizes descent and ascent. Jesus has come from above and will return to his Father. The Johannine Son of Man sayings, therefore, speak not of Jesus' return to earth as judge in the future but of his return to heaven. For John the important truth is not the "second coming" but the astounding good news that the expected judge and messiah has already come.

The ascension of Jesus was not for John the prelude to his future authority, as it is in the Synoptics. It was the completion of his divine mission to reveal the Father. Three sayings in particular speak of the exaltation of the Son of Man (3:14; 8:28; 12:32). These form a subgroup of the Johannine Son of Man sayings and should be studied together. The "lifting up" or exaltation of the Son of Man does not occur after his humiliation on the cross, as in the Pauline confession in Philippians 2:5-11; the cross is instead the first step in his exaltation. When John speaks of Jesus' being "lifted up," therefore, it is speaking as much of his death as of his ascension. The ascension, after all, is not narrated in John. The result is that the Son of Man sayings which predict Jesus' exaltation are the Johannine counterpart to the Synoptic passion predictions.

Moving from one saying to another, the reader can see that John progressively defines his understanding of the Son of Man. In response to acclamations from his first disciples, Jesus announces that they will see the angels of God ascending and descending upon the Son of Man (1:51). Since this announcement recalls Jacob's dream vision of a ladder reaching to heaven with angels ascending and descending on it (Gen 28:12), the implication is that Jesus is the new Bethel, the new meeting place between heaven and earth. Jesus' role as heavenly Revealer is secure because only the Son of Man has descended from heaven and no one else has ascended to heaven (3:13).

There will be something paradoxical about his ascension, however. The Son of Man must be lifted up like the serpent in the wilderness (3:14). When Moses prayed that the people of Israel might be delivered from a plague of fiery serpents, the Lord commanded that he set a bronze serpent on a pole. Then, if a serpent bit one of the Israelites, that person could look to the bronze serpent and live (Num 21:3-9). Jesus' exaltation would therefore provide life for those who looked to him in faith.

The next reference (5:27) explains that the Son not only has the power to give life but also has authority to judge; this is the role of the Son of Man which is emphasized in the Synoptic Gospels. Because Jesus has descended from above, like the personification of Wisdom, he can invite those who accept him to drink living water and eat the bread of life (6:27; cf. Prov 9:1-6).

A verse from Isaiah unifies important Johannine themes: "See, my servant shall prosper; he shall be *exalted* and *lifted up*, and shall be very high" (52:13; cf. John 6:62). But only when the Son of Man has been lifted up will his identity and divine authority be apparent (8:28). When Jesus asks, "Do you believe in the Son of Man?" (9:35), the blind man to whom he has given sight asks who the Son of Man is. With delightful wit Jesus says to the man born blind, "You have *seen* him!"

When the Greeks come and ask to see Jesus, he realizes that the hour has come for him to be glorified (12:23). The third of the lifting up sayings promises that he will draw all people to himself when he is lifted up (12:32). Although Jesus has not mentioned the Son of Man at this point, the crowd responds asking the identity of the Son of Man (12:34; see also 3:14; 8:28). The hour has come, and quickly the events that will lead to Jesus' death are set in motion. When Judas goes out to betray him, Jesus announces, "Now the Son of Man has been glorified, and God has been glorified in him" (13:31). For John that is the essential truth about Jesus. The Son of Man has already come. He has been lifted up and glorified, and the judgment is determined by how we respond to his revelation.[17]

THE NATURE OF FAITH

The Gospel of John contains perhaps the New Testament's most probing treatment of the experience of faith. Why is it that some respond to the revelation in Jesus with faith while others reject it? The false loves that characterize those who refuse to believe have already been treated in the discussion of sin. The Gospel balances free will and determinism. Alone neither is sufficient to explain either belief or unbelief.

On one hand, Jesus issues an invitation for all to believe. The familiar John 3:16 makes the point: "... so that *everyone* who believes in him may not perish but may have eternal life" (cf. 3:15). Similarly, the living water is offered to all, even a Samaritan woman: "... *whoever* drinks of the water that I shall give him will never thirst" (4:14 RSV). "Let anyone who is thirsty come to me" (7:37). The invitation is offered to all, but not all accept.

On the other hand, those who believe have been drawn, called, or given by the Father. The initiative remains with God.

Free Will and Determinism in John

Is it not true that only he whom the Father "draws" comes to Jesus (6:44), only he to whom it is "given" by the Father (6:65; *cf.* 6:37, 39; 17:2, 6, 9, 12, 24)? Is it not said that only he can "hear his voice" who is "of the truth," who is "of God" (18:37; 8:47)—that only he can believe who belongs to his "sheep" (10:26)? And is it not solely "his own" whom he calls to himself (10:3f.), whom he knows and who know him (10:14, 27)? And does not the prophet's word (Isa 6:10) confirm the opinion that unbelief rests upon the hardening imposed by God (12:39f.)?[18]

John, therefore, retains an emphasis on God's sovereignty and initiative. Here the theology of John parallels that of Ephesians: "... and this is not your own doing; it is the gift of God" (2:8).

The revelation brings division, sifting out persons according to how they respond to it. Each of the characters around Jesus represents a type of response to him. By surveying the entire scheme of characterization in the Gospel, we see the whole range of responses to the revelation and the consequences of these responses.[19] Long before the current interest in "stages of faith," the Johannine evangelist wrote a penetrating analysis of the stages one may experience as he or she comes to faith in Jesus Christ. For John, believing is not a static response; it is a way of life. Those who believe can change, both for better and for worse. Ultimately, however, their response reveals whether they are from above or from below, one of the children of God or one of the children of the devil. In the process of reading the Gospel, therefore, we are challenged to reexamine our own response, to lay aside inadequate responses, and move on to an authentic faith.

Signs Faith

The lowest level of faith is represented by those who believe because they see the signs that Jesus does. The disciples begin at this point (2:11), but Jesus would not give himself to those in Jerusalem who believed when they saw the signs that he did (2:23-24). The defection of the crowds who followed him because they saw the signs which he did (6:2) shows why the Gospel challenges those whose faith requires signs to move on to a higher level of faith. Nevertheless, the signs confirm that the Father was working through Jesus: "Even though you do not believe me, believe the works, so that you may know and understand that the Father is in me and I am in the Father" (10:38; cf. 14:11).

At the end of the Gospel, Jesus accepts the faith of Thomas that is based on seeing and then pronounces a final beatitude on all who will come later and believe without seeing: "Have you believed because you have seen me? Blessed are those who have not seen and yet have come to believe" (20:29).

Faith in Jesus' Word

The next higher level of faith is represented by those who come to Jesus because of what they hear in his words. Jesus is the Word that reveals the Father, and those who receive his words are drawn to faith. Some, like Nicodemus, cannot understand even earthly things (3:12). Others, like the royal official and the Samaritan woman, believe without seeing a sign. The royal official returns home. The Samaritan woman moves by stages to the expectant question, Can this be the Christ? (4:29). The Samaritans too "believed because of his word" (4:41) and exclaimed, "we have heard for ourselves, and we know that this is truly the Savior of the world" (4:42).

The Gospel of John has become the means by which the Word of Jesus is conveyed to those who were not eyewitnesses. It is the further work of the Paraclete, the Spirit of Truth, speaking through the Beloved Disciple and the Evangelist. Those who come to faith as a result of reading the Gospel, therefore, are like the Samaritans who hear for themselves and believe. They are Jesus' sheep, whom he calls by name; they hear his voice and follow him (10:4-5, 16, 25-26; cf. 11:43; 20:16).

The Model of Faith

The highest level of faith is illustrated by those who know, love, and bear witness. The Beloved Disciple is the prime exemplar of this response. He is introduced as one who was in the bosom of Jesus (13:23), just as Jesus was in the bosom of the Father (1:18). The goal of faith, therefore, is a knowledge of God that brings a unity between believer and Lord like that between Jesus and the Father. The world did not know Jesus (1:10-11). Only through faith can one "know and understand that the Father is in me and I am in the Father" (10:38). Freedom comes to those who abide in this knowledge (8:31-32), and those who know God have eternal life (17:3).

Believers are also sent to bear witness to the truth in Jesus Christ, just as Jesus himself was sent by the Father (20:21). The goal of their mission is that "the world may know" (17:23). From John the Baptist (1:19ff.) and the first two disciples of Jesus to the Beloved Disciple (19:35; 21:24), the Gospel emphasizes the importance of confessing, or bearing witness.

Jesus is the model for the ethic of the Johannine community. The mark of Jesus' followers is that they live "just as" Jesus lived (see the use of "just as" [*kathos*] in 13:15, 34; 15:10, 12; 17:18; 20:21; 1 John 2:6, 27; 3:3, 7). They share in his peace (14:27; 20:19, 21) and his joy (16:20, 22, 24), and they keep his command to love one another in Jesus' name (13:34; 15:12).

THE CHURCH: THE CHILDREN OF GOD

The word *church* does not appear in the Gospel of John, but the Gospel is rich in images that serve as metaphors and models for the church.[20] The first and most important of the Johannine metaphors appears at the center of the prologue:

> But to all who received him, who believed in his name, he gave power to become children of God. (1:12)

The question of who were the children of God was disputed among the Essenes, Samaritans, Pharisees, and early Christians.[21] The Johannine community laid claim to this title, and the Gospel reinforced that self-understanding of the community. Like the Essenes at Qumran, who saw themselves as the "sons of light" in conflict with the "sons of darkness," the Johannine community found in this self-understanding a secure identity amid conflict with the world.

Once the theme of the "children of God" is introduced in 1:12, it is developed in significant passages throughout the Gospel. The identity of the believers is finally certified by the risen Lord, who sends Mary Magdalene to tell his "brothers" (that is, the disciples; 20:17-18) that he was ascending "to my Father and your Father, to my God and your God" (20:17).

A new birth, "from above," sets the children of God apart from the world (3:3, 5). Nicodemus misunderstands, thinking that in some way he must be born again physically. The birth from above, however, is a birth by the Spirit that gives the believer eternal life. This life is marked by the believer's knowledge of God and obedience to his commands. The children of God "keep Jesus' word" (cf. 8:51, 52, 55; 14:23), and the Spirit abides in them.

The life of the children of God is sustained by bread and water the world cannot see. Just as Jesus had food "that you do not know about" (4:32), so those who receive him have living water (4:10, 14; 7:37-39) and bread of life (6:27, 33, 35, 51). The bread and drink Jesus gives are his own body and blood (6:53). Unless one eats his body and drinks his blood one can have no part in him. The insight that holds this obscure reasoning together is that the revelation Jesus embodies and gives to those who will receive it nourishes one's spiritual life as surely as bread nourishes the physical body. The language clearly evokes the Lord's Supper and gives it a distinctively Johannine meaning, but the Gospel is more concerned to emphasize the importance of accepting Jesus in faith than to command observance of the Lord's Supper.

On the other hand, the Gospel of John is not antisacramental, as some have supposed. According to D. Moody Smith, Bultmann maintained that the evangelist feared "ecclesiastical misunderstanding and misuse" of baptism and the Lord's Supper, but the ecclesiastical redactor added sacramental references to make the Gospel more acceptable to the church.[22]

It is striking that John does not contain the words of institution but instead reports the foot washing. Passages such as John 6:51-58 and 15:1-11 were probably used as homilies at observances of the Lord's Supper. Similarly, instruction on the meaning of baptism is conveyed in John 1:31-33 and 3:3-8, and the practice of baptism is mentioned in John 3:26 and 4:2. For John, however, the observances of baptism and the Lord's Supper, like the signs that Jesus did, pointed beyond themselves to the life of the children of God in Christ. They had been born from above, and they lived by the revelation and the Spirit that Jesus had given them.

Similarly, the community probably practiced foot washing as a sign pointing to Christ's death, their obedience to his commands, and their new relationship to one another. A common meal of bread and fish could also point to the reality of the resurrection, and a charcoal fire could symbolize forgiveness (21:9; cf. 18:18).

Because all believers had been born from above, and all possessed the Spirit of Truth, the Johannine church was exceptionally egalitarian. The twelve disciples held no special authority ("the twelve" appears in 6:67, 70, 71; 20:24), and even the elder, the author of the Johannine Epistles, seeks to exert influence by appealing to the tradition of the community rather than by exercise of his personal authority. As a community, the children of God practice the love that Jesus commanded. They are one, just as Jesus is one with the Father. They are the sheep of the good shepherd, so they know his voice, and they follow him. They are the branches of the vine, and they bear fruit by their obedience to Jesus' commands. They are "friends" (11:11; 15:14-15; 3 John 15), so they are to lay down their lives for one another "just as" Jesus did for them (15:13).

The children of God, therefore, live in a community which is very egalitarian. Women are received as persons of equal standing and faith (for example, Mary and Martha, Mary the mother of Jesus, and Mary Magdalene). All have beheld Jesus' glory; all possess the Spirit; so none is distinguished with greater authority. On the contrary, they are to wash one another's feet, *just as* Jesus washed the disciples' feet.

The children of God are also called to a task. They are to continue the mission of Jesus, so that the world may know that he was sent by the Father. Integral to that mission are the roles of fishing and shepherding. The final chapter of the Gospel paints a symbolic picture of the disciples fishing. By following his command (and fishing in light rather than darkness), they enclose a great catch of fish, 153 in all (a number that some think represented every known species).[23] Still, the net is not torn. The unity of the community of believers is maintained, and the apostle Peter drags the net full of fish to the risen Lord, who has prepared a meal of fish and bread. Peter is then commissioned as a shepherd who will feed the sheep and eventually lay down his life for them. The Beloved Disciple, likewise, has an authorized role, following Jesus and bearing witness to the truth.[24]

THE PROMISE OF LIFE

Two distinctives of Johannine thought, both relative to the Johannine understanding of the life of believers, remain to be considered. These are the Holy Spirit and the hope for the future.

Five passages in the farewell discourse speak of the promise of the Paraclete, the Spirit of Truth (14:16-17, 26; 15:26; 16:7-11, 13-14; cf. 7:39; 20:22). The term *parakletos* comes from the words meaning "to call beside." It has therefore been translated as "comforter" or "advocate" (picking up on the legal connotations of the term). The Spirit will continue Jesus' revelatory work in the world through the disciples. Through the Spirit, the Father and the Son abide with the believer (14:23ff.). The Spirit will both remind the community of what Jesus said and be the means by which further truth comes to it (14:26). This understanding of the Spirit leaves open the possibility of further revelation while insisting that any new revelation will necessarily be consistent with what the community has already received from Jesus. This principle may originally have served as the criterion by which the community evaluated the words of prophets in their midst who claimed to speak at the direction of the Spirit.

The Spirit also bore witness for the community before the world (15:26; 16:7-11), guiding the community in times of persecution. In all likelihood, the community that asserted that the Beloved Disciple's witness was true (19:35; 21:24) believed that the Spirit had worked through him in their own time. Their understanding of the work of the Spirit was influenced by their relationship to the Beloved Disciple, and his teachings were treasured. The Gospel became the Word of God for the Johannine church because it contained the words and works of Jesus handed down to them by the Beloved Disciple under the leadership of the Holy Spirit.[25]

Reflection on the significance of the new life of the children of God also produced a distinctive Johannine eschatology. Just as the Gospel preserves echoes of a more traditional understanding of the atonement, so also it contains allusions to the more apocalyptic, future eschatology that was common in early Christianity. Jesus promises a coming resurrection and judgment:

> Do not be astonished at this; for the hour is coming when all who are in their graves will hear his voice and will come out—those who have done good, to the resurrection of life, and those who have done evil, to the resurrection of condemnation. (5:28-29)

Four times in John 6 Jesus promises that he will raise up those who believe in him at "the last day" (6:39, 40, 44, 54). John repeatedly affirms that those who believe in Jesus have "eternal life" (3:15, 16, 36).

Alongside these references we find a reinterpretation of the Christian hope for the future. Judgment is based on one's response to the revelation in Jesus. Therefore, the judgment occurs now, in the present, in each person's response to Jesus:

> Those who believe in him [the Son] are not condemned; but those who do not believe are condemned already, because they have not believed in the name of the only Son of God. And this is the judgment, that the light has come into the world, and people loved darkness rather than light because their deeds were evil. (3:18-19)

Because those who believe are born from above, they have already "passed from death to life" (5:24; cf. 1 John 3:14). That is the theme of the raising of Lazarus. Martha believed in the resurrection, which was taught by the Pharisees, but she did not yet understand that Jesus himself was the resurrection and life (11:25): "Those who believe in me, even though they die, will live, and everyone who lives and believes in me will never die" (11:25-26). Eternal life is not something that believers will receive in the future; it is that quality of life that begins when one receives Jesus as the revelation of God. "Eternal life" for John marks a quality, not just a quantity, of life. It is life lived in fellowship with God, as one of his children: "And this is eternal life, that they may know you, the only true God, and Jesus Christ whom you have sent" (17:3).

When the purpose of the Gospel is stated—"so that you may come to believe that Jesus is the Messiah, the Son of God, and that through believing you may have *life* in his name" (20:31)—we readily understand that John is a Gospel that brings true life to all who will respond to it with faith in Jesus, the Son in whom God the Father is revealed. John, the "spiritual Gospel," makes the Word of God immediately present and calls for faith from all who read it.[26]

PART TWO

INTERPRETING
THE
JOHANNINE
WRITINGS

CHAPTER 6

INTERPRETING THE FOURTH GOSPEL JOHN 1–4

The real fascination of the Gospel of John becomes evident only in the process of reading it. The foregoing exploration of John as history, literature, and theology, intriguing as it may be, is only preparation for reading the Gospel itself. Similarly, the notes that follow may guide and inform your reading, but they are no substitute for reading the Gospel itself.

THE PROLOGUE (1:1-18)

We will spend a disproportionate amount of time on the prologue, the first 18 verses of John, because its announcement of Jesus as the Logos is the key to understanding all that will follow. The issues that it presents to the reader are also exceptionally important and engaging.

Introduction

By any standard the prologue to the Gospel of John is one of the most profound passages in the Bible. As simple as its language and phrases are, its description of Jesus as the Logos has exerted a lasting influence on Christian theology. In order to appreciate the distinctiveness of the prologue, however, one must compare it with the beginnings of the three Synoptic Gospels.

Mark begins with John the Baptist and emphasizes the fulfillment of scripture. John is presented as a prophet. Mark 1:1 is important because it may well offer a summary of the gospel: Jesus is the Christ (Peter's confession at Caesarea Philippi, Mark 8:29) and the Son of God (the centurion's confession at the cross, Mark 15:39). The same two titles occur in the purpose statement at the end of the Gospel of John (20:31). Mark characterizes John as "the baptizer" who is not worthy to untie the thong of Jesus' sandals, but in the verses that follow, John baptizes Jesus (Mark 1:9-11). Neither the baptism nor the temptation of Jesus are reported in the prologue to John, or anywhere else in that Gospel (on the baptism of Jesus, see below, John 1:29-34).

Matthew begins by tracing the genealogy of Jesus, the son of David, the son of Abraham. This introduction is followed by an account of Jesus' birth and infancy. The beginning of Matthew thereby emphasizes Jesus' Jewish origin, his fulfillment of the Moses typology, and his identity as the Son of God. Of these, only the last is prominent in John. John does not contain a genealogy, a birth narrative, or any account of Jesus' infancy.

Luke also offers an account of Jesus' birth and infancy, but goes beyond Matthew in several respects. Luke describes the birth of John the Baptist as well as Jesus' birth. He includes accounts of the annunciation of each birth. And he links the infancy account to the rest of the Gospel by including the story of Jesus in the Temple at the age of twelve and by delaying the report of Jesus' genealogy until Luke 3. The genealogy also augments Matthew's account in that it extends Jesus' lineage back to Adam, the "son of God." Throughout the infancy narrative Luke demonstrates Jesus' superiority to John the Baptist, a theme that the Gospel of John will develop in its own way both in the prologue and later in the Gospel.

All of the prologues, therefore, serve to educate or prepare the reader for the rest of the Gospel. Important themes are signaled, and the identity of Jesus is established at the very outset by means of Christological titles, divine portents, or the manner of Jesus' birth. Whereas Mark begins with the baptism of Jesus, at which the voice from heaven calls Jesus "my Son, the Beloved" (Mark 1:11), Matthew and Luke affirm that Jesus was born the Son of God. John declares that the Word was in the beginning with God and was God long before becoming flesh. All of the prologues, therefore, are Christological affirmations, but John is the only Gospel to speak of Jesus' preexistence as the Logos and the only Gospel to include a poetic prologue.

The Structure of the Prologue

Source theories regarding the origin of the prologue abound. The first five verses have a distinctive poetic quality, whereas verses 6-8 read like the beginning of an Old Testament story. Allusions to the Old Testament set the prologue in a larger scriptural context. The first words echo Genesis 1:1. The Johannine concept of "the Word" is deeply indebted to the Wisdom literature, and reminders of the role of Moses and the giving of the Law are also clear.

It has often been suggested, therefore, that the prologue is based on a Christian adaptation of a hymn to Wisdom. Still, there is no consensus as to whether the remnant of the hymn is to be found in verses 1-5 only or whether any or all of verses 9-12, 14, 16, and 18 were part of the hymn also. If verses 14, 16, and 18 were part of the hymn, then the hymn had already been adapted for Christian use.

The hand of the Johannine evangelist or redactor is most clearly evident in verses 6-8, 12c-13, 15, and 17. It has been suggested, with some merit, that the Gospel originally began with verses 6-8 and 15. These verses lead directly into verse 19, and if they were once the beginning of the Gospel, then it originally began much like the Gospel of Mark—with John's testimony to Jesus. These passages also reflect a polemic against false understandings of the role of John the Baptist and Moses, and explain who the true children of God are. John is presented solely as a witness to Jesus (1:19-34; 3:26-30; 10:41). As the Gospel unfolds, the opposition between followers of Jesus and followers of Moses increases, and Jesus is presented as the "Prophet like Moses" in fulfillment of Deuteronomy 18:18-19. He is like Moses, but greater than Moses. Finally, this conflict leads to Jesus' death. In the end, Jesus authorizes those who respond to his revelation: they are the true children of God (1:12), while those who oppose Jesus are exposed as children of the devil (cf. 8:44).

Several beautifully intricate structures can be found in this carefully composed opening to the Gospel. Hebrew poetry used couplets with various kinds of parallelism between the two lines: synonymous, antithetical, and stair-step parallelism.

**Synonymous and Stair-Step Parallelism
in Psalm 96:12-13**

Then shall all the trees of the forest sing for joy before the LORD;
    for he is coming,
    for he is coming to judge the earth.
He will judge the world with righteousness,
    and the peoples with his truth.

The progression from lines 2 to 3 and 3 to 4 illustrate stair-step parallelism, while the repetition of the same thought in lines 4 and 5 illustrates synonymous parallelism.

John 1:1-5 can be analyzed in the same fashion. The second noun in each line becomes the first noun in the next line: a beautiful example of stair-step parallelism. When the pattern is traced further, we see that it doubles back on itself, a structure called a *chiasm*.

The Poetic Structure of John 1:1-2

In the beginning (A) was the Word (B),
and the Word (B) was with God (C),
and what God (C) was, the Word (B′) was.
This one (B′) was with God in the beginning (A′). (author's translation)

The repetition of the central element, "God" (C) in the last line is hardly a flaw. It sums up the verse and brings it to a fitting conclusion.

The chiastic structure of the opening lines of the prologue alerts us to the chiastic structure of the whole prologue. As the prologue progresses, however, its poetic structure becomes less clear. Various suggestions regarding its structure have been offered based on the length of its lines, the number of accents per line, and the coordination of lines. The following arrangement of the prologue highlights features of the text discussed below.

THE PROLOGUE

First Strophe: The Word and God

1 In the beginning was the Word,
and the Word was with God,
and what God was, the Word was.
2 This one was with God in the beginning.

Second Strophe: The Word and Creation

3 All things came into being through him,
and without him not one thing came into being.
4 What has come into being in him was life,
and the life was the light of all people.
5 The light shines in the darkness,
and the darkness did not overcome it.

Interpolation: The Word and John

6 There was a man sent from God, whose name was John. 7 He came as a witness to testify to the light, so that all might believe through him. 8 He himself was not the light, but he came to testify to the light.

Third Strophe: The Word and the World

9 The true light, which enlightens everyone,
was coming into the world.
10 He was in the world,
and the world came into being through him;
yet the world did not know him.
11 He came to what was his own,
and his own people did not accept him.
12 But to all who received him,
he gave power to become children of God,

—who believed in his name, 13 who were born, not of blood or of the will of the flesh or of the will of man, but of God.

113

Fourth Strophe: The Word and the Community

14 And the Word became flesh and lived among us,
and we have seen his glory,
the glory as of a father's only son,
full of grace and truth.

15 (John testified to him and cried out, "This was he of whom I said, 'He who comes after me ranks ahead of me because he was before me.'")

16 From his fullness we have all received,
grace upon grace.

17 The law indeed was given through Moses;
grace and truth came through Jesus Christ.
18 No one has ever seen God.
It is God the only Son,
who is close to the Father's heart,
who has made him known. (NRSV, vv. 1, 2, and 12 modified to highlight structure of the Greek)

It is often suggested that the prologue contains hymnic material that can be separated into several strophes or verses. This arrangement is suggested both by the form and by the content of the verses. A chronological order can be detected, though it has been interpreted differently by various scholars.

**The Chronological and Topical Organization
of the Prologue**

Strophe 1: The preexistence of the Word
Strophe 2: From Creation through the history of Israel
Interpolation: John the Baptist's announcement
Strophe 3: The Incarnation
Strophe 4: The response of the community

Johannine scholars have debated the point at which the Incarnation is first mentioned. Ernst Käsemann found the incarnation at verse 5,[1] but others find it in verse 9 or 14. Rudolf Bultmann contended that although the Incarnation is hinted at earlier, it is first mentioned in verse 14.[2] Raymond E. Brown, however, concluded that verses 10-12*b* refer to the earthly ministry of Jesus.[3]

Alternately, a pattern of topical organization is suggested by the concentration on the various roles and relationships of the Word which reveal his character. Note the strophe titles used above: The Word and God, the Word and Creation, the Word and John, the Word and the World, and the Word and the Community.

So strong is the consensus among scholars that verse 15 interrupts the flow of the prologue that it is put in parentheses in the NRSV. Verses 6-8 also describe John as a witness to the light, and their style is noticeably flatter and more prosaic than that of verses 1-5. If an early hymn lies behind the present prologue, it can hardly have contained verses 6-8 or verse 15.

Verses 12c-13 and verse 17 have also often been identified as interpolations. Upon close examination, the interpolations not only have a different style and interrupt the flow of the hymn but are also characterized by an interest in defending against false understandings of the role of John the Baptist, Moses, and the children of God. John's only role is to bear witness to Jesus. In contrast to those who do not believe in Jesus, whose father is the devil (8:44), the children of God continue to believe in Jesus' name. Jesus is also superior to Moses in that while the Law came through Moses, grace and truth have come through Jesus (v. 17).

Several early Christian hymns or confessions have been identified in the New Testament (see Phil 2:6-11; Col 1:15-20; 1 Tim 3:16). Philippians 2:6-11 is particularly important as a parallel because it contains a clear pattern of descent and ascent: Jesus was equal to God, humbled himself, took the form of a servant, and was obedient to death, even death on the cross. Then the action turns upward: God highly exalted him and gave him a name that was above every name, so that every creature should bow and confess that Jesus is Lord to the glory of God. John's prologue is similar but admittedly not as clear: In the beginning the Word is equal to God, then he became involved in creation, he shined in darkness, he is heralded by a mere man, the world knew him not, and his own people would not receive him. At the beginning of verse 12 the action turns: *But* some did accept him, and to them he gave authority to become children of God. Jesus is greater than Moses, having the glory of the only Son, and the prologue ends with the declaration that he is in the Father's bosom and has revealed the Father.

Various interpreters, following M. E. Boismard,[4] have also detected an elaborate chiastic structure in the prologue. A chiasm is a crossing or reversing pattern (as seen earlier, p.112 in reference to 1:1-5).

The Chiastic Structure of John 16:28

(A) I came from the Father
  (B) and have come into the world;
  (B´) again, I am leaving the world
(A´) and going to the Father.

The chiastic structure of the prologue is far more intricate, but the following parallels can be detected in vocabulary, subject, or theme.

The Chiastic Structure of the Prologue

1-2	18	The Word with God
3	17	What came through the Word
4-5	16	What was received from the Word
6-8	15	John announces the Word
9-10	14	The Word enters the world
11	13	The Word and his own people
12a	12c	The Word is accepted
	12b	The Word's gift to those who accepted him.

The pivot of the prologue, therefore, is the conferring of the status "children of God" on those who believed in Jesus.[5] In the debate with the synagogue authorities, such a designation may have had a particular importance for the Johannine community. It defined their status and identity as the true community of the children of God.

The Relationship of the Prologue to the Rest of the Gospel

The most important function of the prologue is to prepare readers to read the rest of the Gospel. In the prologue, the narrator speaks, introducing the reader to the protagonist (Jesus), clarifying his origin and identity, and foreshadowing the plot and themes of the story that is about to be told. Jesus is introduced as the divine Logos, and throughout his public ministry he will do "signs" that point to his identity. The prologue affirms that all things were made through him, so when Jesus changes water to wine or walks on water later in the Gospel, what he does confirms what the narrator has said about who he is. The result is that the narrator's credibility grows, and the reader is led to believe "that Jesus is the Messiah, the Son of God" (20:30-31).

After affirming the creative role of the Logos, the prologue introduces the witness to the light, the entry of the light into the world, and the rejection of the light. The plot is therefore foreshadowed in metaphorical terms. Only at the end of the prologue does the narrator use the name of Jesus (v. 17), and even then the reader must draw the connection between Jesus and what has been said about the Logos, the light, and the only Son. In many respects, the prologue is comparable to a table of contents for the Gospel. The first part of the Gospel (John 2–12) tells of the witness of John the Baptist, the coming of Jesus, the rising hostility toward him, and his rejection by his own people. The second part (John 13–20) tells of his ministry to "his own": he washes their feet, teaches them, prays for them, and then goes out and dies for them. His death is his return to the Father.

Bultmann compared the prologue to a musical overture: "And yet the prologue is an introduction in the sense of being an *overture,* leading the reader out of the commonplace into a new and strange world of sounds and figures, and singling out particular motifs from the action that is now to be unfolded."[6] The importance of the themes that are announced in the prologue and taken up later in the Gospel can be seen in the following list:

Preexistence of the Logos: "He was in the beginning with God." (vv. 1-2)

> John 17:5—". . . glorify me in your own presence with the glory that I had in your presence before the world existed."

Life: "What has come into being in him was life." (v. 4)

> John 5:24—". . . anyone who hears my word and believes him who sent me has eternal life, and does not come under judgment, but has passed from death to life." (cf. 5:25-26)

> John 11:25—"I am the resurrection and the life."

> John 14:6—"I am the way, and the truth, and the life."

117

Light: *"And the life was the light of all people."* (vv. 4 and 9)

John 8:12—"I am the light of the world." (cf. 9:5)

The opposition of light and darkness: *"The light shines in the darkness, and the darkness did not overcome it."* (v. 5)

John 3:19—"And this is the judgment, that the light has come into the world, and people loved darkness rather than light ..."

John 12:46—"I have come as light into the world, so that everyone who believes in me should not remain in the darkness."

John's witness: *"He came as a witness to testify to the light."* (vv. 7-8, 15)

John 1:19—"This is the testimony given by John ..."

(cf. 1:19-34; 3:26-30)

John 10:41—"... everything that John said about this man was true."

The world's opposition: *"... yet the world did not know him."* (v. 10)

John 14:17—"This is the Spirit of Truth, whom the world cannot receive ..."

John 14:19—"In a little while the world will no longer see me, but you will see me."

John 15:18—"If the world hates you, be aware that it hated me before it hated you."

Children of God: *"But to all who received him, who believed in his name, he gave power to become children of God."* (v. 12)

John 11:52—"... to gather into one the dispersed children of God."

Born of God: *"who were born, not of blood or of the will of the flesh or of the will of man, but of God."* (v. 13)

John 3:3—"... no one can see the kingdom of God without being born from above."

Beholding his glory: *"... and we have seen his glory, the glory as of a father's only son ..."* (v. 14)

John 17:5—"... glorify me in your own presence with the glory that I had in your presence before the world existed."

The only Son: "... the glory as of a father's only son ..." (v. 14)

John 3:16—"For God so loved the world that he gave his only Son ..."

Moses: "The law indeed was given through Moses ..." (v. 17)

John 5:45-46—"Your accuser is Moses, on whom you have set your hope. If you believed Moses, you would believe me, for he wrote about me."

John 6:32—"I tell you, it was not Moses who gave you the bread from heaven, but it is my Father who gives you the true bread from heaven."

John 9:28-29—"You are his disciple, but we are disciples of Moses. We know that God has spoken to Moses, but as for this man, we do not know where he comes from."

Seeing God: "No one has ever seen God." (v. 18)

John 5:37—"You have never heard his voice or seen his form."

John 6:46—"Not that anyone has seen the Father except the one who is from God; he has seen the Father."

Because so much of the vocabulary and so many of its themes introduce strands of thought that will be important in the body of the Gospel, it is significant that some elements of the prologue do not recur later. "The Word" is not used later as a title for Jesus. Two significant terms—*grace* and *fullness*—do not appear again in the Gospel. Furthermore, the poetic quality of the prologue is not equaled anywhere else in the Gospel.

The prologue plays an important role in orienting the reader to the Gospel story that follows. The narrator speaks authoritatively, introducing the divine Logos and describing the role of the pre-existent Logos in the creation. The prologue, therefore, provides the lens through which, or the perspective from which, the reader views Jesus. From the outset, the reader understands Jesus in light of his origin with God, his role in creation, the Incarnation, and his mission to reveal the Father. Jesus' role is also defined in relation to Moses and John the Baptist, who will bear witness to him. The opposition is established between those who reject Jesus and those who believe on his name, and the latter are identified as the "children of God."

The authoritative voice of the narrator, the privileged informa-

119

tion that is conveyed in the prologue, the scriptural allusions, the "primacy effect" of this perspective on Jesus—all these powerfully condition the way in which the reader will respond to the rest of the narrative. The reader is drawn to the narrator's confession that the divine Logos was incarnate in Jesus. All that follows in the Gospel's account of what Jesus does and says serves to confirm the prologue's declaration that "the Word became flesh and lived among us" (1:14).

JOHN 1:19-51

John 1:19-51 (or 1:19–2:11) constitutes a second, narrative introduction to the Gospel. Just as the Gospel seems to have two conclusions (at the end of John 20 and at the end of John 21), so it has two beginnings.

The narrative beginning of the Gospel introduces the testimony of John the Baptist and the calling of the first disciples. The themes sounded in the prologue begin to be developed in the narrative. This section has numerous contacts with the Synoptic Gospels—the preaching of John, Jesus' baptism, and the calling of the disciples—but it does not depend directly on any of them. Traditional material is developed in characteristically Johannine form, reflecting both on the ministry of Jesus and on the situation of the Johannine community. What happened in the ministry of Jesus provides direction for understanding the present, especially through reflection on the Christological significance of the historical events.

This section falls into two parts (1:19-34 and 1:35-51), and each part has two subsections (19-28, 29-34; 35-42, 43-51).

The Testimony of John the Baptist (1:19-34)

The testimony of John introduces two significant elements: the trial motif and the fulfillment of messianic expectations. John was introduced in the prologue as a witness, and here he begins to fulfill that function. "The Jews from Jerusalem" sent emissaries to John. The wording reminds us that John too had been sent (cf. 1:6). The question is, "Who are you?" The expected answer is a claim to be one of the expected messianic figures, but John denies each one, thereby leaving the fulfillment of these figures to Jesus. The narrator's emphatic description of John's response calls attention to the importance of confession: "He confessed and did not deny it, but confessed" (1:20). He was not the Messiah. He was not Elijah (cf. Mal 3:1; 4:5). And he was not *the* prophet (the expected "prophet like Moses"; cf. Deut 18:18-19). The interrogation of John already foreshadows the opposition to Jesus. The trial motif pervades the whole ministry of Jesus, so the precrucifixion trial before the Jewish authorities is abbreviated in John because most of that material has been pulled forward into the account of the ministry of Jesus.

Having denied that he was a messianic figure, John identifies himself positively as a witness to Jesus (fulfilling what is said about John in the prologue, 1:6-8, 15). The fact that John baptized is subordinated to his role as a witness (cf. v. 28). The clear implication is that anyone who claimed to be a disciple of John should heed his witness and accept Jesus as the one greater than John.

John's Witness to Jesus (1:29-34)

The witness of John continues in the form of a flashback. Whereas Mark reports the baptism of Jesus without any hesitancy, and Matthew and Luke each deflect possible claims that John was greater because he baptized Jesus, John does not report the baptism. Instead, John the Baptist recalls the coming of the Spirit upon Jesus.

John's title for Jesus is "the Lamb of God who takes away the sin of the world." The title can be interpreted in three contexts: the lamb as the apocalyptic leader of the flock (Ezekiel), the lamb as the servant lamb of Isaiah (Isa 53:7), or the Passover lamb. The one who had sent him had told John that the one on whom he saw the Spirit descend was the one who would baptize in the Holy Spirit. The paragraph ends with a second confession: Jesus is the Son of God (v. 34).

The First Disciples (1:35-42)

This section begins with the same notice as verses 29 and 43: "The next day." These three references mark off four days in John 1:19-51, and John 2 begins "On the third day," which makes a week. Interpreters speculate that this week either recalls the week of creation in Genesis 1 or balances the week in John 20:26.

The brief conversation between Jesus and the two disciples

educates readers in what to expect from this Gospel because the conversation moves on two levels. The first words that Jesus speaks in the Gospel are addressed to the two disciples. Jesus asks, "What are you looking for?" This is a natural question to ask if two people are following you. At a deeper level, of course, it is one of the great existential questions of life: What are you searching for? Does the reader hear more in the question than the characters do? The two disciples respond, apparently naively, "Rabbi, where are you staying?" Again, a natural question in the context of this story. John has pointed Jesus out as the Lamb of God; the disciples want to know where they can find him. Where was he staying (Greek, *meno*)? Again however, we notice something deeper, for *meno* (also translated "abiding") is an important theme in John: "The word became flesh and lived among us" (1:14). In chapter 14, Jesus will tell the disciples that he is going to prepare an abiding place for them. In John 14:23, Jesus finally reveals the answer to their initial question. Ironically, the answer is that he will abide with them. In John 1, though, Jesus issues the invitation, "Come and see." Already we note that Jesus typically does not answer questions directly. Instead, he pushes his conversation partners to a deeper level of understanding or response: "Come and see." Again, the response can be understood on two levels. On the surface, it means come and see where I am staying, but the reader suspects that this is an invitation to discipleship. Seeing and believing is another important theme in the Gospel of John, and by the end of the Gospel, Jesus will call the disciples from believing in response to what they have seen (the signs) to believing without having seen (20:29). This conversation makes us aware that in John things often mean more than surface appearance suggests, and words often have double meanings.

One of the first two disciples, Andrew, brings his brother Simon to Jesus, and Jesus gives Simon a new name: *Cephas* (which is translated Peter). As readers, we are alerted to the significance and meaning of names and to the pattern that one learns his or her true identity when he or she discovers who Jesus is. In the Synoptic Gospels, Peter's great moment comes at his confession of Jesus at Caesarea Philippi. In response to the question, "Who do you say that I am?" Peter answers, "You are the Messiah" (Mark 8:29; Matt 16:16-19; Luke 9:20). In the Gospel of John, however, Peter's brother steals his scene in the first chapter. Andrew finds Simon and tells him, "We have found the Messiah" (1:41). John does not give Peter primacy among the disciples. This scene fits the pattern that we will observe in later chapters where John elevates the role of the Beloved Disciple, sometimes at Peter's expense.

The Calling of Nathanael (1:43-51)

By this point, the reader's introduction to the narrative is nearly complete.[7] The narrator has led the reader from the beginning of time in the prologue to the day John the Baptist pointed Jesus out to his disciples. We are ready to begin to test what we have been *told* about Jesus against what we are about to be *shown*.

"The next day" (cf. 1:29, 35), Jesus calls Philip. A new scene is introduced by a temporal reference and the introduction of a new character. Jesus' words to Philip are familiar to a reader of the other Gospels: "Follow me." While this is the first use of this command in John (cf. 12:26; 21:19), the term "follow" *(akolouthein)* was used three times in the previous scene (1:37, 38, 40), so it has already been identified as a technical term for discipleship. Philip's origin from Bethsaida, which was also the hometown of Andrew and Peter, is reported by the narrator.

Philip's action is reported using the formula of discovery and witness from the previous scene:

> v. 41 He first *found* his brother Simon,
> *and said to him,*
> *"We have found* the Messiah."
> v. 45 Philip *found* Nathanael,
> *and said to him,*
> *"We have found* him about whom Moses in the law
> and also the prophets wrote,
> Jesus son of Joseph from Nazareth."

The repetition invites comparison and contrast with the previous scene. We are not told what Philip's relationship to Nathanael was. Neither are we told where Nathanael was from. The role of the disciples is defined at this early stage by the pattern of each one bringing another to Jesus. Similarly, the repetition of the pattern amplifies the designation "the Messiah" by means of the

123

much longer and more specific identification: "him about whom Moses in the law and also the prophets wrote, Jesus son of Joseph from Nazareth." While the extraordinary circumstances surrounding the birth of Jesus are alluded to later (John 7:42; 8:41), there is no narrative of the virgin birth in John. Philip's identification of Jesus in verse 45 is the fifth of seven titles attributed to Jesus in this narrative introduction to the Gospel (1:19-51).

The Titles for Jesus in John 1:19-51

"Lamb of God" (1:29, 36)
"Son of God" (1:34, 49)
"Rabbi" (1:38)
"Messiah (which means Christ)" (1:41)
"Him about whom Moses in the law and also the prophets wrote"
   (1:45)
"King of Israel" (1:49)
"Son of man" (1:51)

Many of the lofty titles that the church applied to Jesus are used in this first chapter in John. In Mark, in contrast, the disciples do not confess that Jesus is the Christ until Peter's confession at Caesarea Philippi (Mark 8:29), and no one confesses that Jesus is the Son of God until his death (Mark 15:39).

Nathanael's response, "Can anything good come out of Nazareth?" provides our first clue to his character, aside from his name. The narrator uses indirect characterization here. He does not tell us about Nathanael in advance but lets the reader draw his or her own conclusions from what Nathanael says and does and from what Jesus says to him. Nathanael's response signals provincial snobbery on one level, but also raises the question of Jesus' origin. Since so much attention has been given to Jesus' origin from God in the prologue, the reader cannot miss the contrast. We know who Jesus is because we know where he is from; Nathanael does not have the information given in the prologue. All he knows is what Philip told him: "Jesus son of Joseph from Nazareth." The gap between the reader's knowledge and the information available to the character allows the narrator to exploit the ironic potential of the narrative situation. The reader is drawn to the lofty heights of the narrator's perspective while watching the character fumble in ignorance. The choice between identifying with the narrator or Nathanael is easy: the reader will choose the narrator's view of Jesus over that of Nathanael. We know that Jesus did not actually come from Nazareth. The Christian reader probably knows that Jesus was born in Bethlehem, because the debate between Jesus and the authorities plays on this point later (7:42). The real point, however, is that Jesus comes from above (3:31).

At this point the issue becomes how Philip will respond to such skepticism. Will he turn away from Nathanael as a hopeless skeptic? Will he debate the Scriptures or the merits of Nazareth as a prophet's hometown? With disarming simplicity, Philip repeats the invitation Jesus gave a few verses earlier: "Come and see" (v. 46; cf. v. 39). Implied is a confidence that if Nathanael will just come to meet Jesus, he will see that what Philip has said is true: "We have found him about whom Moses in the law and also the prophets wrote" (v. 45).

The narrator moves directly to Jesus' words to Nathanael. We are told nothing more about where Philip met Nathanael or how long it took them to find Jesus. Jesus announced Nathanael's coming even before he reached him. His words tell us who Nathanael is, or at least who he can become: "An Israelite indeed, in whom is no guile!" (v. 47 RSV). This is the first demonstration of Jesus' divine knowledge. As the incarnate Logos, he "needed no one to testify about anyone; for he himself knew what was in everyone" (2:25). Two key terms in Jesus' announcement catch our attention: *Israelite* and *guile*. This is the only reference to an Israelite in the Gospel of John (but see the references to Israel in 1:31, 49; 3:10; 12:13). Israel, of course, was the name given to Jacob and eventually to his descendants. Guile (or deceit), moreover, is the character trait with which Jacob is tagged in the Genesis narratives:

Jacob's Guile

When Esau heard the words of his father, he cried out with an exceedingly great and bitter cry, and said to his father, "Bless me, even me also, O my father!" But he said, "Your brother came with *guile*, and he has taken away your blessing." Esau said, *"Is he not rightly named Jacob?"* (Gen 27:34-36a RSV)

Jacob's name was later changed to Israel (Gen 32:24-29). These passages not only show that Jesus' identification of Nathanael is meant to echo a familiar passage from the Torah, they also set the expectation that those who are true Israelites will come to Jesus, while those who reject him show that they are actually not of Israel. For this hostile response John often uses the term *Ioudaioi*, which at times seems to mean the authorities rather than all Jews.[8]

Nathanael's question, "How do you know me?" (RSV) underscores the wonder of what has just happened. Jesus' response drives the point home. He saw Nathanael when he was under the fig tree, before Philip called him. Interpreters have debated the significance of this response.

The Significance of Jesus' Reference to the Fig Tree

"Does it fulfill a legal convention by identifying under what sort of tree an offense occurred (Susanna 54, 58)?

"Does it evoke recognition that the fig tree was a conventional place for the study of Torah? Or is it an allusion to Hosea 9:10, where God said, 'Like grapes in the wilderness, I found Israel. Like the first fruit on the fig tree ... I saw your ancestors'?

"Alternatively, does Jesus' remark recall the vision of 'all of them under their vines and fig trees' (1 Kgs 4:25; Mic 4:4; Zech 3:10)?

"Zechariah 3:8 voices the expectation of a messianic figure called the Branch. The passage concludes, 'On that day, says the LORD of hosts, you shall invite each other to come under your vine and fig tree' (Zech 3:10). Nathanael identifies Jesus in royal terms appropriate to the messianic 'Branch,' and Jesus identifies Nathanael in terms appropriate to Jacob or 'Israel,' promising that Nathanael, like Jacob, would see God made manifest."[9]

The closing verses of John 1 contain Nathanael's confession and Jesus' promise. Nathanael's confession culminates the series of titles applied to Jesus in John 1: "Rabbi, you are the Son of God! You are the King of Israel!" The identification of Jesus as the Son of God echoes the words of the prologue: "We have seen his glory, glory as of a father's only son" (1:14). Jesus' relationship to God as Son to Father is one of the hallmarks of John's Christology (cf.

5:19-27). At the end of the Gospel of John the narrator will explain that the Gospel was written to lead the reader to make the same confession that Nathanael made at the outset, that Jesus is the Son of God (20:30-31).

The title, "King of Israel," sets up John's later development of the theme of Jesus' kingship. Whereas the Synoptic Gospels report Jesus' teaching on the kingdom of God, the Gospel of John gives far greater emphasis to Jesus' role as king (6:15). Jesus enters Jerusalem as the King of Israel (12:13-15). Pilate questions Jesus' kingship (18:33, 37-39), presents Jesus to the crowd as their king (19:3, 12-15), and eventually fixes the title, "the King of the Jews," over his cross (19:19-22). In contrast to Nathanael (the "true Israelite"), "the Jews" in John ultimately confess, "We have no king but Caesar" (19:15 RSV).

Jesus responds to Nathanael's confession with a question and a promise: "Do you believe because I told you that I saw you under the fig tree? You will see greater things than these" (1:50). The question probes the source and authenticity of Nathanael's belief. For the reader of the Gospel it also raises for the first time the question, What constitutes authentic faith? Jesus seems to be elevating Nathanael as a worthy model for others since he professed belief in response to what Jesus had said. All through the Gospel the narrator will lift up first one response to Jesus, then another, encouraging the reader to compare and assess the various responses. The Gospel of John can therefore be viewed as a series of episodes, in each of which a different character meets Jesus and must decide how he or she will respond to him.[10] Like John the Baptist, Nathanael serves as an early and exemplary response, in comparison with which other responses in subsequent chapters (Nicodemus, the man at the pool of Bethesda, and the crowds in Galilee) will be deficient, incomplete, or inauthentic.

Playing on the relationship between seeing and believing, Jesus assures Nathanael that because he has believed he will see even greater things. What these greater things are is not explained, but it is often surmised that they are the signs, including the death and resurrection of Jesus, recorded later in the Gospel.

The scene concludes with Jesus' promise: "Very truly, I tell you, you will see heaven opened and the angels of God ascending and descending upon the Son of Man" (1:51). This is the first of twenty-five sayings in John that begin with the unprecedented use of the formula, *"Amen, amen,* I say to you."[11] The opening of the heavens was associated with the baptism of Jesus (Mark 1:10) in early Christian tradition. This saying, however, evokes another scene from the story of Jacob: his dream at Bethel of the ladder from heaven to earth and the angels descending and ascending (Gen 28:12). The effect of this allusion to Scripture is to affirm that Jesus is the new Bethel, the new meeting place between heaven and earth. Yet another of Israel's hopes for the future, the coming of the Son of man, has been fulfilled in Jesus.

JOHN 2–4

John 2–4 is the beginning of John 2–12, the public ministry of Jesus. This section of the Gospel is marked by a series of "signs" or mighty deeds that point to Jesus' identity and advance his mission as the Revealer. It is also characterized by Jesus' journeys to Jerusalem for the major Jewish festivals.

The Festivals in John 2–12		
Festival	*Time of Year*	*Context in John*
Passover	March/April	John 2:13ff.
An unnamed festival		John 5:1
Passover	March/April	John 6
Tabernacles	October	John 7–8
Hanukkah	December	John 10:22
Passover	March/April	John 12ff.

From John 5 on, the conflict between Jesus and the religious authorities escalates dramatically.

Chapters 2–4 stand out within John 2–12 as a distinct unit that is marked off geographically and thematically. John 2 begins in Cana of Galilee (2:1) with the first of Jesus' signs, and John 4 brings the unit to a conclusion, again in Cana of Galilee (4:46) with the second of Jesus' signs. The references to the signs are explicit (2:11; 4:54), and these are the only two signs that are numbered.

The geographical settings of these chapters parallel the spread of the church in the first part of Acts in an intriguing way. The pattern may be a coincidence. On the other hand, it may be a part of the two levels that J. Louis Martyn detected: the Gospel tells of the ministry of Jesus at one level and the life of the Johannine community on the other.[12]

Geographical Patterns in John and Acts		
Acts 1:8	*Acts 1–10*	*John 2–4*
Jerusalem	Jerusalem (5:16, 28)	Jerusalem (2:13–3:21)
Judea	Judea (8:1)	Judea (3:22–30)
Samaria	Samaria (8:4-25)	Samaria (4:1-42)
Ends of the earth (the Gentiles; cf. Acts 13:47; Isa. 49:6)	Gentiles (8-10) Ethiopian (8:26-38) Apostle to Gentiles (9:15) Cornelius (10)	Galilee Nobleman (4:46-54; cf. 12:20-21)

John 2–4 is also marked off thematically: it develops the theme of Jesus as the giver of life. The prologue introduces the Word as Life (1:4), and the purpose statement near the end of the Gospel urges readers to believe, so that "you may have life" (20:31). The theme of Jesus as the source of life comes to the fore in this section.

Jesus as the Giver of Life
John 2:1-12—Jesus makes wine at a wedding. Both wine and weddings celebrate the goodness of life.
John 2:13-25—Jesus explains that he will raise the temple in three days, referring to his death and resurrection to life.
John 3:1-21—Jesus challenges Nicodemus to be born again/from above, and John 3:16 explains that Jesus came to give life.
John 3:22-36—Whoever believes has eternal life (v. 36).
John 4:1-45—Jesus offers living water.
John 4:46-54—Jesus gives life to the nobleman's son. Note the interweaving of believing and living in this paragraph.

The Wedding at Cana (2:1-12)

The story of Jesus changing the water to wine is the first of a series of acts and pronouncements in which Jesus offers himself as the fulfillment of traditional Jewish ceremonies and festivals. He replaces the water used for cleansing with wine at the marriage ceremony. Then, in the Temple he offers his body as the new Temple, the new place where one meets God.

The Gospel of John contains fewer miracle accounts than the Synoptics, and these are treated as "signs" that point to Jesus' true identity as the Logos incarnate. The miracle at the wedding at Cana, therefore, serves to confirm the affirmation of the prologue that the Logos was God's agent in creation and that the Logos became incarnate in Jesus. It is as the Logos incarnate that Jesus is able to continue to exercise power over or within the created order; hence the perceptive insight of the medieval quip that "the water recognized its creator and blushed."[13] The miracle is clearly symbolic. All interest is focused not on the miracle but on its meaning and significance.

The Structure of the First Sign

John 2:1-12

1. A supplicant presents Jesus with a request: "They have no wine" (2:3).
2. Jesus rebuffs the request: "Woman, what concern is that to you and to me?" (2:4).
3. The supplicant persists: "Do whatever he tells you" (2:5).
4. Jesus gives instructions that will grant the request: "Fill the jars with water" (2:7).
5. The other person complies with Jesus' order, and the sign is accomplished: the servants fill the jars, draw from them, and carry it to the chief steward (2:8-9).
6. The sign is verified by a third party: "Everyone serves the good wine first ... But you have kept the good wine until now" (2:10).
7. There is a response of faith: "and his disciples believed in him" (2:11).[14]

The miracle is set "on the third day," perhaps signaling that it is to be understood from a post-Easter perspective. This is the only scene in which Jesus' mother appears until his death on the cross, and here Jesus responds, "My hour has not yet come" (2:4), which in the Johannine idiom, as we learn later, is a veiled reference to the time of Jesus' death. Jesus' rebuff of his mother's request, though it seems harsh, fits a pattern in John in which Jesus refuses to do what someone asks him to do, and then later does it of his own accord and in his own time (cf. 7:3; 11:3). Jesus is never coerced into doing anything in John; even when he does what he is asked to do, he does so of his own free will.

The reader will notice that John uses water in a number of different contexts: John's baptizing (1:26-28), ritual cleansing (2:6-7), new birth (3:5), living water (4:10-15), healing water (5:2-7), and Jesus walking on water (6:16-21).[15] The six water pots were used by the Jews for ritual cleansing, as John explains—either for emphasis or as necessary information for Gentile readers. The number six may symbolize the incompleteness of the traditional ritual, which Jesus then literally fills (that is, fulfills) and replaces. His command to fill the pots may have been puzzling, since no one could get into a pot that was filled to the brim without causing it to overflow. The size of the pots conveys the great quantity of wine that is produced. Wine was a powerful symbol that occurs in the Hebrew scriptures in reference to physical and spiritual joy (Eccl 9:7; Gen 27:28); future hope (Zech 10:6-7; Isa 25:6; Joel 2:19); and abundance (Joel 2:24; 3:18; Amos 9:13). The red color also made association with blood common. Therefore, wine was secondarily associated with suffering and death. Nevertheless, the eucharistic significance of this event is probably secondary. The wedding scene could also have eschatological overtones, evoking images of the great eschatological banquet (see Isa 25:6-8; Mark 2:18-20; Rev 19:7-9).

The surprise, and the whole point of the passage, comes with the chief steward's declaration that the host has kept the good wine for last when it was customary to serve the good wine first. The wine, of course, had not come from the host but from Jesus. Jesus' coming as the fulfillment of Israel's hopes and eschatological expectations is therefore reflected in the provision of a bountiful amount of good wine, "kept until now," at a wedding. It had not been kept by any person *(anthropos)* but by the Lord. Good irony, like good wine, is delicious!

131

The Replacement of the Temple (2:13-25)

The cleansing of the temple is recorded in all four Gospels, but the Synoptics place it at the end of Jesus' ministry, whereas in John it is his first public act. John may have moved the scene to the beginning of the ministry to establish the fulfillment/replacement theme early, to introduce the allusion to Jesus' death and resurrection after three days, or to allow the raising of Lazarus to be the climactic sign of his public ministry. On the other hand, the Synoptics may have placed the event late in his ministry because they only record one trip to Jerusalem, at the end of Jesus' life.

Verse 13 marks the first of three journeys from Galilee to Jerusalem (cf. 5:1; 7:10). Passover was one of the annual pilgrimage festivals, when thousands of faithful Jews traveled to Jerusalem. Two other Passovers in the Gospel of John (see John 6 and 12ff.) provide the basis for thinking that Jesus' ministry lasted about three years, or at least more than two years. Laws requiring that only unblemished animals be used for sacrifices meant that most pilgrims purchased the animals for sacrifice after they arrived in Jerusalem. The prohibition of coins bearing human images meant there was also an active trade in currency. Money changers and merchants had set up shop in the temple area, though this may have been a recent development. Only the Gospel of John mentions a whip, but it was hastily made of cords, not a bull whip, and the Gospel does not say that Jesus used it on the merchants.

Two pronouncements, each followed by a parenthetical reference to what the disciples remembered later, guide the reader's understanding of this event. In verse 16, Jesus says, "Stop making my Father's house a marketplace!"—probably an allusion to Zechariah 14:21, "And there shall no longer be traders in the house of the LORD of hosts on that day." Malachi 3:1 may also lie in the background. Verse 17 interprets Jesus' pronouncement by saying that his disciples remembered Psalm 69:9, "Zeal for your house will consume me." The authorities respond by asking what *sign* he could show them. Even the authorities speak in a Johannine idiom at this point, using the same word the narrator used in verse 11 to describe the Cana miracle.

Jesus responds by pointing the authorities to the ultimate sign, his death and resurrection. Jesus' second pronouncement has parallels in Mark 14:58; 15:29—"Destroy this temple, and in three days I will raise it up." But Mark and Matthew say these were the words of false witnesses. The ambiguity of Jesus' words in the first chapter deepens here, as he makes a deliberate play on words that the authorities do not grasp. In this instance the narrator pauses to be sure that the reader does not miss the meaning also. The authorities assume Jesus was speaking of the actual temple structure that had been under construction since 20/19 B.C., 46 years. The narrator, however, explains that Jesus was speaking of his own body. English translations obscure the subtle progression of terms that are used in this scene: "temple" (vv. 14, 15), "house" (vv. 16, 17), "sanctuary" (vv. 19, 20, 21).

In verse 22 the narrator adds a further comment that clarifies the evaluative point of view from which the entire Gospel is written: (1) a retrospective, post-Easter perspective, "after he was raised from the dead"; (2) one informed by what the disciples remembered—and we will learn later of the primary role of the Beloved Disciple in this regard; (3) one informed by reflection on Jesus' words, some of which probably form the foundation for the Johannine discourses; and (4) an interpretation of what Jesus did and said that is informed by the study of scripture. The tradition of the disciples will be traced to the Beloved Disciple (21:24), and the process of recalling and reinterpreting the tradition will be understood as the work of the Paraclete (see 14:26). The Gospel, by its own admission, is therefore not an unvarnished account of what the eyewitnesses saw and heard (cf. 12:16), but a later, post-Easter reflection on the significance of Jesus' ministry in the light of his resurrection, the development of the tradition in the church's teaching and worship, and the study of the scriptures.

The end of chapter 2 presents a further challenge for the reader. The narrator reports that "many believed in his name because they saw the signs that he was doing" (2:23), but that Jesus would not entrust himself to them because he knew what was in them. Jesus, as the incarnate Logos, knew both the true (Nathanael) and the uncommitted (Nicodemus). The prologue assures the reader that "all who received him, who believed in his name" he empowered as "children of God" (1:12). The disciples "believed in him" when they saw the sign he did at Cana, but Jesus did not receive the faith of those who responded to the signs he did in Jerusalem. The issue with which we are confronted, therefore, is to understand what constitutes an acceptable response to Jesus. The Gospel warns against shallow, fickle responses and calls for readers to move on to deeper levels of understanding and commitment.

The Dialogue with Nicodemus (3:1-21)

Readers have been told a great deal about Jesus to this point: The prologue establishes that he was the Logos; John the Baptist declares that he is "the Lamb of God that takes way the sin of the world"; the wedding at Cana demonstrates that he is, or at least provides, the good wine that has been kept "until now"; and the cleansing of the temple allows Jesus to reveal that he is the new sanctuary in which the faithful will meet God. We have also seen the initial responses to Jesus, from his disciples, from his mother, from the authorities in Jerusalem, and from the people in Jerusalem who believed because of his signs. John 3 will extend both the characterization of Jesus and the responses to him.

The chapter begins with only a slight transition signaled by the introduction of a new character (Nicodemus) and a new setting (night). Jesus is still presumably in Jerusalem, and Nicodemus may be representative of those who had seen the signs he did there. Nicodemus is characterized *directly* by what the narrator says about him:

a man of the Pharisees—the group of Torah-observant Jews who would subsequently lead and redefine Judaism after the destruction of Jerusalem
named Nicodemus—a Greek name that means "Conqueror of the People"
a ruler of the Jews—from the ruling class in Jerusalem, probably a member of the Sanhedrin, and therefore a mature man

And *indirectly* by the setting and what he does:

came to Jesus by night—which may signal Nicodemus's desire for secrecy, his courage in coming to Jesus, or his lack of understanding.

Nicodemus is also characterized by what he says and what Jesus says to him. The figure of Nicodemus is therefore partially

134

defined, but open enough to allow readers to interpret him as a representative of the Pharisees, a representative of those who believed because of Jesus' signs, a seeker of unusual courage, a religious insider investigating a radical upstart, a secret believer who lacked the courage to declare his faith openly, or an oppressor who had to decide whether or not to side with the oppressed.[16]

Once Nicodemus has been introduced, the scene advances through the dialogue until it gives way to monologue, and Nicodemus disappears from the narrative until he reappears in 7:50-52 and 19:38-42. The conversation opens with Nicodemus confidently asserting that the group he represents knows that Jesus is "a teacher who has come from God." The conversation proceeds in typically Johannine fashion, with Jesus responding metaphorically. The responses seldom really connect with what has just been said. As one wag put it, in the Gospel of John "Jesus seems to be congenitally incapable of giving a straight answer."[17]

John 3:3 is a traditional saying with a parallel in Matthew 18:3. Again, in typically Johannine fashion, John will take a traditional saying and build an entire discourse around it. How does one enter the kingdom of God? Is it sufficient to be born Jewish, to be a Pharisee, or a ruler of the people? Jesus dismisses the traditional view that one's relationship with God is based on birth rights. Who one is by birth does not matter. One must be born *anōthen,* a word that can mean either "again" or "from above." Nicodemus takes the literal sense, "again," and therefore misunderstands what Jesus means. One cannot be literally born again when one is old, but one who would enter the kingdom must be born "from above." John 3:3 and 5 are the only references to the kingdom of God in John, although this is the most common theme of Jesus' sayings in the Synoptic Gospels. Being born from above means being born "of water and Spirit." Christian readers would have detected the baptismal reference here, but the primary emphasis is birth through the Spirit.

Nicodemus, who was introduced as one with great dignity, learning, and position, and who began confidently, saying, "We know ..." disappears from the scene after Jesus shows that he really cannot grasp the most elementary things even though he is a teacher of Israel. What he said about Jesus was correct, but he has not been "born from above." The children of God, after all,

135

are born "not of blood or of the will of the flesh or of the will of man, but of God" (1:13). In the verses that follow, the discourse picks up themes introduced by the traditional or core saying in John 3:3: flesh and Spirit (3:6-8), and the distinction between earthly and heavenly things, above and below (3:11-12). Jesus, as the Son of Man who descended from heaven, can therefore mediate between the two realms and reveal what he has seen and heard from the Father. The Spirit is like wind (the double entendre of the Greek *pneuma*); it blows where it will, and one does not know where it is from or where it is going. Ironically, like the serpent that Moses lifted up on a pole to give healing to the people of Israel, Jesus too will be lifted up on a pole (3:14; cf. Num 21:9; Isa 52:13).

John 3:16 is an integral part of the discourse. The verse explains the giving of eternal life, another important element of Johannine thought, as a result of God's love for the world, through the revelation of God in Jesus. The paragraph that follows then explains this core saying or maxim of the Johannine community. Verse 17 explains God's sending, verse 18 the relationship between believing and not perishing, and verses 19-21 the significance of Jesus' coming as the light. The incarnation brings judgment because Jesus reveals those who belong to the light and those who are of the darkness.

The structure of John's dualism emerges much more clearly in John 3:1-21.

Categories of Johannine Dualism in John 3	
light	darkness (night)
above	below
Spirit	flesh
heavenly	earthly
life (eternal life)	death (perish)
saved	condemned
love	hate
deeds done in God	evil deeds
those who believe	those who do not believe

The discourses in the Gospel extend, interpret, and play on the relationship between these and other terms, calling readers to turn from the things below and accept the revelation that has come through Jesus by believing in him.

More of John's Testimony (3:22-30)

The remainder of the chapter consists of two units: 3:22-30, which extends John the Baptist's testimony to Jesus; and 3:31-36, which extends the discourse that follows Jesus' dialogue with Nicodemus. The scene changes in 3:22, and Jesus and his disciples go to the Judean countryside. In contrast to the Synoptic Gospels (cf. Mark 1:14-15), John records a period during which John and Jesus ministered and baptized simultaneously before John was put in prison. John is ambiguous, if not contradictory, on the question of whether Jesus baptized others (cf. 3:22, 26; 4:2), leading many interpreters to treat John 4:2 as a later gloss.

When a dispute over purification arises between John's followers and a Jew, John's disicples observe that more people are going to Jesus than to John. John answers with five affirmations:

1. One can receive only what God has given.
2. He had said that he was not the Messiah—a reminder to his followers (and by implication any of his followers who might hear this gospel).
3. He was not the bridegroom but the bridegroom's friend, who heard the bridegroom's voice.
4. His joy has therefore been fulfilled.
5. And, Jesus must increase while he must decrease.

John, again in his own words, has fulfilled the role defined for him in the prologue (1:6-8, 15). He has borne witness to Jesus (cf. 1:19-34), and he has pointed his followers away from himself and toward Jesus.

Part of a Discourse on the Earthly and the Heavenly (3:31-36)

This paragraph seems to be so oddly placed that interpreters have debated whether it originally followed immediately after 3:21. No new speaker is introduced, so one might assume that John the Baptist is still speaking. But verses 31-36 do not read like a continuation of John's testimony to Jesus. Instead, they seem to be a doublet of 3:11-21. Verse 31 returns to the contrast between the earthly and the heavenly (cf. v. 12). The themes of bearing witness to what one has seen and heard in verse 11 are echoed in verse 32. The reference to the one whom God has sent in verse 34 parallels verse 16, as do the affirmations that "the Father loves the Son" (v. 35) and that the one who "believes in the Son has eternal life" (v. 36). As in 3:19-21, the discussion of eternal life in verse 36 leads to its corollary: the judgment (here "wrath of God") rests on those who refuse to believe.

Since the content of 3:31-36 returns to themes articulated in Jesus' discourse earlier in the chapter, one should probably assume that Jesus is speaking here, but it is also possible that the narrator is now speaking in a voice that is scarcely distinguishable from Jesus'. In spite of the ambiguity of the identity of the speaker, precisely because they are a doublet of earlier material verses 31-36 bring the chapter to a satisfying conclusion by recapping some of its leading themes.

Jesus' Dialogue with a Samaritan Woman (4:1-42)

The story of Jesus meeting the Samaritan woman at a well is a beautiful development of type scene, character, irony, and theme. A type scene is a scene that the reader will recognize from past associations.[18] Because everyone knows what is expected, variations on the theme provide novel and interesting twists.

Well Scenes in the Old Testament		
Passage	*Hero*	*Character Trait*
Genesis 24:1-61	Isaac	Isaac is absent (passive); Rebekah is dominant.
Genesis 29:1-20	Jacob	Jacob wrestles the stone.
Exodus 2:15-21	Moses	Moses delivers the shepherd girls and provides water in the wilderness.

In the stories of the patriarchs and Moses, the hero meets his bride at a well in a "far country." The scene always serves to highlight some aspect of the hero's character. Isaac, who is the passive patriarch—the child sacrifice and the digger of wells

138

who would move on rather than fight to defend them (cf. Gen 22; 26:15-33)—is not even present. His father sends a servant to find Isaac a wife. Jacob, the trickster, is running away from his brother. He has spent a night at Bethel, with a stone for a pillow, and he will have to work 14 years for Rachel. At the well, he has to wrestle the stone from the opening. Moses, was the great deliverer of his people, their guide in the wilderness. At the well, he delivers the shepherd girls and provides water in the wilderness, foreshadowing his future role. For those accustomed to the type scenes of the Hebrew scriptures, therefore, a story of Jesus meeting a woman at a well would have held great interest.

The Samaritan woman is in many ways the opposite of Nicodemus. He was a Jew; she was a Samaritan. He was a respected leader; she was village peasant with five husbands in her past. The tension between Jesus and the Samaritan woman crosses four levels: gender, nationality, race, and religion. In the course of the conversation, all four barriers are crossed and community is created. This story, therefore, is the Johannine equivalent of the story in Acts 8 about how the gospel reached the Samaritans.

The first three verses explain the reason for Jesus' travel through Samaria. Often Jewish travelers went around Samaria so as to avoid contact with the Samaritans. The Gospel of John differs from the Synoptics in that the early part of Jesus' ministry overlaps the end of John's ministry. When Jesus hears that the Pharisees have been told that he is baptizing more followers than John, he resolves to leave Judea and return to Galilee, just as he will later withdraw from conflict in 7:1; 8:59; 10:39-40. Contradicting the earlier report in John 3:22, the narrator explains that only Jesus' disciples were baptizing (4:2). While on one level Jesus' departure from Judea may have been to avoid conflict with the Pharisees, at another level his journey through Samaria was necessary because it was the Father's direction (4:4). The stage directions are completed with the report that Jesus was sitting at Jacob's well near Sychar, about the sixth hour. He was alone because his disciples had gone to buy food (v. 8). Following the Jewish reckoning of time, the sixth hour would have been noon, but a good case can be made for counting the hours from noon so that it would have been six in the evening.[19]

The story is a recognition scene (see above, chapter 4). The dialogue carries all the action as the woman comes step by step to grasp who Jesus is. The first part of the conversation (4:7-15) focuses on their common need for water and Jesus' offer of "living water." Jesus initiates the conversation on the level of common physical need: "Give me a drink." The request carried radical implications because Jesus, a Jewish man, was offering to drink from the vessel of a Samaritan woman. In doing so, Jesus was setting aside powerful social conventions and ignoring centuries of hostility between Jews and Samaritans. The conversation progressively addresses and transcends each of the barriers that separate Jesus and the woman, while Jesus develops the symbolism of "living water," and the woman grows in her perception of who Jesus is.

Jesus' reference to "living water" is ambiguous (as was *anōthen*, "again" or "from above" in 3:3) because its literal meaning would have been running or flowing water. The woman responds with a statement of the obvious problem and then two questions: Jesus has nothing with which to draw water, and the well was deep. After all, he had asked her for a drink; now he was offering her "living water." Where would he get "living water?" Jacob had dug the well to provide them water. Was he greater than the patriarch? The second question is ironic because it presumes a negative response, but the reader who was introduced to Jesus by the prologue knows that indeed Jesus is greater than the patriarch. The theme of fulfillment and replacement continues.

Water was a precious and essential commodity in this hot, arid climate. Jewish apocalypses picture paradise as a lush garden with streams and rivers. Water was also a symbol for eschatological cleansing: "On that day living waters shall flow out from Jerusalem" (Zech 14:8), and water will flow from the temple (Ezek 47:1-12). But Jesus has already demonstrated that he would be the new temple (cf. 2:13-22). Those who thirst will drink from the water that flows from him (7:37-39; 19:34). Similarly, in the Qumran scrolls, the well represents the Torah, which the scholars dig and which provides living water that sustains the community.

"Living Water" in the Qumran Scrolls

But God remembered the covenant of the very first, and from Aaron raised men of knowledge and from Israel wise men, and forced them to listen. And they dug the well: *Num 21:18* "A well which the princes dug, which the nobles of the people delved with the staff." The well is the law. And those who dug it are the converts of Israel, who left the land of Judah and lived in the land of Damascus, all of whom God called princes.... (CD 6:2-6)

He disclosed (these matters) to them and they dug a well of plentiful water; and whoever spurns them shall not live. (CD 3:16-17)

And thus, all the men who entered the new covenant in the land of Damascus and turned and betrayed and departed from the well of living waters, shall not be counted in the assembly of the people and shall not be inscribed in their lists.... (CD 19:34).

[I give thanks, Lord,]
because you have set me in the source of streams in a dry land,
in the spring of water in a parched land,....
Trees of life in the secret source,
hidden among the trees of water.
They must make a shoot grow
in the everlasting plantation, to take root before it grows.
. . . .
For it [the flame of searing fire] sees, but does not know,
notices, but does not believe,
in the spring of life....
But you, my God,
you have placed in my mouth as it were early rain for all [...]
spring of living water; ... (1QH 16(=8):4, 6-7*a*, 13*b*-14*a*, 16).[20]

After the woman asks for some of the water Jesus has offered (v. 15), the conversation enters its second phase (vv. 16-26). Living water is not mentioned again. Instead, the conversation focuses on the woman's marital background, Jesus' identity, and the differences between Jewish and Samaritan worship. The second part of the conversation, like the first, is initiated by Jesus, who tells the woman to go and get her husband (v. 16). When she responds that she has no husband, Jesus further demonstrates that he knows what is in the heart of each person (1:48; 2:24-25) by confirming that she has spoken the truth. She has had five husbands, and the man she is living with is not her husband, or perhaps not *her* husband because the

141

Greek pronoun is in the emphatic position. It has often been suggested that the reference to five husbands is an allusion to the five nations that were settled in Samaria (2 Kgs 17:24). More immediate is the characterization of the woman as one who has been victimized by a series of marriages that for whatever reasons did not last, and who is now living with a man out of wedlock.

The woman's first response to Jesus was abrupt, using no title of respect (4:9). Thereafter, she addressed him as "sir" (4:11, 15, 19), and in verse 19 she volunteers that he is a prophet. Nevertheless, she uses this perception to test Jesus' response on the divisive issue of the differences between Jewish and Samaritan worship practices. The two cultic centers—Mt. Gerizim and Jerusalem—had spurred hostilities for generations. Again, Jesus transcends the divisive issue by elevating the conversation to a new level. True worship is not defined by a geographical or cultic center but by "spirit and truth." The first person plural, "we worship what we know" in verse 22 may be another example of the voice of the narrator, speaking for the Johannine community, merging with the voice of Jesus in the Gospel (see 1:14; 3:11; 21:24). "The hour" has already appeared in the narrative in Jesus' response to his mother (2:4), and will later be defined more precisely as the time of Jesus' death and resurrection (4:21, 23; cf. 7:30; 8:20; 12:23, 27; 13:1; 16:32; 17:1; 19:14, 27). When the woman alludes to the coming of the Messiah, Jesus says, "I am he" (4:26).

The scene shifts with the return of the disciples in verse 27. They marvel not that Jesus was talking with a Samaritan, but that he was talking with a woman. The narrator reports that when the woman returned to the city, she left her water jug. This detail may convey her excitement and haste, or more profoundly it may symbolize that as Jesus had said, because she had accepted the living water she would no longer need to come to the well to draw (vv. 14-15). The narrator also reports what was going on in the city while Jesus was talking with the disciples at the well, so in narrative form the reader is given a split screen with two simultaneous scenes. The woman calls people in the city to come see Jesus (cf. 1:39, 46), asking "Can this be the Christ?" (v. 29 RSV). Her recognition of Jesus has moved another step. Her faith is like that of Nathanael (1:48-51); she believed because of Jesus' insight into her life.

Verse 31 returns the reader to the well. Just as water can have symbolic significance, so too can food. Jesus has bread to eat that the disciples do not know of, not literal bread but doing the will of the one who sent him (v. 34). Two agricultural proverbs follow.

Two Proverbs
"Four months more, then comes the harvest." (v. 35) "One sows and another reaps." (v. 37)

The time is now, and Jesus sends his disciples to gather the harvest. Their commission will become clearer in later scenes (17:18; 20:21), but here it clearly means that the Samaritans are to be included in the community of those who receive the gospel.

Verses 39-42 are the climax of this intricate story. The woman functioned as an effective witness for her people and brought them to Jesus. The disciples had brought Jesus lunch, but the woman brought the entire city! The woman's testimony to her townspeople is repeated: "He told me everything I have ever done" (4:29, 39). The prophet knew all she had ever done and still accepted her. The story that began with one woman ends with the whole village. It began when the woman met a stranger at the well near a particular city, moved through the barriers between Jews and Samaritans, and ends with the confession that Jesus is "the Savior of the world." Again, the recognition of Jesus is the focal point on which the story ends. Belief that was based on the woman's testimony has been confirmed by their own hearing (4:42). Theirs is a faith that is based not on signs (cf. 2:11, 23-25; 3:2) but on Jesus' word (4:41).

Steps in the Samaritan Woman's Response		
Verse	*Title*	*Response*
4:9	None	"How is it that you, a Jew, ask a drink of me, a woman of Samaria?"
4:11-12	"Sir"	"Are you greater than our ancestor Jacob?"
4:15	"Sir"	"Give me this water, so that I may never be thirsty."
4:19	"Prophet"	"Sir, I see that you are a prophet."
4:25	"Messiah"	"I know that Messiah is coming."
4:29	"Messiah"	"He cannot be the Messiah, can he?"
4:42	"Savior"	*Townspeople:* "We know that this is truly the Savior of the world."

The Official's Son (4:43-54)

The healing of the official's son marks the end of this section of the Gospel. It is the second numbered sign (cf. 2:11; 4:54), and it returns the narrative to Cana, "where he had changed the water into wine" (4:46). In a more subtle fashion, it advances the theme that has been important throughout this section: Jesus is the one who gives life.

Jesus as the Giver of Life		
The Prologue	1:1-18	"In him was life." (1:4)
The Wedding at Cana	2:1-12	Jesus provides wine at a wedding. Both wine and weddings were associated with the celebration of life and with eschatological hopes. Jesus' coming meant new life.
The Cleansing of the Temple	2:13-25	When Jesus was raised from the dead, his disciples would see that he was the new temple.
Conversation with Nicodemus	3:1-21	The necessity for new life: "You must be born [again/from above]." (3:7) God sent his only Son, so that "whoever believes in him may have eternal life." (3:15-16)
John's Testimony	3:22-30	Jesus is the bridegroom. (3:29)
Discourse	3:31-36	"Whoever believes in the Son has eternal life." (3:36)
The Samaritan Woman	4:1-42	"The water that I will give will become in them a spring of water gushing up to eternal life." (4:14)
The Official's Son	4:43-54	"Your son will live." (4:50)

Verses 43-45 record Jesus' return to Galilee. The saying that a prophet is not without honor except in his own country is found in all three Synoptic Gospels (Matt 13:57; Mark 6:4; Luke 4:24). The tension between the proverb in verse 44 and the report that he was welcomed in Galilee (v. 45) has led to debate among interpreters as to whether John considers Jesus' "own country" to be Nazareth, Galilee, Judea, or Jerusalem—or whether verse 44 must be a gloss inserted at a later time. At least it is clear that in this Gospel, Jesus is welcomed in Galilee but rejected in Jerusalem.

The account of the healing of the official's son has parallels in the healings at a distance in the Synoptics: the healing of the centurion's servant (Matt 8:5-13; Luke 7:1-10) and the healing of the Syrophoenician woman's daughter (Matt 15:21-28; Mark 7:24-30). In each case Jesus heals at a distance, and when the one who made the request returned home, the servant or daughter was well. Nevertheless, the healing John records also follows the form of the Johannine miracle accounts:

The Form of the Healing of the Official's Son

John 4:46-54

1. A supplicant presents Jesus with a request: A royal official "went and begged him to come down and heal his son." (4:47)

2. Jesus rebuffs the request: "Unless you see signs and wonders you will not believe." (4:48)

3. The supplicant persists: "Sir, come down before my little boy dies." (4:49)

4. Jesus gives instructions that will grant the request: "Go; your son will live." (4:50)

5. The other person complies with Jesus' order, and the sign is accomplished: "The man believed the word that Jesus spoke to him and started on his way." (4:50)

6. The sign is verified by a third party: ". . . his slaves met him and told him that his child was alive." (4:51)

7. There is a response of faith: "So he himself believed, along with his whole household." (4:53)

145

In John's account, the official traveled from Capernaum to Cana, a distance of about 15 miles. He asks Jesus to come and heal his son, who was "at the point of death." Death is the problem, not a particular illness. As in the changing of water to wine, Jesus at first rebuffs the request, this time on the basis that unless the people see "signs and wonders" they will not believe (cf. 2:23-25). The official repeats his request, and again the issue is death (v. 49). Whereas in the Synoptic accounts the centurion says that Jesus does not have to go to his house—he has only to give the command—here the official begs Jesus to come with him, and Jesus sends him home with only the assurance that his son will live. The man believes Jesus, and as he is on his way home he is met by servants who tell him that his son recovered at the very hour when Jesus said, "Your son will live." So, he and his whole household believe. One can hardly miss the interplay between believing and living in this story. The story drives home the theme: Jesus gives life to those who believe in him.

Believing and Living in John 4:46-54

Death	*Belief*	*Life*
His son was at the point of *death*. (v. 47) "Come down before my little boy *dies*." (v. 49)		
	"Unless you see signs and wonders you will not *believe*." (v. 48)	
		"Your son will *live*." (v. 50)
	The man *believed* the word that Jesus spoke to him and started on his way. (v. 50)	
		His slaves met him and told him that his child was *alive*. (v. 51)

> ... the hour when
> Jesus had said to
> him, "Your son
> will *live*."
> (v. 53)
>
> So he himself
> *believed* along
> with his whole
> household. (v. 53)

The characters in John 1– 4 have modeled various responses to Jesus. Nathanael mistook Jesus' origin, thinking that he was from Nazareth, but he came to Jesus nevertheless, as an Israelite in whom there is no guile. Nicodemus models the necessity of being born "from above"; he cannot understand because he is "from below" and sees only earthly things. John the Baptist bears a self-less witness to Jesus, saying that he must decrease while Jesus increases. The Samaritan woman moves step by step to recognize that Jesus is the expected Messiah, and the Samaritans confess that Jesus is the "Savior of the world." The official at the end of this section believes without any sign, and finds that Jesus has given life to his son. The theme of Jesus as the giver of new life has been clearly established, as has the variety of responses to Jesus and the various stages of faith that they represent. While these themes continue in John 5–12, others will also be developed in the coming chapters.

CHAPTER 7

INTERPRETING THE FOURTH GOSPEL JOHN 5–12

J ohn 5–12 is marked by cycles of increasing hostility against Jesus set in the context of Jewish festivals. The progression of festivals is evident in the following references. At each festival Jesus does or says things that show that he is the fulfillment of what the festival celebrates.

Jewish Festivals in John 5-12

John 5:1	An unnamed festival
John 6:4	Passover
John 7:2	The Jewish festival of Booths
John 10:22	The festival of the Dedication (Hanukkah)
John 12:1	Passover

This section of the Gospel begins with a healing at the pool of Bethesda and ends with the raising of Lazarus and Jesus' entry into Jerusalem for the Passover celebration. The rising hostility is introduced by the explanation in John 5:16: "Therefore the Jews started persecuting Jesus, because he was doing such things on the sabbath." And 5:18: "For this reason the Jews were seeking all the more to kill him, because he was not only breaking the sabbath, but was also calling God his own Father, thereby making himself equal to God." These statements introduce and foreshadow the role of "the Jews" in the rest of the Gospel. The discourse that follows cites the witnesses to Jesus (5:19-47) as though Jesus were already on trial. In the next episode (John 6) the people murmur against Jesus (6:41) and then fight with one another (6:52). The reader is warned that "the Jews" are seeking to kill Jesus (7:1). The level of hostility escalates in the ensuing debate. The authorities seek to arrest Jesus. Then, there is a division among the people (7:43). John 8 contains the most hostile exchange between Jesus and "the Jews," in which Jesus declares that their father was the devil (8:44). "The Jews" respond that Jesus is a Samaritan and has a demon (8:48), and they attempt to stone him (8:59). In response to the healing of the blind man, there is division among the Pharisees (9:16). "The Jews" take official action against Jesus' followers (9:22). Division among "the Jews" follows again (10:19), with some saying that he is demonic and others defending him. When "the Jews" again take up stones against Jesus (10:31, 33), he withdraws from Jerusalem (10:40). Mary and Martha send for Jesus because Lazarus is at the point of death. Jesus delays, then returns, asks Martha if she believes that he is "the resurrection and the life" (11:25), and then raises Lazarus from the dead. The section ends with the authorities plotting to put Jesus to death, and Jesus' soliloquy at the end of his public ministry (12:44-50).

JOHN 5

John 5 is composed of three units: the healing of the man at the pool of Bethesda (5:1-18), Jesus' discourse on the authority of the Son (5:19-30), and a discourse on the witnesses to Jesus (5:31-47).

The Man at the Pool (5:1-18)

The man at the pool is one of the most enigmatic of John's characters. He only appears in this scene, and his response to Jesus is open to debate.

The Form of the Healing of the Man at the Pool

John 5:1-18

1. A supplicant presents Jesus with a request. Instead, Jesus takes the initiative: "Do you want to be made well?" (5:6)
2. Jesus rebuffs the request. Instead, the man is evasive: "Sir, I have no one to put me into the pool when the water is stirred up." (5:7)
3. The supplicant persists. Instead, Jesus persists.
4. Jesus gives instructions that will grant the request: "Stand up, take your mat and walk." (5:8)
5. The other person complies with Jesus' order, and the sign is accomplished: "At once the man was made well, and he took up his mat and began to walk." (5:9)
6. The sign is verified by a third party: "So the Jews said to the man who had been cured, 'It is the sabbath; it is not lawful for you to carry your mat.'" (5:10)
7. There is a response of faith. Instead, "the man went away and told the Jews that it was Jesus who had made him well." (5:15)[1]

The pool of Bethesda, which lay on the north side of the temple, was a gathering place for the sick. Jesus initiates the conversation, asking the man if he wants to be well. The man evades Jesus' question, blaming his condition on the fact that he could never get to the pool first when the waters were stirred. John 5:4 is a textual gloss that explains that after an angel stirred the waters the first one in the pool would be healed. The verse does not appear in the best manuscripts, and it does not appear in any manuscript before the fifth century.[2] Jesus commands the man to rise, take up his pallet, and walk. Parenthetically, this command is the longest verbatim parallel between John and the Synoptics (cf. Mark 2:9). The man has been entirely passive through this process. He did not ask Jesus to heal him. He did not say he wanted to be well, and he blamed his condition on others.

Only when the man has been healed are we told that it was the sabbath (5:9). This delayed information introduces the issue of a possible violation of sabbath law, either in the matter of healing or carrying a load on the sabbath. "The Jews" enter the scene, charging that the healed man was violating the sabbath. Again, he blames his action on someone else—the one who had healed him. And after 38 years by the pool, he did not even know his healer's name. When Jesus finds him and charges him to sin no more, the man reports to "the Jews," who appear here as the religious authorities, that Jesus was the one who healed him. Was he thereby bearing witness to Jesus, or was he absolving himself of suspicion by implicating Jesus? There is no statement that he believed (contrast 2:11; 4:53). Instead, the man appears to be acting in character, still making sure that he was not blamed by reporting Jesus to the authorities. Nothing about this miracle has followed the expected form. As a result of this encounter, the religious authorities sought to kill Jesus. The charges against him were twofold: sabbath violation (5:16) and blasphemy (5:18).[3]

The Son's Authority (5:19-30)

As we have seen, the Johannine miracle accounts in the previous chapters have been very similar to the Synoptic miracle stories. They are brief, self-contained units. At this point the evangelist's technique changes and a discourse is appended to the miracle that unpacks some of its themes. In this case, the discourse reports Jesus' response to the charges against him: his authority to heal and his relationship to the Father.

Miracle Accounts, Dialogues, and Discourses in John		
John 2:1-12	The Wedding at Cana	No dialogue or discourse follows.
John 4:46-54	The Official's Son	No dialogue or discourse follows.
John 5:1-18	The Man at the Pool	Discourse on Jesus' authority and the witnesses to Jesus (5:19-47)
John 6:1-14	The Feeding of the 5,000	Discourse on the bread from heaven (6:22-59)

John 6:16-21	The Walking on the Water	No dialogue or discourse follows.
John 9:1-8	The Healing of the Blind Man	A series of dialogues in six ensuing scenes (9:9-41)
John 11:1-44	The Raising of Lazarus	Dialogues with 1. the disciples (11:7-16), 2. Martha (11:20-27), and 3. Mary (11:28-37) unpack the significance of the miracle as it is being narrated.

The discourse on Jesus' authority as the Son opens with an allusion to what was probably a common proverb regarding an apprentice son's relationship to his father: "the Son can do nothing on his own, but only what he see the Father doing."[4] Jesus' authority, therefore, comes from the Father, and he promises that he will do even greater works. Fulfilling expectations about the apocalyptic Son of Man, he will raise the dead and give life. Jesus' claim extends the theme of Jesus as the giver of life in John 1–4, and it foreshadows the raising of Lazarus in John 11. In Jewish law, the one sent was due the same respect as the sender (5:23). Like the Son of Man, Jesus will raise the dead and execute judgment. Eternal life begins here and now, and those who hear Jesus and believe already have eternal life. Nevertheless, Jesus also looks ahead to the time when all the dead will hear his voice and rise, either to life or to condemnation (cf. 5:29 and Dan 12:2). Verse 30 concludes this section of the discourse by reiterating the principle with which it began: "I can do nothing on my own.... I seek to do not my own will but the will of him who sent me."

The Witnesses to Jesus (5:31-47)

Having defended his authority to heal on the sabbath and call God his Father, Jesus now calls forth witnesses to his defense. The whole discouse, therefore, takes on the atmosphere of a trial scene in which accuser bring charges, the accused is asked to respond, and then witnesses are summoned. By law, testimony had to be confirmed by two witnesses (Deut 19:15), but Jesus has several authoritative witnesses.

Witnesses to Jesus		
John 5:33-35	John the Baptist	He testified to the truth. He was a burning and shining lamp
John 5:36	Jesus' works	A testimony greater than John's. The works testify that the Father has sent Jesus.
John 5:37-38	The Father	"You have never heard his voice or seen his form, and you do not have his word abiding in you...."
John 5:39	The Scriptures	"... it is they that testify on my behalf."
John 5:45-47	Moses	"Your accuser is Moses, on whom you have set your hope. If you believed Moses, you would believe me, for he wrote about me."

Jesus probes further into the nature of unbelief. Earlier, he said that the judgment had already come with the coming of the light. Some loved darkness because their works were evil (3:19-21). Now, he charges that his accusers refuse to come to him because they do not have the love of God in them (v. 42), and they seek glory from one another and not from God (v. 44). The reasons for unbelief, like the nature of faith, will be explored further, later in the Gospel (cf. 8:21-59; 9:39-41; 10:1-18; 12:43; 15:18–16:4). The reference to Moses prepares for the Mosaic overtones of the feeding of the multitude in the wilderness and the crossing of the sea in the next chapter.

JOHN 6

This chapter presents Jesus as the Bread of Life. It may once have been an independent homily, since it is closely related to Exodus 16, Numbers 11, and other Old Testament passages.

Rudolf Bultmann suggested that chapters 5 and 6 were originally reversed because the geographical notices in chapters 5–7 flow more smoothly when the chapters are reversed.[5] The present order, however, allows chapter 6 to develop the theme of the witnesses to Jesus introduced in the discourse in chapter 5 (God, Scripture, Jesus' works, and Moses). Each of these plays a powerful role in John 6. Jesus fulfills the role of Moses (or the expected prophet like Moses; Deut 18:15, 18) by feeding the multitude in the wilderness and crossing the sea.

The discourse that follows is based on the sign. Interestingly, the discourse treats only the giving of the bread. Jesus' walking on the water is not developed. Its inclusion in the chapter may therefore show that it was firmly linked to the feeding of the five thousand in the oral tradition. This is the only miracle related in all four Gospels. Raymond E. Brown has charted the parallels between Mark and John as follows:[6]

The Multiplication of the Loaves in Mark and John		
Multiplication for 5000	John 6:1-15	Mark 6:30-44
Walking on the sea	16-24	45-52
(Then skipping to the end of Mark's second multiplication account which is found in Mark 8:1-10)		
Request for a sign	25-34	8:11-13
Remarks on bread ·	35-59	14-21
Faith of Peter	60-69	27-30
Passion theme; betrayal	70-71	31-33

Feeding the Multitude (6:1-15)

The first four verses set the scene: the other side of the Sea of Galilee (or Tiberias, the best known landmark in the area), the multitude following Jesus, up on a mountain, at the time of Passover. The Passover motif is emphasized. While crowds of pilgrims are making their way to Jerusalem, another crowd is thronging around Jesus in Galilee. John explains that the crowds came because of the signs that Jesus had done in healing the sick. The reader is reminded of the healings in John 4 and 5, but the crowd also represents those who have a "signs faith." By the end of the chapter they will have left Jesus. The reference to going up on a mountain with his disciples is reminiscent of Matthew's introduction of the Sermon on the Mount (Matt 5:1-2), but both passages evoke memories of the Sinai event. The sign itself follows the typical Johannine pattern.

The Form of the Feeding of the Multitude

John 6:1-15

1. A supplicant presents Jesus with a request:
   The request is absent, or implicit at best: Jesus "saw a large crowd coming toward him." (6:4)
2. Jesus rebuffs the request:
   "Where are we to buy bread for these people to eat?" (6:5)
3. The supplicant persists:
   Andrew: "There is a boy here who has five barley loaves and two fish. But what are they among so many people?" (6:9)
4. Jesus gives instructions that will grant the request:
   "Make the people sit down." (6:10)
5. The other person complies with Jesus' order, and the sign is accomplished:
   "So they sat down, about five thousand in all. Then Jesus took the loaves, and when he had given thanks, he distributed them to those who were seated; so also the fish, as much as they wanted." (6:10)
6. The sign is verified by a third party:
   "When the people saw the sign that had been done, ..."
7. There is a response of faith:
   "they began to say, 'This is indeed the prophet who is to come into the world.'" (6:14)

In John there is no temptation scene, as in Matthew and Luke, in which Jesus is tempted to make bread. Instead, here Jesus tests Philip. The issue is similar: bread to feed the multitudes. John emphasizes, however, that Jesus knew what he was going to do. John allows no doubt or suspicion that Jesus' actions are directed by others. A denarius was a laborer's daily wage, so two hundred denarii would have been about eight months' income.

As in John 1 and 12, Andrew is Philip's companion and comes off better than Philip. John is the only Gospel to mention that the loaves were *barley* loaves. Barley ripened earlier than wheat, and since it was cheaper, it was used for bread by the poor (Judg 7:13; Ezek 4:12) and as feed for animals (1 Kgs 4:28). Its significance here, however, is as an echo of the barley loaves in the account of Elisha's feeding a multitude.

Elisha Feeds a Multitude with Barley Loves

2 Kings 4:42-44

A man came from Baal-shalishah, bringing food from the first fruits to the man of God: twenty loaves of barley and fresh ears of grain in his sack. Elisha said, "Give it to the people and let them eat." But his servant said, "How can I set this before a hundred people?" So he repeated, "Give it to the people and let them eat, for thus says the LORD, 'They shall eat and have some left.'" He set it before them, they ate, and had some left, according to the word of the LORD.

The feeding of the multitude—in the wilderness, at the time of Passover, with barley loaves—is therefore a clear affirmation in narrative form that Jesus is the fulfillment of Moses and the prophets. He is the expected Prophet like Moses (Deut 18:15-18) who will again deliver his people.

The language of taking, blessing, and giving is evocative of the Eucharist, but the institution of the Eucharist is not recorded in John. The fish became an early Christian symbol. The gathering of the left-over bread may have been noted for various reasons: it confirms the abundance of bread that was produced; the number twelve was important in relation to the tribes of Israel; it corresponds to the gathering of the manna and the record that there was some left after Elisha fed the one hundred on barley loaves; or it may be symbolic of the gathering of the church (as in Didache 9.4). Whatever the symbolic meaning, it continues John's pattern of mentioning a significant physical detail in the narration of a sign: six water pots filled (2:6-7), a water jug left behind (4:28), a mat carried by one who had not been able to walk (5:8-12), and now twelve baskets of bread fragments.

The sign was revelatory, as are all the signs in John. The peo-

156

ple understood what had been done as a disclosure of Jesus' messianic identity: "This is indeed the prophet who is to come into the world" (6:14). He was not just *a* prophet in their eyes (cf. 4:19), but *the* prophet—the expected Prophet like Moses (Deut 18:15-18). Because Jesus knew that they were about to try to make him a political king (6:15), he withdrew to the mountain alone. The reference to the mountain forms an inclusion with the reference at the beginning of the scene (v. 3).

Walking on the Water (6:16-21)

Having fed the people as Moses did in the wilderness, Jesus now performs a sea miracle, like the parting of the sea at the Exodus. This miracle, however, does not follow the seven-part pattern that is typical of the Johannine signs, and the discourse that follows is concerned only with Jesus as the Bread of Life, not with the meaning of the walking on the sea. The walking on the water is recorded in Mark 6:45-52 and Matthew 14:22-33 also, so it was probably already attached to the feeding of the multitude as a fulfillment of the Exodus typology in the oral tradition before it reached John. Walking on water, like the multiplication of loaves, again demonstrates Jesus' sovereignty over the created order as the creative Logos incarnate. Both creation and Exodus motifs are prominent in the Old Testament passages evoked by this event.

Walking on the Water in the Old Testament	
Job 9:8	[God] who alone stretched out the heavens and trampled the waves of the Sea.
Ps. 77:15-20	With your strong arm you redeemed your people, the descendants of Jacob and Joseph. When the waters saw you, O God, when the waters saw you, they were afraid; the very deep trembled.... Your way was through the sea, your path, through the mighty waters; yet your footprints were unseen. You led your people like a flock by the hand of Moses and Aaron.

Isaiah 43:2-3   When you pass through the waters, I will be with
you;
and through the rivers, they shall not over-
whelm you; ...
For I am the LORD your God,
the Holy One of Israel, your Savior.

When the disciples saw Jesus walking on the water and were frightened, Jesus reassured them, saying, "It is I; do not be afraid." The admonition not to fear is typical of theophanies and angelophanies (see Judg 6:23; Tobit 12:16-17; Luke 1:13, 30). The words "It is I" (Greek, *ego eimi*) can also mean "I am," the formula of divine self-disclosure (Exod 3:14; cf. Judg 13:11; Isa 43:3, 11-13; 51:12). The walking on the water, therefore, is once more a revelatory event that discloses that Jesus is the incarnate Logos, one greater than Moses. The sea was a place of chaos in Hebrew literature, but Jesus delivers his disciples from the chaos: "... immediately the boat reached the land toward which they were going." As this brief account demonstrates, both Jesus' words and his works are revelatory in this Gospel.

The True Bread of Life (6:22-59)

John 6:22-59 is a profound and beautifully developed discourse on the identity of Jesus as the Bread of Life. Like many other sections of the Gospel, it is intricately structured and repays close study and repeated readings. Various patterns have been suggested: that of a synagogue sermon, elaborate chiastic structures, John 6 as the center of the entire Gospel, movement from Jesus as Wisdom to the eucharistic significance of Jesus as the Bread of Life, and source critical theories that have identified John 6:51-58 as the work of the redactor. The following analysis of the structure attempts to show the progression of the discourse along thematic lines.

The Structure of John 6:22-59

The Setting for the Discourse: Capernaum (vv. 22-24)

Introduction (vv. 25-31)

The Crowd (v. 25):   "Rabbi, when did you come here?"

Jesus (vv. 26-27):	Introduces the contrast between physical bread and bread from heaven—"Do not work for the food that perishes, but for the food that endures for eternal life."
The Crowd (v. 28):	"What must we do to perform the *works* of God?"
Jesus (v. 29):	"This is the *work* of God, that you believe in him whom he has sent."
The Crowd (vv. 30-31):	"What sign are you going to give us?... Our ancestors ate manna in the wilderness; as it is written, '*He gave them bread from heaven to eat.*'"

I. Who gave them the bread from heaven? (vv. 32-34)

Jesus (vv. 32-33):	"Very truly, I tell you, it was not Moses who gave you the bread from heaven, but it is my Father who gives you the true bread from heaven." The bread from heaven gives life.
The Crowd (v. 34):	"Sir, give us this bread always."

II. What is the bread from heaven? (vv. 35-51)

Jesus (vv. 35-40):	"I am the bread of life." (v. 35) "... that all who see the Son and believe in him may .have eternal life." (v. 40)
The Jews (vv. 41-42):	began to grumble—"Is not this Jesus, the son of Joseph ... How can he now say, 'I have come down from heaven?'"
Jesus (vv. 43-51):	"No one can come to me unless drawn by the Father who sent me; and I will raise that person up on the last day." (v. 44) "I am the bread of life." (v. 48) "I am the living bread that came down from heaven. Whoever eats of this bread will live forever; and the bread that I will

give for the life of the world is my flesh."
(v. 51)

III. How does one eat the bread from heaven? (vv. 52-58)

The Jews (v. 52):   "How can this man give us his flesh to eat?"

Jesus (vv. 53-58):   "Very truly, I tell you, unless you eat the flesh of the Son of Man and drink his blood, you have no life in you. Those who eat my flesh and drink my blood have eternal life, and I will raise them up on the last day." (vv. 53-54)

Conclusion (v. 58)

"This is the bread that came down from heaven, not like that which your ancestors ate, and they died. But the one who eats this bread will live forever." (v. 58)

The setting: the synagogue at Capernaum (v. 59)

John 6:22-24. These verses set the stage for the discourse, but they are unusual because they give so much space to what seems to be inconsequential movement and stage setting. The description of the multiplication of the loaves as "after the Lord had given thanks" (Greek, *eucharistēsantos*) may already foreshadow the eucharistic interpretation in verses 51-58. These verses also set up the crowd's opening question, "Rabbi, when did you come here?" (v. 25). The crowd is mystified because they do not know of Jesus' walking on the water. "Seeking" Jesus is a significant and recurring theme in the Gospel because Jesus is elusive and must be sought.[7]

John 6:25-31. Characteristically, Jesus does not answer their question but moves the conversation to another level. Jesus says that the crowd does not even have a signs faith; they just want another meal. His response points to the contrast between physical bread and the bread of life that he offers them: one perishes while the other endures (cf. Isa 55:2). This contrast, based on a metaphorical use of "bread of life" (or some variation thereof), serves as the basis for the entire discourse that follows. The crowd has not grasped the significance of the multiplication of the loaves because they do not understand that Jesus himself is the bread that sustains life—"in him was life" (1:4).

The crowd picks up on Jesus' admonition that they should work and asks how they can do the works of God. The question assumes the importance of doing good works. Jesus subordinates the doing of good works to the priority of the one good work, believing in him (v. 29), just as later we will see that individual sins are subordinated to unbelief, the foundation of all sin.

Then the crowd asks for a sign that will demonstrate his authority (cf. Mark 8:11-12). The reader knows that Jesus, ironically, has just done a sign for the crowd—precisely the kind of sign they are now asking for—and they did not grasp it. As justification, the crowd recalls that their ancestors ate manna in the wilderness (remember that this was occurring at Passover, 6:4), and they quote a verse of scripture: "(1) He gave them (2) bread from heaven (3) to eat" (v. 31). This quotation does not reproduce any known verse of the Old Testament exactly, but it has close contacts with Exodus 16:4, 15 and Psalm 78:24. In its present form, however, the verse provides the three-part structure for the rest of the discourse, which becomes an extended homily or exposition of the meaning of this verse that the crowd quoted as a challenge to Jesus. First, Jesus explains that Moses did not give their ancestors the bread from heaven—God did (vv. 32-34). Second, Jesus is the true bread from heaven that gives life (vv. 35-51). And third, eating the bread of life means eating Jesus' body and drinking his blood (vv. 52-58). Verse 58 concludes the discourse by recapping the exposition of the verse. The reference to the ancestors in verse 58 forms an inclusion with the reference to the ancestors in verse 31.

John 6:32-34. The first part of the body of the discourse reinterprets the ambiguous subject of the verse quoted in John 6:31. The crowd has misunderstood. It was not Moses who gave their ancestors bread in the wilderness but God. Moreover, it was not a onetime event in the past. God *gives* the true bread from heaven. The reference in verse 33 to coming down recalls the earlier contrast between what is above and what is below. As the bread of life, Jesus gives life to the world (cf. 3:16-19). The crowd responds by asking for this bread, just as the woman at the well had asked for the living water so that she would not have to come to the well to draw water each day.

John 6:35-51. This section of the discourse takes up the second element of the sentence from scripture quoted in verse 31. The real bread of life is Jesus, not the manna that was given to their ancestors. This part of the discourse explains how Jesus serves as the bread of life. The response of "the Jews" in verses 41-42 divides this section into two parts. The first begins with Jesus' claim, "I am the bread of life." Those who come to him will not hunger or thirst, but will have eternal life. This claim introduces the issue of who can come to Jesus. If mankind is divided into two groups, each stamped by its origin, and one is either "of God" or "of the devil," "from above" or "from below," how can one come to Jesus? The Gospel affirms the priority of God's election over human response, as Bultmann's classic statement makes clear:

> Is it not true that only he whom the Father "draws" comes to Jesus (6:44), only he to whom it is "given" by the Father (6:65; cf. 6:37, 39; 17:2, 6, 9, 12, 24)? Is it not said that only he can "hear his voice" who is "of the truth," who is "of God" (18:37; 8:47)—that only he can believe who belongs to his "sheep" (10:26)? And is it not solely "his own" whom he calls to himself (10:3f.), whom he knows and who know him (10:14, 27)?[8]

Nevertheless, "everyone has the possibility of letting himself be drawn by the Father (and also the possibility of resisting)."[9] So faith is not the result of our initiative but of God's initiative with us. Moreover, in spite of John's emphasis on the present crisis of decision and his realized eschatology, the Gospel still asserts that Jesus' work will only be culminated in the future: "... that all who see the Son and believe in him may have eternal life; and I will raise them up on the last day" (v. 40, cf. vv. 39, 44, 54).

The narrator's report that "the Jews" began to grumble (the Greek word is wonderfully onomatopoeic: *egoggyzon*) echoes the murmuring of the Israelites in the wilderness (Exod 16:2, 7-8). Not only has Jesus fulfilled the role of Moses, the crowd is acting out the rebelliousness of their ancestors in the wilderness. The issue again concerns Jesus' origin. They think they know where Jesus is from. Therefore, he cannot have "come down from heaven." At the end of this section, Jesus reaffirms that he is "the bread of life" (v. 48). Their ancestors ate the manna and died, but those who receive the bread of life will not die. How then does one "eat" the bread that Jesus offers? Verse 51 introduces the issue for the final section of the discourse: the bread that Jesus offers for the life of the world is his flesh.

John 6:52-58. The third section of the discourse treats the final part of the verse quoted in John 6:31: "He gave them bread from heaven *to eat.*" The grumbling among "the Jews" escalates to quarreling or fighting among themselves. This is the beginning of a theme we will find developing in the next several chapters: the more clearly Jesus reveals his identity, the more division it brings among the people. How could Jesus give his flesh? Believers who know the Gospel story know immediately how Jesus will give his flesh, both at the table and at the cross, but for those who do not know, Jesus' words are those of a madman. Jesus' demand that they "eat the flesh of the Son of Man and drink his blood" (v. 53) continues the metaphorical language of eating and drinking, but now has clear eucharistic overtones. Verses 52-58, therefore, probably reflect the Johannine community's use of this material in connection with the observance of the Lord's Supper. "Eating" the bread means receiving Jesus and the life he offers. Participating with the community of believers in the Lord's Supper when the community was being persecuted and ostracized would have been an open and public declaration of one's faith. Bultmann and others have concluded that the overt sacramentalism of this section means that it did not come from the Evangelist but from a later redactor. On the other hand, the way in which it concludes the exposition of John 6:31 shows that it is in fact an integral part of the whole discourse (John 6:22-59).

Verse 58 serves as a conclusion for both the third section and the whole discourse. The reference to the ancestors serves as an inclusion with the reference in verse 31, and the last two sentences summarize the whole discourse: Jesus is the true bread from heaven, and anyone who eats this bread has eternal life.

The End of Jesus' Ministry in Galilee (6:60-71)

Verses 60-71 record the response of the crowd of Jesus' disciples (vv. 60-65) and of the inner group of twelve (vv. 66-71). Reflecting back on the whole discourse (and probably especially the third section), they say, literally, "This is a hard word." Jesus continues to challenge them with a prediction that the Son of Man will ascend again and a warning that only the spirit gives life. But, the narrator reports, Jesus knew from the beginning that some of them did not believe (see 2:23-25). He also knew who would betray him (Judas).

As a result, many of those who had followed Jesus "because they saw the signs that he was doing" (6:2) now withdrew from him: "He came to what was his own, and his own people did not accept him" (1:11). The twelve are mentioned for the first time in John in verse 67 where they appear without introduction, almost as though they are the ones who are left after the rest of Jesus' disciples turn away from him. There is no appointment of the twelve in John or list of their names, as there is in each of the Synoptic Gospels. "The twelve" appear only in this paragraph and in John 20:24. Probably because the Beloved Disciple was *the* apostle of the Johannine community, the twelve are not as important in John as they are in the Synoptic Gospels. Simon Peter is the spokesman for the group, as he often is in the Synoptics, and just as Peter confesses that Jesus is the Christ at Caesarea Philippi (Matt 16:16-19), so here he says, "Lord, to whom can we go? You have the words of eternal life. We have come to believe and know that you are the Holy One of God" (6:68-69). This confession picks up key themes from the preceding discourse, especially believing and eternal life. The title "the Holy One of God" occurs elsewhere in the Gospels only in Mark 1:24 and Luke 4:34. Jesus chose the Twelve, but one of them would betray him (6:70-71).

John 6, therefore, reports the sifting of the crowd of disciples who followed Jesus because of the signs that he did. It is like an "Operation Gideon" (cf. Judg 7:2-8, where the Lord tells Gideon that he has too many troops and to send most of them home). It is much harder to believe Jesus' words than his signs: This is a hard word! (v. 60). Some remain with Jesus, and Peter confesses that his word is life, but the chapter ends with a foreshadowing of Judas's betrayal of Jesus.

JOHN 7–8

When Jesus goes to Jerusalem for the feast of Tabernacles, the hostility toward him escalates dramatically. The language is ominous: *kill* (7:1, 19-20, 25; 8:37, 40), *hate* (7:7), *arrest* (7:32, 44), *devil* (8:44), *murderer* (8:44), *demon* (8:48), and *stones* (8:59). Dissension among "the Jews" leads to a heated exchange, attempts to arrest Jesus, and people taking up stones against him. The controversy with the religious authorities in John 5 seems to continue in John 7, leading some interpreters to think either that John 5 and 6 once appeared in reverse order or that John 6 was added to the Gospel in the second edition so that John 7 once followed directly after the end of John 5. Because discourses are always more difficult to follow than narratives, previewing the structure of chapters 7 and 8 helps the reader to make sense of their various parts.

The Structure of John 7–8		
John 7:1-13	Jesus travels to Jerusalem for Tabernacles	
John 7:14-52	Two teaching episodes lead to two attempts to arrest Jesus:[10]	
7:15-36		*7:37-52*
15-24	Jesus' teaching	37-39
25-31	Speculation among the people	40-44
32-36	Attempt to arrest Jesus	45-52
[John 7:53–8:11	A secondary gloss: The story of the woman caught in adultery]	
John 8:12-59	A debate in the temple with the Pharisees and "the Jews who had believed in him"	
8:12-20	"I am the light of the world": Jesus' testimony and the witnesses to him	
8:21-30	"I am going away": Their inability to comprehend Jesus' departure	
8:31-59	"The truth will make you free": Sons and slaves—a paternity suit	

The feast of Tabernacles, or Booths, commemorated the Exodus and God's care for the Israelites in the wilderness. The images of water and light were important for this celebration, and both appear prominently in these two chapters. Jesus claims that he is the source of living water (7:37-39) and that he is the light of the world (8:12). In essence, he is the fulfillment of that which the people in Jerusalem were celebrating, just as in the previous chapter he demonstrated that he was the real "Bread from Heaven."

The Feast of Tabernacles (7:1-13)

The stage directions in verse 1 require some interpretation. Jesus has been in Galilee throughout chapter 6, and the reference to the "Jews" (here evidently meaning either "Judeans" or the religious leaders) must harken back to the debate in John 5. Jesus' brothers, who we are told did not believe in him, challenge Jesus to go up to Jerusalem for the feast of Tabernacles—a seven-day harvest festival that had been given religious meaning and had become one of the most popular pilgrimage festivals. The brothers' challenge is not unlike the temptation in Matthew and Luke for Jesus to throw himself off the pinnacle of the Temple: "Show yourself to the world" (7:4). Jesus responds that his *kairos* (time) has not come, but "the world" (here meaning all that is opposed to him) hates him because he testifies that its works are evil (cf. 3:19-21; 15:18-25). Perhaps with some play on words, Jesus says that he is not "going up" (one always went *up* to Jerusalem, but here it may also imply that he is not ascending to the Father at this festival). He stays in Galilee, but then goes up to Jerusalem in secret. Jesus always acts in accord with his own time, not the demands that others make on him (cf. 2:4; 11:3-7). The Jews are looking for the elusive messiah—"Where is he?" (7:11). Some said he was a good man, but others that he deceived the crowd (a charge that can be found in later Jewish and Christian sources). "The Jews" in verse 13 must refer to a specific group of leaders because this verse reports that the people who had gathered in Jerusalem for the festival (all of whom were Jews) feared "the Jews" (cf. 19:38; 20:19).

Two Teaching Episodes and Two Attempts to Arrest Jesus (7:14-52)

When Jesus arrives in Jerusalem, the debate with the authorities in John 5 seems to continue without interruption.

Parallels Between John 5 and John 7:15-24		
John 5		*John 7:15-24*
5:47	"letters" or what is written (Greek, *grammata*)	7:15
5:31	speaking on his own behalf	7:17
5:44	seeking glory from God	7:18
5:45-47	Moses gave the Law	7:19-23
5:18	seeking to kill Jesus	7:19-20
5:1-18	the healing of the man at the pool —the "one work" (?)	7:21
5:1-18	"I healed a man's whole body on the sabbath"	7:23
5:9	the sabbath	7:23

Jesus' authority is challenged when he teaches in the Temple (as in the Synoptics: Mark 11:27-28; Luke 19:47-48). What was the source of his teaching? His teaching is that of the One who sent him and whose glory he seeks. One of the reasons for unbelief is that people seek their own, rather than God's, glory. Moses gave the Law, but they did not keep it (cf. Acts 7:38-39; 15:10). They charged Jesus with violating the sabbath when he healed a man's whole body on that day (cf. Mark 3:1-6), but they allowed circumcision on the sabbath.

Jesus' teaching leads to speculation among the people (7:25-31). The more Jesus teaches, the more his teaching sifts the people, inflaming the opposition of some of the crowd and leading others to believe. The crowd speculates about Jesus' identity and whether the authorities may actually know that he is the Messiah because they allow him to teach openly. Debate again focuses on Jesus' origin. They assume they know where Jesus is from and therefore conclude that he cannot be the Messiah. Ironically, they do not know Jesus' origin or the One who sent him. Speculation leads to an effort to arrest Jesus, but it is futile because his "hour" has not yet come (cf. 8:20). Those who believe point to the signs that he has done—if not because of his words, at least they believe because of his signs (cf. 14:11).

The chief priests and the Pharisees (who are probably "the Jews" referred to in 7:13) send the temple police to arrest Jesus (7:32). Jesus responds with a *mashal* or riddle: "I will be with you a little while longer, and then I am going to him who sent me. You will search for me, but you will not find me; and where I am, you cannot come" (7:33-34; cf. 8:21-22; 13:33). Seeking the Lord and seeking Wisdom are common themes in the Hebrew Scriptures.[11]

Seeking and Finding the Lord/Wisdom	
Deut 4:29	"From there you will seek the LORD your God, and you will find him if you search after him with all your heart and soul."
Job 28:12	"But where shall wisdom be found?"
Prov 1:28	"They will seek me diligently, but will not find me."
Isa 55:6	"Seek the LORD while he may be found."
Hos 5:6	"With their flocks and herds they shall go to seek the LORD, but they will not find him; he has withdrawn from them."

| Bar 3:14-15 | "Learn where there is wisdom ... Who has found her place?" |
| Wis 6:12 | "Wisdom is radiant and unfading, and she is easily discerned by those who love her, and is found by those who seek her." |

This is a passion prediction (cf. Mark 8:31; 9:31; 10:32-34) in Johannine language. "The Jews" misunderstand, thinking, again ironically, that he is going to the Dispersion (where the Johannine community was probably located) to teach Greeks.

A somewhat shorter unit follows, repeating the structure of John 7:15-36—Jesus teaches (7:37-39), the crowd speculates about his identity (7:40-44), and the temple police return to the chief priests and Pharisees (7:45-52). The setting for Jesus' teaching in verses 37-39 is one of the climactic events of the celebration at Tabernacles. Each year, water was carried in a golden pitcher from the pool of Siloam to the Temple:

> " 'The Water-libation, seven days'—what was the manner of this? They used to fill a golden flagon holding three *logs* [about one and a half pints] with water from Siloam. When they reached the Water Gate they blew [on the *shofar*] a sustained, a quavering and another sustained blast." (*m. Sukkah* 4.9)[12]

On the last day of this festival, Jesus cried out, "Let anyone who is thirsty come to me." The quotation from scripture that follows does not reproduce any known verse exactly, and the word "his" may mean either Jesus or the believer (7:38).

The Quotation in John 7:38

| Ps 105:40-41 | "... and [he] gave them food from heaven in abundance. He opened the rock, and water gushed out; it flowed through the desert like a river." |
| Ps 78:15-16 | "He split rocks open in the wilderness, and gave them drink abundantly as from the deep. He made streams come out of the rock, and caused water to flow down like rivers." |

Zech 14:8	"On that day living waters shall flow out from Jerusalem."
Isa 44:3	"For I will pour water on the thirsty land, and streams on the dry ground; I will pour my spirit upon your descendants, and my blesssing on your offspring."
Isa 58:11	"... and you shall be like a watered garden, like a spring of water, whose waters never fail."
Joel 3:18	"In that day ... all the stream beds of Judah shall flow with water; a fountain shall come forth from the house of the LORD...."
Sir 24:21*b*	"and those who drink of me will thirst no more."

These passages recall both the water that flowed from the rock in the wilderness and the promise that water would flow from the Temple in Jerusalem. Verse 39 clarifies that Jesus was speaking of the Spirit, which those who believe in him will receive (cf. 19:30, 34).

Once again, Jesus' words provoke consternation (7:40-44). This time the speculation among the people concerns Jesus' Galilean origin. Jewish tradition held that the Messiah would be a descendant of David and would come from Bethlehem: "But you, O Bethlehem of Ephrathah, who are one of the little clans of Judah, from you shall come forth for me one who is to rule in Israel, whose origin is from of old, from ancient days" (Mic 5:2). The evangelist is probably playing on the irony that Christian readers knew of Jesus' birth in Bethlehem (which is not a part of John's Gospel), but his opponents charge that he cannot be the Messiah because he comes from Galilee and not Bethlehem. Debate now leads to division among the crowd.

Some want to arrest Jesus, but the temple police return to the chief priests and Pharisees (cf. v. 32). When they say they have never heard anyone speak like Jesus, the Pharisees charge that Jesus has deceived them and the ignorant crowd. No authorities have believed in him have they? In fact, of course, the reader knows of Nicodemus's conversation with Jesus, and Nicodemus immediately steps forward again to suggest that a hearing should be held before Jesus is condemned (cf. 19:39). The authorities then turn on Nicodemus and ask derisively whether he is a Galilean also, claiming that no prophet ever came from Galilee—which is not accurate since Jonah was a Galilean (2 Kgs 14:25).

The Story of the Woman Taken in Adultery (7:53–8:11)

The story of Jesus, the woman taken in adultery, and her accusers is an interpolation. It appears to be an early, free-floating unit of tradition that did not find a secure home in the written Gospels, perhaps because some feared that it would lead to leniency in dealing with adultery. It does not appear in the Greek manuscripts of John before about 900, and then some insert it after 7:36, after 21:25, or after Luke 21:38, instead of at this point.[13]

The story itself has held great fascination for interpreters, some of whom have found its center in: the opposition between Jesus and the woman (Augustine: "a wretch and Mercy [*miseria et misericordia*]"); the words that Jesus wrote on the ground (J. D. M. Derrett, Exod 23:1*b* and 23:7; J. N. Sanders, the Ten Commandments; and R. E. Brown, "doodling"); or in the parallel scenes in verses 6*b*-7 and 8-11 in which Jesus challenges the scribes and the Pharisees, as well as the woman (G. R. O'Day).[14]

Verses 7:53–8:2 provide the setting: early morning, Jesus teaching in the Temple (cf. Mark 11:20, 27-28; Luke 19:47–20:2). Verses 3-6*a* introduce the characters, the charge against the woman, and the trap that is set for Jesus, which pits him against the Law. Twice Jesus stoops and writes on the ground, and twice he speaks. Whether the structure is interpreted as two parallel scenes or a chiasm with Jesus' pronouncement in verse 7 at its center, the words that Jesus speaks form the climax of the story. O'Day diagrams the relationship between Jesus' two pronouncements as follows:

The one who is without sin   X *throw the first stone at her* (v. 7*b*)
Neither do I condemn you. Go   *from now on sin no more* (v. 11*b*)

The story vividly depicts Jesus' grace toward the woman taken in adultery. He challenges both the woman and her accusers to lay aside the question of guilt or innocence and to enter into a new life in which one's regard for self and one's relationship to others are based on grace and mercy.[15] There are good reasons, therefore, why the church chose to make a place for this story in the Gospels, even though it was not originally part of the Gospel of John.

A Debate in the Temple (8:12-59)

The debate with the crowd at the end of John 7 continues in this section. Many of the themes in this debate were first sounded in John 5. In chapter 5, Jesus said he did only what the Father gave him to do and that the Father bore witness to him (5:19, 36-37). These issues are now explored in greater detail. The main issue is that of paternity. Who is Jesus' father, and who is his opponents' father? Underlying this debate is the Semitic principle that the child will be like the father. The responses of "the Jews" and a progression of topics serve to break up the discourse and provide a minimal structure.

John 8:12-20. Just as Jesus had claimed that he was the source of living water (7:37-39), so now he picks up the other image that was associated with the celebration of Tabernacles, and claims: "I am the light of the world" (8:12; cf. Isa 9:1-2; Zech 14:7-8). Once again, Jesus' claim is tantamount to saying that he himself is the fulfillment of that Jewish festival, as the following description of the festival from the Mishnah suggests.

The Lighting of Candles at the Festival of Tabernacles

At the close of the first Festival-day of the feast they went down to the Court of the Women where they made a great amendment. There were golden candlesticks there with four golden bowls on the top of them and four ladders to each candlestick, and four youths of the priestly stock and in their hands jars of oil holding a hundred and twenty *logs* which they poured into all the bowls.

They made wicks from the worn out drawers and girdles of the priests and with them they set the candlesticks alight, and there was not a courtyard in Jerusalem that did not reflect the light of the Beth ha-She'ubah. (*m. Sukkah* 5.2-3)[16]

According to the Talmud, the candlesticks were fifty cubits high, and many think that the "treasury of the Temple" (v. 20), where Jesus made this pronouncement, was located in the Court of the Women.

The verses that follow reintroduce issues from chapter 5. First, is Jesus testifying on his own behalf, and is his testimony true? Earlier, Jesus had said that if he (alone) testified on his behalf, his testimony would not be true (5:31). Jesus' position vacillates between that of the accused and the judge in these verses. Both his testimony and his judgment are true because he acts by the authority of the one who sent him, his Father. The law that testimony had to be confirmed by two witnesses is an allusion to Deuteronomy 19:15. Because Jesus claims that his Father testified on his behalf, the authorities ask, "Where is your father?" (v. 19). They thereby introduce the main issue for the rest of the chapter. Once more they attempt to arrest him, but they cannot (cf. 7:30, 32, 44-45).

John 8:21-30. Having raised the question of Jesus' origin, the discourse turns again to the question of his destiny. Just as he has come from the Father, he will return to his Father. They will search, but they cannot go where he is going (see above, 7:33-36). "The Jews'" puzzled attempts to understand Jesus' words are ironic. Jesus will lay down his life in the process of returning to the Father, so he was speaking of his death, but he will not kill himself—they will seek his death (cf. 5:18; 7:1). Jesus speaks of his future in spatial terms. They cannot follow him because they are from below and he is from above. Jesus charges that they will die in their sin (v. 21) or sins (v. 24). For John, the cardinal sin and the root of all sins is failure to believe in Jesus (v. 24). His death will reveal once and for all that he did what his Father sent him to do. The three "lifted up" sayings serve as Johannine passion predictions (cf. Mark 8:31; 9:31; 10:32-34).

The Johannine "Lifted Up" Sayings

John 3:14	"And just as Moses lifted up the serpent in the wilderness, so must the Son of Man be lifted up, that whoever believes in him may have eternal life."
John 8:28	"When you have lifted up the Son of Man, then you will realize that I am he, and that I do nothing on my own, but I speak these things as the Father instructed me."
John 12:32	"And I, when I am lifted up from the earth, will draw all people to myself."

John 8:31-59. These verses contain the heart of the debate over the paternity, and therefore the identity, of Jesus and his opponents. The debate is bracketed by references to Abraham (vv. 33, 57-58). The debate opens with Jesus' claim that if the Jews who believed in him would continue in his word they would know the truth and be free. They respond by maintaining that they are descendants of Abraham and have never been slaves (overlooking the enslavement of the Israelites in Egypt).

Jesus responds by asserting that sin enslaves (cf. Rom 6:6-23). The saying about the difference between a slave and a son (8:35) may have been a traditional maxim. Those who have freedom through the son, therefore, are free (again the thought here has parallels in Rom 7 and Gal 3–4). Although they are Abraham's children, they do not believe in him (cf. Gen 15:6; Rom 4:3; Gal 3:6). Because they seek to kill him, they show that they are really acting out the impulses of the devil (8:44). The works that one does are the real test of one's identity. Underlying all this debate is the claim that the believers—the Johannine community—are the true children of God because they have believed in Jesus (cf. 1:12).

The debate reaches a shrill point here, and one that has led to terrible atrocities in the name of Christianity. Care must always be taken to interpret John's references to "the Jews"—who as we have seen (7:13) are often only the religious leaders—in the context of the Johannine community's debate with the synagogue and the narrative function of "the Jews" in the Gospel. John says nothing that condemns Jews of subsequent generations.

Jesus' opponents reply with slander regarding his birth, saying that *they* are not illegitimate, while implying that Jesus is. Again it appears that John knows more of the tradition of Jesus' birth than is narrated (cf. 7:40-42).

Those who keep Jesus' word will not see death either (v. 51). This claim echoes claims from previous chapters—a characteristic of the tapestry of the Johannine discourses. In John 3 Jesus said that whoever believed in him would have eternal life. In John 4 he offered "living water." In John 5 he said that whoever believed in him had already crossed over from death into life. And in John 6 he offered the bread of life (unlike the manna that their ancestors had eaten, because they died). Jesus' opponents reply that Abraham and the prophets had died. Like the woman at the well who asked if Jesus were greater than Jacob, they now ask ironically if he is greater than "our father Abraham" (v. 53). Jesus' glory, however, comes from his Father. The reference to Abraham seeing Jesus' day, although it is difficult to relate to a specific event in Abraham's life, is consistent with the claims for preexistence that John makes for Jesus and his claims that Old Testament figures foresaw his coming (cf. 12:41). Here as elsewhere, Jesus' "I am" sayings serve as a divine claim.

JOHN 9

This chapter is a delightful short story in itself, but one with links to the rest of the Gospel. Having revealed himself as "the light of the world," Jesus now gives sight to a blind man. John 9 is also the window through which many interpreters have peered into the history of the Johannine community, because it describes the blind man's expulsion from the synagogue. For the history it seems to reflect, see chapter 3 above.

John 9 explores the meaning of sin. What is sin? Who is guilty? The new character in this story is a man who was born blind. In the commonly accepted theology of the time, God punishes the wicked and rewards the righteous. Conversely, suffering was a sign of God's judgment. The question then, raised by the disciples, was "Who sinned, this man or his parents, that he was born blind?" (9:2). Lurking behind this question is the more basic one, What is sin? In the course of the story, the blind man receives his sight, while the blindness of the Pharisees is exposed.

The chapter is best approached as a sequence of seven scenes each of which is marked by a change of characters. The principle of duality, that John prefers scenes with two principal characters, is clearly evident in this chapter.

The Structure of John 9

Scene 1: The Healing of the Blind Man (9:1-7)

Scene 2: The Neighbors and the Blind Man (9:8-12)

Scene 3: The Pharisees Question the Blind Man (9:13-17)

Scene 4: The Pharisees Question the Blind Man's Parents (9:18-23)

Scene 5: The Pharisees Question the Blind Man a Second Time (9:24-34)

Scene 6: Jesus Questions the Blind Man (9:35-39)

Scene 7: Jesus Responds to the Pharisees (9:40-41)

The Healing of the Blind Man (9:1-7)

The disciples enter the Gospel story again for the first time since John 6, but they serve merely to get the action started. They ask, "Who sinned, this man or his parents, that he was born blind?" Their question assumes that the man's congenital blindness was the result of sin. Jesus denies that the man's blindness is the result of either his or his parents' sin but affirms that he was born blind so that God's works might be revealed in him. This response shifts the problem of providence and suffering but does not resolve it. Nevertheless, Jesus reveals that God's works relieve human suffering, and he sets about immediately, "while it is day," not merely to heal the man but, in an act of new creation, to create sight for him. Jesus makes clay with his spittle. No doubt the beggar knew about spittle, but this man's spittle would bless rather than curse. The making of clay is reminiscent of God's creation of humanity in Genesis 2:7 (cf. John 20:22). Then, he sends the man to wash in the pool of Siloam. John does not miss the opportunity to alert the reader that "Siloam" means "Sent," playing on the Johannine motif of Jesus as the one sent from God. The washing also echoes the story of the healing of Naaman, who was sent by Elisha to wash in the Jordan (2 Kgs 5:10-14). The first scene, therefore, is similar to a Synoptic healing miracle, but John will follow it with six related scenes that develop the significance of this sign. In form it is also strikingly similar to the story of the man at the pool of Bethesda (John 5:1-18). The miracle itself is related with surprising brevity, "he went and washed and came back able to see" (9:7).

The Neighbors and the Blind Man (9:8-12)

This scene verifies that a miracle has indeed occurred; there is no mistake in the man's identity. The reaction starts at the outer edge, with the neighbors and passersby. Just as earlier the crowd in Jerusalem had debated Jesus' identity (John 7:12), so now some say the man who can now see had been blind, while others say he is a different man. The man who had received his sight confirms that it is he, echoing Jesus' Johannine claim "I am" (*ego eimi*; 9:9). He does not know how it happened, but he knows who made it happen—a man called Jesus. Note that each time the miracle is recounted it is told with even greater brevity. To the important question of where Jesus may be found, the man says, again characteristically, "I do not know."

The Pharisees Question the Blind Man (9:13-17)

Only now are we told that the healing occurred on the Sabbath (9:14; cf. 5:9). The neighbors therefore take the man to the Pharisees. In response to their questioning, the man gives the briefest account yet of the miracle: "He put mud on my eyes. Then I washed, and now I see" (v. 15). The reader knows all the important details and does not need to hear them again. The interest is not in how the cure happened but in the issue of sin and faith as it relates to each character in the story. Is the blind man a sinner? Are the Pharisees righteous? And is Jesus an impostor or one sent from God? The Pharisees are hung on a dilemma. Jesus has done work that they understood was forbidden on the Sabbath, but he has done a wonder! A man sent from God would keep the Sabbath, and a sinner could not do wonders. Making clay, anointing, healing chronic conditions, and washing were all considered work that violated the Sabbath (m. Sabbat 7.2; 14.3; m. Moed 8.6). Revelation again brings division, with some saying that Jesus was sent from God and others saying that he is a sinner. The previous scene ended with the man responding, "I do not know." This scene ends with the man's first step toward understanding, "He is a prophet." The double meaning of receiving sight is beginning to emerge.

The Pharisees Question the Blind Man's Parents (9:18-23)

Scene four is the center of the sequence of seven scenes. The Pharisees continue their search for a solution to the dilemma by interrogating the man's parents. If he were not born blind or if he were not their son, the Pharisees could show that the healing was a hoax. The parents fear reprisals. They confirm that the man is indeed their son and that he was born blind, but they do not know how he can now see. For any further information, the authorities will have to ask the man himself, for "he is of age" (9:21). The narrator pauses to explain the parents' fear of "the Jews" (here, the Pharisees, the religious leaders) by telling the reader in an aside that "the Jews" had agreed that anyone who confessed Jesus should be put out of the synagogue. J. Louis Martyn argued that this is a ref-

176

erence to an action taken by the rabbis at Jamnia.[17] At a minimum, it appears to be an anachronistic reference that reflects actions taken by the leaders of the synagogue in the area of the Johannine community at the time the Gospel was written. It therefore gives us an important glimpse of the social context of the Gospel of John.

The Pharisees Question the Blind Man a Second Time (9:24-34)

The Pharisees come to the man a second time and impose an oath on him. "Give God the glory" means "swear to tell the truth." They then confidently declare that they know that Jesus is a sinner. The contrast between the Pharisees' exaggerated confidence and the man's pleas of ignorance sets up a classic contrast between a braggart (an *alazon* in Greek drama) and the ironist (an *eiron*). With delightful subtlety, the narrator shows us the man's insight and exposes the Pharisees' blindness:

Contrasting Responses in John 9	
The Blind Man	*The Pharisees*
"I do not know." (v. 12)	"This man is not from God." (v. 16).
"I do not know whether he is a sinner.	"We know that this man is a sinner." (v. 24)
One thing I do know, that though I was blind, now I see." (v. 25)	"We know that God has spoken to Moses, but as for this man, we do not know where he comes from." (v. 29)

When the authorities persist in searching for proof of violation of the sabbath by asking about the means by which Jesus healed the man, he responds with delightful sarcasm: Why do they want to hear the story again? Do they also want to become his disciples? In response, the authorities draw the line. He may be Jesus' disciple, but they are disciples of Moses. For them, the two are mutually exclusive, but John has already shown that Moses is one of the witnesses to Jesus (cf. 5:45-46).

The man begins to taunt his accusers. What a marvel that here is a man who does wonders, but they do not know where he is from! Of course, in the context of this Gospel, had they known where Jesus was from they would have known his true identity (cf. Nathanael in John 1:46). If Jesus were not from God, surely he could not have given him his sight. The Pharisees, however, return to their understanding of sin. The man was born blind, under God's judgment. Therefore, he could not teach them. Consequently, they drove him out, just as the adherents of the Johannine community had evidently been driven out of the synagogue because of their confession of Jesus.

Jesus Questions the Blind Man (9:35-39)

So far, the story has progressed like a detective story. An alleged crime has been committed, and the Pharisees, the defenders of the Law, have questioned the witnesses to expose the guilt of the offender. Now, Jesus comes to the man who has been cast out by the authorities, and he tests the man's vision. How clearly could he see? Fourteen questions are asked in this chapter, but this one is the most important: "Do you believe in the Son of Man?" When the man asks who this is, Jesus answers with more delightful irony, "You have seen him." He, who had previously seen no one, has now seen the Son of Man! Immediately, and in marked contrast to the man at the pool of Bethesda, the man responds, "Lord, I believe." Like the woman at the well, he has come step by step to confess Jesus: "the man called Jesus" (v. 11); "he is a prophet" (v. 17); "if this man were not from God, he could do nothing" (v. 33); and "Lord, I believe" (v. 38).

Jesus Responds to the Pharisees (9:40-41)

With the story of the blind man resolved, the narrator turns again to the Pharisees. Jesus declares that he came to bring judgment, so that those who were blind might see and those who could see might become blind. When the Pharisees hear this they ask, tellingly, "Surely we are not blind, are we?" To which Jesus responds, "[Because] you say, 'We see,' your sin remains." The double reversal has been completed. The man who was blind has come to sight, and the blindness of the seeing Pharisees has been exposed.

In the course of the story the nature of sin has also become clear. Sin lies not in being born blind but in refusing to see when one is confronted with the light. The blind man is therefore a model for every person. All are born blind, and all are called to believe when they are confronted by the one sent from God. Sin consists not in being born unbelieving but in refusing to believe when one has seen the power of God at work.

JOHN 10

Chapter 10 follows the end of chapter 9 without any interruption or indication of a lapse of time, change of place, or introduction of new characters. Nevertheless, the opening verses introduce a new set of metaphors that are the focus of Jesus' words in verses 1-21. The latter half of the chapter (vv. 22-42) reports Jesus' words in the Temple at the time of Hanukkah and the response of "the Jews." When they try to arrest him again, Jesus withdraws across the Jordan.

The Good Shepherd and His Sheep (10:1-21)

The first five verses of this section are a Johannine parable, a riddle that characterizes the shepherd, the gate, the thief, the gatekeeper, and the sheep. The following verses interpret each of these elements further. The imagery is rich, rooted in the Old Testament, and common to the Synoptics. However, its meaning here is open to various interpretations. The primary background for this passage is Ezekiel 34, where the prophet castigates the religious leaders as poor shepherds. In the Synoptics Jesus offers the parable of the lost sheep (Luke 15:3-7; Matt 18:12-14) and the scattering of the sheep (Mark 14:27).

Ezekiel 34

The word of the LORD came to me: Mortal, prophesy against the shepherds of Israel: prophesy, and say to them—to the shepherds: Thus says the Lord GOD: Ah, you shepherds of Israel who have been feeding yourselves! Should not shepherds feed the sheep?... You have not strengthened the weak, you have not healed the sick, you have not bound up the injured, you have not brought back the strayed, you have not sought the lost, but with force and harshness you have ruled them. So they were scattered, because there was no shepherd; and scattered, they became food for all the wild animals.... For thus says the Lord GOD: I myself will search for my sheep, and will seek them out. (vv. 1-5, 11)

The problem that faces the interpreter of these metaphors in John is one of context. Should the riddle (Greek, *paroimia*) be interpreted historically in the context of Jesus' ministry, ecclesiologically in the context of the Johannine community, or cosmologically in the context of John's interpretation of Jesus as the Logos?[18] Viewed historically, as words of the historical Jesus, the riddle depicts Jesus as the shepherd, the Jews as the sheep, his own as the believers, and the Jewish leaders as the thieves and robbers. In the evangelist's context at the time the Gospel was written, the shepherd would be Jesus or by extension the Christian leaders, the sheep and his own would be the Johannine community, and the thieves and robbers the leaders of the synagogue. In the context of John's depiction of the coming of the Logos to "his own," the shepherd is the Logos, the sheep humankind, his own the believers, the sheepfold the world, the thief Satan, and the doorkeeper John the Baptist. The images are rich, therefore, but it is difficult to determine the context in which they are to be read, especially in this chapter.

The riddle in the first five verses and its interpretation in the following verses also illustrate the generative power of figurative speech. The riddle appears to be drawn from traditional material, as are the aphorisms and parables of Jesus in the Synoptic Gospels. The traditional unit generated Christological reflection, and successive interpretations of the riddle appear in verses 6-10, 11-13, 14-18, and 26-29.

Scholars have debated whether verses 1-5 constitute one figurative discourse or truncated sections of two parables. Regardless of which view one takes, these verses provide the imagery for much of the rest of the attached discourse. The first verse identifies the thief or bandit as one who does not enter the sheepfold through the gate. By contrast the shepherd enters by the gate. His identity is recognized by the gatekeeper, who opens the gate for him, and by the sheep, who respond to his voice. The statement that the shepherd calls his sheep by name resonates with various other passages in John (1:42; 5:25, 28-29; 11:43; 20:16). The verb translated "leads out" in verse 4 is the same as that in 9:35 "cast out." The blind man may therefore serve as a representative of those who have been led out of the sheepfold by the shepherd. The sheep are "his own" (1:11; 10:12; 13:1). They will not follow a stranger because they do not know his voice (v. 5). The riddle, therefore, contrasts the shepherd and the thief on the basis of the manner in which each comes into the sheepfold and whether the sheep recognize their respective voices or not. Not incidentally, the issue of who is recognized as the shepherd underscores the pattern of recognition scenes that is vital to the plot of the Gospel.[19]

Verses 7-10 pick up the image of the gate and use it as a metaphor for understanding Jesus' life-giving function. The sheep come in and go out to pasture through the gate. Others, now those who came before Jesus (false prophets or false messiahs), are thieves and robbers (now plural). Again recognition plays a vital role because the thieves steal and kill while the shepherd gives life.

The next point of comparison is obvious: Jesus is the shepherd—the good shepherd (vv. 11-13). The good shepherd is distinguished from the impostor (now a hireling rather than a thief) in two ways: (1) he lays down his life for the sheep, and (2) he cares for the sheep and does not run away when he sees the wolf coming. The wolf is a dynamic metaphor for evil (cf. Gen 4:7; Matt 10:16; Acts 20:29; 1 Pet 5:8).

Verses 14-18 provide further commentary on Jesus' role as the good shepherd. Recognition and relationship are again the key elements. He knows his sheep, and they know him; furthermore, his relationship to them reflects his relationship with the Father. The other sheep that he has, which must be brought together so that there may be one flock and one shepherd (cf. 11:52), are either Gentile believers or Jewish believers in other communities. Finally, the Christological reflection turns to the way in which the good shepherd lays down his life. He does so of his own accord; later we will see that Jesus is not seized but goes with his captors. Also, distinctively in John, Jesus is not raised by the Father but lays down his life and takes it up again.

The conclusion to this part of the discourse reiterates that Jesus' words brought division and rejection as well as revelation. Just as in 8:48, some say he is demon possessed, while others point out that a demon could not open the eyes of a blind man. The conclusion, therefore, effectively ties the discourse to the debate in chapter 8 and the healing of the blind man in chapter 9.

Jesus at the Festival of Dedication (10:22-42)

Verse 22 signals the beginning of a new scene by reporting a change of time and place. The scene that follows is set at the festival of Dedication (Hanukkah), in the Temple, in the portico of Solomon (cf. Acts 3:11; 5:12). As at the other Jewish festivals, what Jesus does or says here will point to the way in which he is the fulfillment of what the festival celebrated. The festival of Dedication commemorated the retaking of the Temple from the Seleucids in 164 B.C. and its cleansing and rededication.

The Rededication of the Temple

Then Judas [Maccabeus] detailed men to fight against those in the citadel until he had cleansed the sanctuary. He chose blameless priests devoted to the law, and they cleansed the sanctuary and removed the defiled stones to an unclean place. They deliberated what to do about the altar of burnt offering, which had been profaned. And they thought it best to tear it down, so that it would not be a lasting shame to them that the Gentiles had defiled it. So they tore down the altar, and stored the stones in a convenient place on the temple hill until a prophet should come to tell what to do with them.... They also rebuilt the sanctuary and the interior of the temple, and consecrated the courts.... Then Judas and his brothers and all the assembly of Israel determined that every year at that season the days of dedication of the altar should be observed with joy and gladness for eight days, beginning with the twenty-fifth day of the month of Chislev. (1 Macc 4:41-46, 48, 59)

At the festival of Dedication, the people pressed Jesus to tell them whether he was the expected Messiah or not. Jesus recalls his earlier claim that the works he does testify on his behalf (5:36; 7:21; 9:3-4). They cannot believe, however, because they do not belong to his sheep. This allusion to the preceding discourse about the good shepherd and his sheep opens a further unit of reflection regarding the shepherd's sheep. His sheep hear his voice, he knows them and they follow him, he gives them eternal life, and no one can take them from him (vv. 26-29). No one can take them from him because the Father has given them to him, and no one can take them from the Father. The highest Christological claim in the Gospel appears in 10:30, "The Father and I are one." The Greek numeral here is neuter, not masculine; Jesus and the Father are one entity, not one person.

The sequence of events here echoes that of John 5:16-18. Jesus makes claims regarding his relationship to the Father, and "the

Jews" seek to kill him. Jesus' claim in verse 30 is blasphemous to the Jews, so they take up stones to stone Jesus. The hostility against Jesus has been building since chapter 5. The more clearly Jesus declares who he is, the greater the hostility becomes. When Jesus challenges his opponents to justify their actions, they respond that it is not because of his works but his words, his blasphemy, that they seek to stone him. Jesus responds by citing a psalm that may have been addressed to unjust judges, "I said, you are gods" (Ps 82:6). The argument is obscure, but it appears to challenge those who opposed him to look beyond words and titles to the reality of what God is doing in their midst. He is the one whom the Father has sanctified and sent to them. While they celebrate the sanctification of the Temple, they should be celebrating the coming of the sanctified One sent by the Father! If they will not believe him, at least they should recognize the power of God in the works that he has done. Several important Christological themes cluster here: sanctified, sent, Son of God, the Father in the Son and the Son in the Father, know, and believe.

Again, however, they try to arrest him, so Jesus withdraws across the Jordan, closing a major section of the Gospel. John the Baptist is mentioned again, for the last time. Just as John 2–4 begins and ends in Cana of Galilee, so John 1–10 begins and ends with John the Baptist across the Jordan. Jesus is superior to John, however, because John did no signs. Nevertheless, everything John said was true. The pattern of revelation leading both to recognition and belief and to rejection and hostility has become clear. The stage is now set for the return of Jesus to Judea, where he will give life by laying down his own life.

JOHN 11

The raising of Lazarus is the climactic sign of Jesus' ministry in the Gospel of John. In the Synoptic Gospels the so-called cleansing of the Temple led to the arrest of Jesus, but in John, the raising of Lazarus sets in motion the events that lead to Jesus' death. Source critics have even suggested that the cleansing of the Temple was moved up in John's Gospel to chapter 2 so that the raising of Lazarus could occupy this position. The good shepherd will lay down his life for the sheep (10:11, 15). Later in the Gospel, Jesus will say, "No one has greater love than this, to lay down one's life for one's friends" (15:13).

183

To appreciate the nuances of this episode, the reader needs to recognize how central it is in the development of key Johannine themes. Raising a person from the dead dramatically portrays Jesus as the giver of life. We recall that the prologue opened the Gospel affirming that "in him was life" (1:4). The theme of Jesus as giver of life was highlighted in our exposition of John 2–4, and the discourse in John 6 identified Jesus as the Bread of Life.

Parallel to these references, the Gospel has balanced hope for the future fulfillment of God's redemptive work with claims that those hopes have already been realized in Jesus. The one who believes in Jesus will have eternal life (3:15-16; 6:47). The judgment is not future but present: "And this is the judgment, that the light has come into the world, and people loved darkness rather than light because their deeds were evil" (3:19). On the last day, Jesus will raise those who have come to him (6:39, 40, 44, 54). But the one who hears Jesus' word and believes in him has eternal life and has already passed from death into life (5:24). The Father has given the Son authority to raise the dead and give life (5:21). The dead will hear the voice of the Son of God and those who hear it will live (5:25). The hour is coming, Jesus said, when all who are in the tombs will hear his voice (5:28-29). The raising of Lazarus thus serves to underscore the theme of Jesus as the giver of life while at the same time declaring that those who believe already have life.

The hope for life after death is one that runs deep in human experience and in the Hebrew Scriptures. Job wrestled with the issue of life after death because the ancient Hebrews had only a vague sense of Sheol as the place of the dead. One lived on in memory and in one's descendants. God promised, therefore, to make Abraham's name great and give him many descendants. Job complains that life is short. Even plants bud forth again when there is water, but what about human beings? When they die, do they live again? (Job 14:1-14).

Miguel de Unamuno wrestled with the question in his book, *The Tragic Sense of Life*. An agnostic, he could not resolve his quest to know whether there is more to life than just the short years of our physical lives. His analysis was that human beings have such a driving need to know that there is something beyond death that we spend most of our lives diverting and distracting ourselves from this issue because we cannot know what lies beyond death.

The "tragic sense of life" is that our spirits tell us that it must be, but we cannot know that it is so. He concludes the book saying that he took up his pen to distract us for a while from our distractions, and finishes it saying, "May God deny you peace, but give you glory."[20] Ultimately, his counsel is that one should live in such a way that if there is no life beyond death, it will be an injustice.[21]

In the first century A.D., belief in the resurrection of the dead was a fairly recent development. The first clear affirmation of a hope for resurrection appears in Daniel 12:2. The Greeks believed in the immortality of the human soul, that there is something in the human being that is inherently immortal. But the Hebrew belief was that there is nothing inherently immortal in the human soul. Life beyond death depends entirely on God and the power of God. Belief in God's steadfast love and divine retribution finally led to the affirmation that death is not the end. So recent was this belief that not all first-century Jews had accepted it. The Pharisees and the Essenes believed in the resurrection of the dead, but the Sadducees did not. The story of the raising of Lazarus makes a distinctively Johannine claim: Jesus is "the resurrection and the life" (11:25).

John 11 follows the typical form of a Johannine sign, but with one major difference. In John 5, 6, and 9, the sign was reported briefly and followed by a discourse appended to interpret the sign, but in John 11, three conversations interpret the meaning of the sign before the raising of Lazarus is actually narrated. The chapter has six parts: (1) the request for Jesus to come (vv. 1-6), (2) conversation with Thomas and the disciples (vv. 7-16), (3) conversation with Martha (vv. 17-27), (4) conversation with Mary (vv. 28-34), (5) the raising of Lazarus (vv. 35-44), (6) responses to the miracle (vv. 45-53).

The Form of the Raising of Lazarus
John 11:1-53

1. A supplicant presents Jesus with a request: "Lord, he whom you love is ill." (11:3)

2. Jesus rebuffs the request: "This illness does not lead to death ..." (11:4). He stayed where he was for two days longer.

3. The supplicant persists. In this case Jesus insists on returning to Judea (v. 7) and then insists on being taken to the tomb when the sisters had given up hope.

---

4. Jesus gives instructions that will grant the request: "Take away the stone" (v. 39); "Lazarus, come out!" (v. 43); and "Unbind him, and let him go." (v. 44)

5. The other person complies with Jesus' order, and the sign is accomplished: "The dead man came out." (v. 44)

6. The sign is verified by a third party: many of the Jews saw what Jesus did (v. 45).

7. There is a response of faith: "Many of the Jews therefore, who had come with Mary and had seen what Jesus did, believed in him. But some of them went to the Pharisees and told them what he had done." (vv. 45-46)

The Request for Jesus to Come (11:1-6)

The first scene sets the stage for the miracle. Three new characters are introduced: Lazarus, Mary, and Martha. The name Lazarus occurs in a parable in the Gospel of Luke in which Lazarus is a poor beggar who dies and is taken to the bosom of Abraham. Interestingly, that parable ends with the lament, "If they do not listen to Moses and the prophets, neither will they be convinced even if someone rises from the dead" (16:31). In John, Lazarus is the brother of Mary and Martha, who are mentioned in a separate story in Luke 10:38-42. Here in John, Mary is introduced as the one who anointed Jesus and wiped his feet with her hair, an act that is attributed to a harlot in Luke 7:37-38, and in John the anointing of Jesus is not reported until John 12. The introduction of Mary and Martha by means of reference to the anointing suggests that this story was well known in Christian communities. Lazarus is refered to as "he whom you love" (11:3), which has led some to speculate that Lazarus was the unnamed Beloved Disciple who is introduced in John 13:23. While an interesting case can be made for this identification, in the final analysis the identity of the Beloved Disciple remains unknown to modern readers of the Gospel.[22]

Jesus, who had withdrawn across the Jordan (10:40), responds to the news that Lazarus is ill by declaring that God will be glorified through Lazarus's illness and by remaining where he is for two days. This enigmatic response continues the pattern of Jesus rebuffing requests and acting only in response to the Father's direction (cf. 2:4; 7:3-10).

Conversation with Thomas and the Disciples (11:7-16)

When Jesus announces to his disciples that he is returning to Judea, they object that it is not safe because his opponents had recently attempted to stone him there. Jesus responds that they must work while there is light, and that Lazarus had "fallen asleep." The euphemism of sleep for death is common, but John uses it here as a typical Johannine misunderstanding. The disciples take Jesus' words literally, so the metaphor serves as an opportunity for further clarification. In this case the narrator explains the misunderstanding, and Jesus declares plainly, "Lazarus is dead." The first conversation, therefore, interprets death as being like sleep. Jesus is going to Bethany to wake Lazarus up. Thomas sees clearly what this means and challenges the others, "Let us also go, that we may die with him."

Conversation with Martha (11:17-27)

Theologically, the conversation with Martha is the most important of the exchanges in this story. Verses 17-20 provide necessary stage directions: Lazarus has been in the tomb for four days by the time Jesus arrives, Bethany is fifteen stadia (two miles) from Jerusalem, many Jews had come to comfort the sisters, and when Martha heard that Jesus had come she went out to meet him. We are not told whether Mary also knew that Jesus had come, or why Martha did not tell Mary, but the device allows Jesus to talk to each of the sisters individually.

Martha opens the conversation, not with a greeting, but with words that express both faith and implied criticism: "If you had been here, my brother would not have died" (v. 21). It is unclear what she wants Jesus to ask God for at this point. Jesus offers nothing, but merely asserts that Lazarus will rise again. Martha apparently understands this assurance in terms of the teaching of the Pharisees and Jesus' own words concerning resurrection at the end of time (Dan 12:2; cf. Jesus' words in John 6:39, 40, 44, 54: "on the last day"). In a move that may surprise the reader as it surprises Martha, Jesus makes a claim that puts death and resurrection in a new perspective: "I am the resurrection and the life" (v. 25). Just as earlier Jesus had articulated a "realized eschatology" in reference to the Last Judgment (3:18-19), so now he pulls the hope of resurrection from the future into the present. Eternal life begins now, so those who believe in him already have life. In that sense, they will not die, and if they die they will live on. Jesus presses once again for his dialogue partner to move to another level of faith. In response, Martha voices the normative Johannine confession: "You are the Messiah, the Son of God" (11:27; cf. 20:31). There is no parallel to Peter's confession at Caesarea Philippi in John, but in some ways Martha's confession stands as the Johannine counterpart to Peter's confession in the Synoptics (cf. 1:41; 6:68-69).

Conversation with Mary (11:28-34)

Jesus' conversation with Mary is not as significant theologically. Instead, it underscores Jesus' love for "his own" and serves as a transition to the raising of Lazarus. Mary appears at the feet of Jesus in each of her scenes. She is introduced as the one who anointed Jesus' feet (11:2), in this scene she falls at Jesus' feet (11:32), and in the next chapter the anointing of his feet is reported (12:3).

The interpretive crux in this scene is the meaning of the Greek verb *enebrimēsato* ("he was greatly disturbed") in 11:33, 38. The verb denotes intense emotion, often either indignation or anger. Jesus shows more emotion in this scene than in any other in the Gospel, but is it grief or anger? Is he angry at death, angry at the people's lack of faith, grieving with or for his friends, or responding to the immediate prospect of his own death? He is "greatly disturbed" and weeps. Those standing by comment on how Jesus loved Lazarus. Others voice the sentiment of the sisters, speculating that Jesus might have prevented Lazarus's death.

The Raising of Lazarus (11:35-44)

Even the conversation seems skewed at this point. Uncharacteristically, Jesus asks for information: "Where have you laid him?" Mary Magdalene will ask this same question repeatedly at the empty tomb in John 20. In response, they say to Jesus, "come and see," which elsewhere is Jesus' invitation (1:39, 46; 4:16).

The scene at Lazarus's tomb is strikingly similar to the story of the empty tomb. There are weeping women, the tomb, a stone lying against it, references to the wrappings around the corpse, and days have passed. Jesus orders them to remove the stone, even when they protest that there will be a stench. Jesus prays, looking to heaven, but it is an odd prayer. Characteristically he does not ask God for anything, but here he merely thanks the Father that the Father always hears him. The implication is that he has already asked the Father to raise Lazarus, so now all that is necessary is to voice gratitude so that the crowd standing by might know that what is about to happen is an act of God.

Then Jesus calls Lazarus out of the tomb, fulfilling his role as the good shepherd who calls his sheep by name and leads them out (cf. 10:3): "My sheep hear my voice.... I give them eternal life, and they will never perish" (10:27-28). The narrator's description of Lazarus emerging from the tomb still bound by the grave wrappings may be symbolically significant in view of the fact that when the disciples enter Jesus' empty tomb, we are told, his grave wrappings had been discarded and left there (20:6-7).

The raising of Lazarus, like the giving of sight to the blind man, should probably be read as illustrative of what Jesus does for all of his own. He calls his sheep by name and gives them eternal life. Those who trust in him already have eternal life, so even if they die, they will still live. The raising of Lazarus, therefore, illustrates a central tenet in John's confession of Jesus as the one who has come to give life.

Responses to the Miracle (11:45-53)

As public as the raising of Lazarus is, it provokes divergent responses from those who witnessed it. Miracles never substitute for faith. Many believed in Jesus. Others reported what he had done to the authorities. Depending on how one understands the response of the man at the pool of Bethesda, these alternative responses repeat the responses of the man at the pool in John 5 and the blind man in John 9. One goes to the authorities; the other believes. These alternative responses may also have special significance for the choices that the initial readers of the Gospel faced.

The chief priests called a meeting of the Sanhedrin. Their words are full of irony as they attempt to sort out their options. They ask what they are to do in response to Jesus' signs. The reader already knows what the proper response is and the futility of any contrary response. They complain that if they allow him to go on doing signs, the Romans will destroy their Temple and their nation. In fact, the reader knows that they killed Jesus, and still the Romans came in A.D. 70 and destroyed the Temple and dispersed the people. Caiaphas ironically judges that it is better for one man to die than for the nation to perish. He intends the words as cold political expediency, but the reader knows that Jesus is the good shepherd who laid down his life for his sheep. The narrator underscores the irony through his comment that the high priest was actually prophesying Jesus' death, though he did not know it. Moreover, he was unwittingly fulfilling his function as high priest by providing the sacrifice for the people. The narrator adds that Jesus did not die for the nation of Israel only but for all the dispersed children of God. Jesus' return to Judea to raise Lazarus, therefore, leads directly to his own death. He lays down his life for his own, as the story of Jesus giving life to Lazarus ends with the council plotting Jesus' death (11:53).

Jesus' Withdrawal to Ephraim (11:54-57)

John 11 begins with Jesus in retreat across the Jordan and ends with him withdrawing to Ephraim. The preparations for Passover begin at the end of John 11. Although there are two previous Passovers in John, the preparations for Passover have not been narrated in detail as they are here: people were traveling to Jerusalem for the celebration and purifying themselves, the people were speculating about whether Jesus would return for the festival (cf. 7:11-13), and the chief priests and the Pharisees gave orders that anyone who saw Jesus should report him so that he could be arrested. The preparations for this particular Passover continue in John 12 with the anointing of Jesus and his entry into the city.

JOHN 12

This chapter brings Jesus' public ministry to a close, marking the end of the first half of the Gospel. John 12 contains the accounts of the anointing of Jesus, his entry into Jerusalem, the coming of the Greeks who wish to see Jesus, and a summary of the teachings of Jesus in a soliloquy at the end of the chapter. Each of these scenes relates preparations for the Passover that was drawing near.

The Anointing of Jesus (12:1-8)

The anointing of Jesus and the entry into Jerusalem that follows pose fascinating questions regarding John's relationship to the Synoptic Gospels. All four Gospels contain an anointing scene, but the differences between them make it difficult to think that John was drawing directly from the Synoptics. The following chart presents the similarities and differences in graphic form.

The Anointing of Jesus

	Mark 14:3-9	Matthew 26:6-13	Luke 7:36-50	John 12:1-8
Place	Bethany the house of Simon the leper	Bethany the house of Simon the leper	Galilee the house of Simon the Pharisee	Bethany the house of Lazarus
Time	two days before Passover	two days before Passover	during Jesus' Galilean ministry	six days before Passover
Woman	unnamed	unnamed	a harlot	Mary
Ointment	an alabaster flask of pure nard, very expensive	an alabaster flask of very expensive ointment	an alabaster flask of ointment	a pound of costly ointment, pure nard
Anointing	poured on his head	poured on his head	wet his feet with her tears, wiped her tears with her hair, anointed his feet	anointed his feet wiped them with her hair
Protest	Some: the wasted	The disciples: the	The Pharisee: If	Judas: the wasted

191

	ointment could have been sold for 300 denarii and given to the poor	wasted ointment could have been sold for a large sum and given to the poor	Jesus were a prophet, he would have known what sort of woman this was	ointment could have been sold for 300 denarii and given to the poor
Response	(1) Let her alone. Why trouble her? (2) She has done a beautiful thing. (3) You always have the poor. (4) She has anointed my body for burying. (5) What she has done will be told in memory of her.	(1) Why trouble her? (2) She has done a beautiful thing. (3) You always have the poor. (4) She has done it to prepare my body for burial. (5) What she has done will be told in memory of her.	(1) The parable of the two debtors (2) You gave me no water for my feet. (3) Her sins are forgiven. (4) Your faith has saved you. Go in peace.	(1) Let her alone. (2) Let her keep it for the day of my burial. (3) You always have the poor.

Various theories have been advanced to explain this complicated set of relationships. One that has much to commend it is that John was drawing on oral tradition of the anointing of Jesus. Jesus had been anointed once, on his head, in Bethany, just before the Passover. During his ministry in Galilee a harlot had wept at his feet and wiped her tears with her hair. In the process of oral tradition, details from the weeping and the anointing were confused because of the similarity of the events. Simon is both a leper and a Pharisee. The harlot had an alabaster flask and anointed his feet after weeping on them. Mary, however, wipes not her tears— as the woman in Luke 7 does—but the ointment from Jesus' feet.

The anointing of Jesus in John takes place in the house of Lazarus, evidently at a meal celebrating Lazarus's return from the dead. The anointing may also serve the kingship motif that will be prominent during the trial and death of Jesus. He is anointed, just as he will ride in procession into the city, but the anointing ironically is an anointing of his feet, not by the high priest but by a woman, and he rides in procession not on a stallion but on a donkey. He will be elevated and enthroned, in a sense, but his lifting up will be on a cross with the inscription over him, "The King of the Jews." The anointing of this king, fittingly, is an anointing of his body for burial.

The Entry into Jerusalem (12:9-19)

The entry into Jerusalem is bracketed by references to Lazarus (vv. 9-10 and 17) that tie the entry to the raising of Lazarus. By contrast, in the Synoptics, the entry is tied to the cursing of the fig tree and the cleansing of the Temple. In John, the crowds come out not only to see Jesus but to see the man raised from the dead. The Pharisees plot, therefore, to put Lazarus to death also. When the crowd hears that Jesus is coming, they take up palm branches and begin to chant the words of Psalm 118, one of the psalms that was sung by pilgrims approaching the city for the major festivals. The narrator interprets the event by quoting from Zechariah 9:9.

The Quotation in John 12:15

John 12:15	*"Do not be afraid, daughter of Zion.* *Look, your king is coming sitting on a donkey's colt!"*
Zechariah 9:9-10	Rejoice greatly, O *daughter Zion!* Shout aloud, O daughter Jerusalem! *Lo, your king comes* to you; triumphant and victorious is he, humble and *riding on* a donkey, on a colt, *the foal of a donkey.* He will cut off the chariot from Ephraim and the war-horse from Jerusalem; and the battle bow shall be cut off, and he shall command peace to the nations; his dominion shall be from sea to sea, and from the River to the ends of the earth.

Because there was no system of chapter and verse numbers at the time—no footnotes, parentheses, quotation marks, or cross references—the evangelist quotes enough of the well-known text to evoke it and its context as a commentary on the event being narrated. Jesus' entry into Jerusalem on a donkey is thereby presented as a fulfillment of the prophets. He will bring peace, and his dominion shall extend to the ends of the earth.

John's distinctive hermeneutic is stated clearly in verse 16. The disciples did not understand the meaning of the event at the time. Only later, after Easter, through the study of the scripture and the leadership of the Paraclete (see 14:26), could they grasp the full meaning of these events. John writes not what they saw or heard but their later understanding of the events of Jesus' ministry (cf. 2:22; 20:9).

The Coming of the Greeks (12:20-26)

The Pharisees' ironic comment that the world has gone after Jesus introduces a scene in which some Greeks come and tell Philip that they wish to see Jesus. The coming of the Greeks is a signal that Jesus' revelatory ministry will extend beyond Israel to all the world, but Jesus knows that he cannot bypass his death and go to the Greeks (cf. 7:33-36; 8:21-22). He responds: "The hour has come for the Son of Man to be glorified." Jesus has referred to his "hour" on earlier occasions (2:4; 7:30; 8:20), but this is the first announcement that his hour has come (cf. 13:1).

The parable of the grain of wheat falling into the earth (12:24) may well be an authentic parable that is not contained in the Synoptic Gospels. Here, it underscores the necessity and life-giving significance of Jesus' death. The saying on loving life and losing it echoes Mark 8:35, Matthew 10:39 and 16:25, and Luke 9:24 and 17:33—showing how the evangelist embeds traditional sayings within distinctively Johannine discourses.

The Johannine Gethsemane (12:27-36)

Jesus now faces the hour of his death. His soul is troubled (cf. 11:33; 13:21; 14:1, 27). This scene, rather than the one in the garden in John 18, more closely approximates the Synoptic account of Jesus' prayer in Gethsemane. Nevertheless, the Johannine Jesus, who is one with the Father (10:30), would never pray "not

194

what I want, but what you want." Instead, he merely entertains the thought of asking the Father to deliver him from his hour and immediately rejects it. Instead, he prays, "Father, glorify your name," and the voice from heaven answers cryptically, "I have glorified it, and I will glorify it again." This is the only voice from heaven in John. Even it, like the signs, is subject to various interpretations and responses. Some say it was thunder, others that they heard the voice of an angel. Jesus underscores that it was for their benefit, not his. The Johannine Jesus needs no such confirmation. He understands that the coming of the Greeks and the voice from heaven mean that the time of his death is near. It means judgment (cf. 3:19) and the defeat of the devil (cf. 14:30; 16:11; Rev 12:8). Jesus himself will be "lifted up." This is the third of the "lifting up" sayings, which metaphorically describe his death and its effects. Characteristically, the crowd does not understand and asks, "How can you say that the Son of Man must be lifted up?" Verse 34 is the only place in the Gospels where those around Jesus use the title "Son of Man." It is all the more notable because Jesus does not use the title in the immediate context. Instead, he said, "when I am lifted up" (v. 32, but cf. 8:28).

The Narrator's Commentary (12:37-43)

The next six verses contain the longest commentary in the Gospel. There is no dialogue, only commentary and two quotations from Isaiah. The narrator reports that Jesus withdrew and hid from the crowds. Their unbelief fulfilled the pronouncement of judgment in Isaiah 53:1 and 6:10. The latter verse was often quoted by the New Testament writers. Jesus uses it to explain the purpose of the parables (Matt 13:14; Mark 4:12; Luke 8:10), it stands at the conclusion of the book of Acts (28:26), and in Romans 11:8 it serves as an explanation for the failure of the mission to Israel. The narrator's quotation of Isaiah's pronouncement of judgment at the conclusion of Jesus' public ministry is therefore comparable to the way it is used elsewhere in the New Testament. Although the people saw signs, they would not believe. Although some of the Pharisees believed, they were "secret believers" who would not confess Jesus publicly. The inauthenticity of their faith, the narrator explains, is due to misplaced love: they loved the praise of others more than God's praise.

195

Jesus' Parting Words (12:44-50)

The first half of the Gospel, Jesus' revelation to the world, ends with a parting soliloquy that summarizes themes from the preceding chapters. The narrator does not tell us where Jesus was, or whether anyone else was present. The Word merely speaks. Jesus' revelation to the world was summarized in the prologue in the words, "He came to what was his own, and his own people did not accept him" (1:11). The narrator has just commented on the people's failure to accept Jesus' revelation. Jesus now proclaims that he has come to reveal the one who sent him. He has come as light to the world, to save the world. But those who do not receive him are judged by the words he has spoken. He has spoken what the Father has given him to say, and his words are the source of eternal life. With this short summary, Jesus' public ministry is ended, and the Gospel turns to the foot washing and Jesus' farewell discourse—his revelation to "his own."

CHAPTER 8

INTERPRETING THE
FOURTH GOSPEL
JOHN 13–21

The second half of the Gospel contains seven major sections: (1) Jesus' last meal with his disciples, which includes the foot washing and the farewell discourse; (2) the arrest of Jesus in the garden; (3) the trial of Jesus before Caiaphas and before Pilate; (4) the cross; (5) the tomb, which was the site of the burial, discovery of the empty tomb, and appearance to Mary Magdalene; (6) the appearances to the disciples in Jerusalem; and (7) the appearance by the lake in Galilee. Each of these major sections is divided into distinct episodes and scenes that depict the significance of Jesus' departure, his kingship, and his death and resurrection.

With his public ministry concluded, Jesus now gathers his disciples. He will wash their feet, instruct them, pray for them, and then go out to die for them. Although the events in John 13–19 all occur in the span of less than twenty-four hours, it is surprising what the reader is not told. The reader is not told where Jesus met for the last meal with his disciples or precisely who was there. Moreover, the words of institution and the giving of the bread and the wine are not a part of this scene. Some of the material in the farewell discourse and in John 6 appears to reflect a tradition that included the Eucharist, but for reasons about which we can only speculate the institution of the Eucharist is not reported in John's account of the Last Supper.

Literary problems in this section have led modern interpreters to postulate that it reflects at least two, and possibly three, stages of composition. A distinct seam in the narrative appears at the end of John 14, where Jesus says, "Rise, let us be on our way." Then he continues talking for two more chapters and prays for a chapter before we are finally told at John 18:1, "After Jesus had spoken these words, he went out with his disciples..." Moreover, there are doublets of material, repetitions, and inconsistencies that support the view that John 13–14 and 15–16 are two different versions of Jesus' farewell discourse—or that there are three strata: (1) 13:31–14:31; (2) 15:1–16:4a; (3) 16:4b–33.[1]

Synopsis of Tensions and Repetitions in John 13:31–16:33		
John 13:31–14:31	*John 15:1–16:4*a	*John 16:4*b-33
Peter: "Lord, where are you going?" (13:36)		Jesus: "None of you asks me, 'Where are you going?'" (16:5)
The Paraclete (14:16-17, 26)	The Paraclete (15:26)	The Paraclete (16:7-15)
The new command (13:34-35)	The new command (15:12)	
keeping and loving (14:15, 21-24)	keeping and loving (15:9-10)	
Jesus' departure (13:33; 14:3-4, 28)		Jesus' departure (16:5, 7, 10, 17, 28)
"a little while" (13:33; 14:19)		"a little while" (16:16-19)
	The world's hostility (15:18-25; 16:1-4a)	The world's hostility (16:25-33)

In addition to the literary puzzle, the *timing* of the Last Supper, the trial, and the crucifixion of Jesus poses a chronological problem for interpreters when the Johannine account of these events is compared with the Synoptic Gospels. All four Gospels agree that Jesus was crucified and buried before sundown on Friday, that the empty tomb was discovered on Sunday morning, and that these events occurred at the time of the Jewish Passover. In Jewish custom, each new day begins at sundown, and the Passover is celebrated on Nisan 15.

**Preparation
of the Passover Lamb**

Exodus 12:3-8

Tell the whole congregation of Israel that on the tenth of this month [Nisan] they are to take a lamb for each family.... You shall keep it until the fourteenth day of this month; then the whole assembled congregation of Israel shall slaughter it at twilight. They shall take some of the blood and put it on the two doorposts and the lintel of the houses in which they eat it. They shall eat the lamb that same night; they shall eat it roasted over the fire with unleavened bread and bitter herbs.

As with our modern calendar, a given day of the month could fall on any day of the week in different years. Every Friday, however, was a day of Preparation for the sabbath. According to the Synoptic accounts, the Last Supper coincided with the Passover meal on the evening beginning Nisan 15: Jesus ate the Passover meal with his disciples, went out to Gethsemane, was arrested, tried, crucified, and buried on the day of Passover. According to John, the Last Supper fell on the evening before Passover; the Jews would not enter Pilate's Praetorium because had they done so they would have been defiled and could not have eaten the Passover that night; and that year the Passover coincided with the Sabbath.

The Chronology of the Last Supper and Crucifixion of Jesus

	The Synoptics	John
Preparation for the meal (Thursday afternoon)	"On the first day of Unleavened Bread, when the Passover lamb is sacrificed, his disciples said to him, 'Where do you want us to go and make the preparations for you to eat the Passover?' ... So the disciples set out and went to the city, and found everything as he had told them; and they prepared the Passover meal." (Mark 14:12, 16; Nisan 14)	
The meal (Thursday evening)	"When it was evening, he came" with the twelve. (Mark 14:17; Nisan 15)	"before the festival of the Passover" (John 13:1; Nisan 14)
The trial (early Friday morning)	"as soon as it was morning" (Mark 15:1; Nisan 15)	"Then they took Jesus from Caiaphas to Pilate's headquarters. It was early in the morning. They themselves did not enter the headquarters, so as to avoid ritual defilement and to be able to eat the Passover." (John 18:28; Nisan 14)
Jesus' death (Friday afternoon)	"At three o'clock" (Mark 15:34; Nisan 15)	"Since it was the day of Preparation, the Jews did not want the bodies left on

200

		the cross during the sabbath, especially because that sabbath was a day of great solemnity." (John 19:31; Nisan 14)
The burial (late Friday afternoon)	"When evening had come, and since it was the day of Preparation, that is, the day before the sabbath" (Mark 15:42; Nisan 15)	"And so, because it was the Jewish day of Preparation, and the tomb was nearby, they laid Jesus there." (John 19:42; Nisan 14)

Both John and the Synoptics remember that Jesus died during Passover, but they find the theological significance of the chronology in different places. For the Synoptics, the celebration of the Last Supper replaces the Passover meal. For John, Jesus—"the Lamb of God who takes away the sin of the world" (1:29, 36)—dies at the very time the Passover lambs were being slaughtered, on the afternoon of Nisan 14. Historically, the case can be made that John is more accurate because it is unlikely that the Jewish authorities would have arrested, tried, and executed Jesus on the day of Passover.

JOHN 13

Chapter 13 develops the recurring theme of knowledge and ignorance as a variation on the conflict between belief and unbelief as responses to Jesus in the plot of the Gospel of John.[2] Here again is a scene in which recognition is possible but not achieved. The chapter reports what Jesus knew and the actions following from that knowledge. The disciples, especially Peter and Judas, do not share Jesus' knowledge, and their ignorance leads to denial and betrayal. John 13 reports the foot washing, Jesus' exhortation to the disciples, the forecast of betrayal, and a final appeal to

Judas. In view of the events that the reader already knows are coming, the whole chapter is filled with pathos.

The Meal Scenes in John 12 and 13		
	John 12	**John 13**
Time	"six days *before the Passover*"	"*before* the festival of the Passover"
Companion	"Lazarus was one of those at the table with him."	"One of his disciples— the one whom Jesus loved—was reclining next to him."
Washing of feet	"Mary took a pound of costly perfume made of pure nard, *anointed Jesus' feet,* and *wiped them* with her hair."	"Then he poured water into a basin and began to *wash the disciples' feet* and to *wipe them* with the towel that was tied around him."
Judas	"But Judas Iscariot, one of his disciples (the one who was about to *betray him*), said, 'Why was this perfume not sold for three hundred denarii and the money given to *the poor*?' (He said this not because he cared for *the poor,* but because he was a thief; he kept *the common purse* and used to steal what was put into it.)"	"The devil had already put it into the heart of Judas son of Simon Iscariot *to betray him....* After he received the piece of bread, Satan entered into him. Jesus said to him, 'Do quickly what you are going to do.' Now no one at the table knew why he said this to him. Some thought that, because Judas had *the common purse,* Jesus was telling him, 'Buy what we need for the festival'; or, that he should give something to *the poor.*"

| Jesus' death | Explicit: "so that she might keep it for the day of my burial" | Implicit: Jesus "took off" his robe and later "put on" his robe (cf. John 10:17-18, where the same verbs are used: "I lay down my life in order to take it up again.") |
| Jesus' departure | "... but you do not always have me." | "Jesus knew that his hour had come to depart from this world" |

The Foot Washing (13:1-5)

The first five verses introduce the scene by reporting its setting and locating Jesus' action in the context of his unique knowledge. John 13:1 marks a major transition in the Gospel, introducing not only the scene of the foot washing but the entire second half of the Gospel. Two systems of time are set in relation to each other in this introduction: the calendar of Jewish festivals (2:13, 23; 4:45; 5:1) and the approach of Jesus' hour (2:4; 4:21, 23; 7:30; 8:20; 12:23, 27). The narrator provides an inside view of what Jesus knew, that his hour had come. Inside views of what Jesus knew are common in John.

What Jesus Knew

Nathanael (1:48)

what is in the hearts of others (2:24-25)

that the testimony about him is true (5:32)

what he is about to do (6:6)

when his disciples grumble about him (6:61)

those who do not believe in him and who his betrayer is (6:64)

the one who sent him (7:29; 8:55)

from whence he came and where he is going (8:14)

that the Father always hears him (11:42)

that the Father's command is eternal life (12:50)

With John 13:1 the reader learns that Jesus' hour is the time for his departure from this world and his return to the Father. Verse 2 serves as a counterpoint to verse 1, but it is problematic because it involves Semitic idiom and because it stands in tension with the report that Satan entered Judas in verse 27. C. K. Barrett resolves the tension by recognizing the idiom and translating the verse "The devil had already made up his mind that Judas should betray [Jesus]."[3] The reader, therefore, knows what is in the mind of Jesus and what is in the mind of the devil.

The extended clauses in verses 1-3 weave together the setting and the report of what Jesus knew, giving the introduction "a most solemn effect."[4] The terminology of verse 4 has thematic significance. The same verbs for taking off and putting on were used in John 10:11, 15, 17, and 18 for the good shepherd laying down his life for the sheep and taking it up again. The description of Jesus' laying aside his garments seems already to suggest the connection between the foot washing and Jesus' death. Jesus, who has already been anointed for his burial (12:7), now interprets the meaning of his death by washing the disciples' feet. He prepares them to follow his example by laying down their lives for others. If these implications were obvious, however, there would be no need for the dialogues that follow. The dialogues with Peter, the disciples, the Beloved Disciple, and Judas serve to interpret the meaning of the action, just as the author has previously used dialogues and discourses to unpack the meaning of Jesus' signs.

The First Conversation with Peter (13:6-11)

The first conversation with Peter involves three statements by Peter and three responses from Jesus. *Peter* (1): "Lord, are you going to wash my feet?" Peter's first statement, expressing amazement and resistance, arises from his acceptance of the social norms that reinforce superior and inferior social standings. By laying aside his garments and washing the disciples' feet, Jesus has displaced those norms. *Jesus* (1): "You do not know now what I am doing, but later you will understand." Since the scene was introduced by the narrator with a report of what Jesus knew, the contrast between Jesus and Peter could not be more sharp. If Peter knew about Jesus' hour and his return to the Father, he would understand the meaning of the foot washing. "Later" Peter will understand (cf. 2:22; 12:16)—after Jesus has completed his mission and returned to the Father. Various characters— Nathanael, Nicodemus, Martha, and Thomas, for example—have misunderstood some aspect of Jesus' mission. Peter does not understand the need for Jesus to die (cf. 13:36-38; 18:10-11). Because Peter does not understand Jesus' imminent death and glorification, he cannot understand the foot washing.

Peter (2): "You will never wash my feet." This statement under-scores that refusing to accept Jesus' love (foot washing/death) is a mistaken response that grows out of ignorance. *Jesus* (2): "Unless I wash you, you have no share with me." The reader can-not literally allow Jesus to wash his or her feet, but the reader can understand that Jesus' death revealed God's love for his own in the world. The foot washing scene, therefore, functions metaphorically and proleptically in relation to Jesus' death, clari-fying the meaning of his death so that the reader may have a part in Jesus and his story.

Peter (3): "Lord, not my feet only but also my hands and my head!" Impulsively, Peter shifts to the opposite extreme, but again Jesus' response demonstrates that Peter's request rises from his lack of understanding. Jesus was not perpetuating the practice of ritual washings. *Jesus* (3): "One who has bathed does not need to wash [except for the feet], but is entirely clean. And you are clean, though not all of you." The difficulties in interpreting this verse have led to the introduction of textual variants which have further compounded the problems facing the interpreter. The basic ques-tion concerns the phrase in brackets, "except for the feet." The shorter reading, omitting this phrase, seems to fit the narrative flow of verses 6-11 better. Jesus' third response affirms that one who has been washed (by Jesus' death, which is interpreted by the foot washing) has no need of any further washings such as Peter was requesting.

The conclusion of this conversation returns to the theme of knowledge. Jesus also knew that Judas would betray him. The reader is drawn into the circle of those who share in Jesus' reve-lation. The narrative's handling of information, therefore, com-plements and supports its development of the theme of knowl-edge (revelation and belief) versus ignorance (rejection and unbelief).

Jesus' Exhortation to the Disciples (13:12-17)

The transitional question again concerns the disciples' knowledge or understanding: "Do you know what I have done to you?" The real audience for this question is not the disciples, who do not yet know about Jesus' death, but the readers of the narrative, who already know of Jesus' death and resurrection, though it has not yet been reported in the narrative.

Jesus clarifies his rejection of the prevailing norms of social standing. First, the foot washing does not mean that Jesus is not to be honored as teacher and Lord (v. 13). Second, because the disciples honor him as their teacher, they are to follow his teaching and example by serving others. The Johannine community may have actually continued the practice of foot washing. The unusual term *hypodeigma* ("example"—v. 15) occurs in the Apocrypha in well-known passages that exhort the faithful to mark an exemplary death.

Exemplary Deaths in the Apocrypha

Eleazar: " 'Therefore, by bravely giving up my life now, I will show myself worthy of my old age and leave to the young a noble example *[hypodeigma]* of how to die a good death willingly and nobly for the revered and holy laws.'... So in this way he died, leaving in his death an example *[hypodeigma]* of nobility and a memorial of courage, not only to the young but to the great body of his nation." (2 Macc 6:27-28, 31)

A mother and her seven sons: "And through the blood of those devout ones and their death as an atoning sacrifice, divine Providence preserved Israel that previously had been mistreated. For the tyrant Antiochus, when he saw the courage of their virtue and their endurance under the tortures, proclaimed them to his soldiers as an example *[hypodeigma]* for their own endurance." (4 Macc 17:22-23)

Enoch: "Enoch pleased the Lord, and was taken up, an example *[hypodeigma]* of repentance to all generations." (Sir 44:16)

Jesus' death means a complete rejection of the world's norms and the conferring of a new set of values under which Jesus' followers will serve one another even to the point of laying down their lives (cf. 15:13; 16:2; 21:19). Consequently, members of the Johannine community should be willing to die for one another: "We know love by this, that he laid down his life for us—and we ought to lay down our lives for one another" (1 John 3:16). Jesus' death, as it is here interpreted through the foot washing, is the norm of life and conduct for the believing community. This is a radical ethic, but one that accords well with the view that the Johannine community experienced persecution and conflict with the synagogue and Roman imperial authority.

The Forecast of Betrayal (13:18-20)

Jesus knew that not all of the disciples would be able to accept the ethic based on his radical love and expressed in the foot washing and in his death. He knew that Judas would betray him, but ironically the betrayal would lead to the completing of Jesus' mission at his death. Verse 20, a Synoptic-like double *amen* saying, like verse 16, authorizes the work of the disciples. The sacrifice required by the radical Johannine ethic is warranted by the promise that those who receive the disciples also receive Jesus.

Jesus and Judas (13:21-30)

This is the last time that Jesus is "troubled in spirit" (cf. 11:33; 12:27). The narrator has prepared for Jesus' confrontation with Judas first by reporting that the devil had decided that Judas should betray Jesus (v. 2), then by an allusion to Judas in verse 10, and again by the proleptic interpretation of the betrayal by means of Jesus' quotation of Psalm 41:9 in verse 18. The disciples do not understand. At this point the Beloved Disciple is introduced for the first time (see the discussion of authorship in chapter 2). Peter signals the Beloved Disciple to ask Jesus who he is talking about. In response to the question, Jesus takes bread, dips it, and gives it to Judas, fulfilling Psalm 41:9. Satan enters into Judas, but it is Jesus, not Satan, who prompts Judas to leave and carry out his betrayal. Judas, like Peter, acts out of his lack of understanding. He responds to the spirit that dwells within him (Satan), in contrast to the other disciples who will respond to the abiding presence of the Holy Spirit.

Immediately, the story returns to the theme of knowledge: "Now no one at the table knew why he said this to him" (v. 28). Judas was able to betray Jesus because the others did not understand what he was doing. Their erroneous assumptions are reported in verse 29, driving home the narrator's report that they did not understand. Judas belongs to the darkness rather than the light, so verse 30 tersely adds, "and it was night." That is all John needs to say about Judas's fate. He left the light and went out into the darkness. The implication is clear: Refusing to accept Jesus' revelatory act places one in the realm of darkness (cf. 3:19-21).

The New Command and the Second Conversation with Peter (13:31-38)

This section reports further instruction—including the new commandment and the second conversation with Peter, both of which have significant connections with the foot washing and with the farewell discourse that follows. Jesus' death is characterized as his glorification. As his glory was veiled in the foot washing, however, the glory of his death will be veiled by the cross. Jesus repeats the *mashal,* or riddle, that he has used on two previous occasions (7:33-36; 8:21-22). This time Jesus does not say that they will not be able to find him (cf. 7:34) or that they will die in their sin (8:21). Neither of these consequences applies to the disciples, but they will not be able to come where he is going.

Jesus' new command has taken on additional significance following the foot washing. The close association of love with the foot washing and Jesus' death conveys the implication that Jesus was charging his disciples to love one another even if such love requires that they lay down their lives for the community. This inference will later be reinforced by the association of keeping the new commandment (15:12, 17) with laying down one's life for one's friends (15:13) and bearing fruit (15:16; cf. 12:24).

Jesus' death is the model for community. The foot washing and the new commandment are two facets of the same instructions: Do (foot washing/serve/love/die) for one another as I am doing for you. By such imitation of the pattern of Jesus' life and death, they will show all people that they are his disciples. This commissioning expresses the divine intent that all may know.

Throughout this chapter, and again in John 18:10-11, Peter is characterized as one who does not understand Jesus' death. He therefore does not understand where Jesus is going (to the Father) or why he cannot follow him. The irony of Peter's pledge

208

of loyalty is pointed. He cannot follow—that is, he cannot discharge his duty as a disciple—because he does not understand the meaning of Jesus' death. Peter's pledge that he would lay down his life is ironic because Peter does not understand that Jesus is laying down his life for the disciples, that Jesus is going to the Father by means of his death, or that eventually Peter would indeed lay down his life (cf. 21:19). Jesus confronts Peter with reality. Because he does not understand, that very night he will deny Jesus three times. The contrast between knowledge and ignorance of the revelation conveyed by Jesus' death is clear. This contrast is fundamental to the plot of the entire Gospel, and it will be developed further in the events leading to Jesus' death.

JOHN 14

The first part of the farewell discourse, which actually begins with John 13:31, continues to the end of chapter 14. It is interrupted four times by the disciples: Peter (13:36), Thomas (14:5), Philip (14:8), and Judas (not Iscariot; 14:22). In this part of the discourse, Jesus reassures the disciples that he is going to prepare a place for them and that he will return to them. He has revealed the Father to them, he will send the Paraclete, and he leaves them his peace.

Jesus' Departure to Prepare a Place for the Disciples (14:1-7)

There is ample reason for the disciples to be troubled: (1) one of them will betray Jesus, (2) Jesus is leaving them, and (3) even Peter will deny Jesus. Earlier, Jesus was troubled (11:33; 12:27; 13:21). Now that Judas has departed, Jesus begins to urge his disciples not to be troubled (14:1, 27). His consolation of the disciples takes the form of assurances that he is going to prepare a place for them where they can be together again. They have seen the Father in him. He will not leave them orphaned but will send the Paraclete, and he and the Father will abide with the disciples.

John does not contain a list of virtues and vices or specific ethical teachings. Instead, it commands that Jesus' disciples should love one another, believe in him, and keep his commandments. It becomes evident in the Johannine Epistles that these general commands leave a great deal of room for differences of interpretation in the Christian community.

Jesus tells the disciples that there are many *monai* in his Father's house (14:2). The word is the plural of a noun related to *menein* ("to abide"). Literally, it means "abiding places." William Tyndale (d. 1536) translated it "mansions." Following his lead, so did the King James Version: "In my Father's house are many mansions." Earlier in the Gospel, Jesus spoke of the temple of his body (2:21), playing on the concept of the Temple as the place where one meets God. John 14:2-3 is often interpreted as a promise that Jesus is going to prepare a place in heaven for the disciples. This may well have been a notion current in early Christian tradition. By the end of the chapter, however, John has brought his own "realized eschatology" to bear on the hope of being with Jesus in this life as well as in the hereafter. The disciples are not concerned about where they will go after they die, but how they will relate to Jesus since he is going away. Jesus assures them that this is not the last "upper room" experience they will have together. He is going out to prepare a place for them, and he will come again to be with them. The reference is probably not primarily to the Second Coming but to post-Easter experiences. The language is sufficiently ambiguous that it sets up a typical Johannine misunderstanding which will be clarified in the remainder of the chapter.

When Thomas objects that they do not know where Jesus is going, Jesus answers with an "I am" saying: "I am the way, and the truth, and the life." The three terms may be related in various ways. *The way* may be the process, *the truth* the means or goal, and *life* the result. The way may lead to truth and life, or truth and life may explain why Jesus is the way. The irony is that the claim is hardly self-evident (the way), the disciples do not understand (the truth), and the next day he will die (life). The claims of Christianity are exclusive, nevertheless: "No one comes to the Father except through me" (see below, chapter 10).

Jesus as the Revelation of the Father (14:8-14)

In apparent exasperation, Philip says, "Lord, show us the Father, and we will be satisfied." The request reflects a misunderstanding of Jesus' function as the Logos and the fundamental reality of the Incarnation. Jesus' answer is emphatic: God may be seen in him. The union between Jesus and the Father may be mystical, moral, or metaphysical. The latter two come closer to Johannine thought because the prologue affirms a metaphysical union and Jesus repeatedly affirms that he acts at the direction of the Father (a moral union). This moral union is also possible for all believers. As in John 5, Jesus appeals to his words and his works as witnesses to the truth of his claims. Because God is revealed in Jesus, knowledge of God through faith is the supreme calling of the believer. The one who believes can then be part of the "greater works" that Jesus will do after his resurrection. The future works will be greater not because they will be better or more spectacular, but because they will be more extensive (the mission and spread of the church). Asking in Jesus' name means asking in fulfillment of his life and character. This qualification rules out asking for mundane things and focuses on Jesus' mission to glorify the Father.

The Promise of the Paraclete (14:15-24)

Not only is Jesus going to prepare a place for them, but he will send another to be with the disciples in his place: the Paraclete. There is no adequate translation for this term, which seems to have a legal background and may mean advocate, intercessor, helper, comforter, or counselor. When Jesus says "another" Paraclete, John evidently intends for the reader to understand Jesus as having been a Paraclete also. The Paraclete will continue doing what Jesus began to do. Moreover, there is an intriguing correspondence between the promised work of the Paraclete and the functions that John attributes to the Beloved Disciple.

Functions of the Paraclete

be with you forever (14:16)

teach the disciples all things and remind them of all that Jesus said (14:26)

testify on Jesus' behalf (15:26)

prove the world wrong about sin, righteousness, and judgment (16:8)

guide the community into all truth (16:13)

not speak on his own but will speak what he hears (16:13)

glorify Jesus (16:14)

take what is Jesus' and declare it to the community (16:14-15)

Like the Paraclete, the Beloved Disciple guided the community, bore witness to Jesus, reminded them of all that Jesus had said, and (probably) defended the community in times of conflict. Naturally, he did not remain with them forever (see 21:23), but the parallels in function are sufficiently strong to suggest that the Johannine community recognized that the Paraclete was at work in the Beloved Disciple. They may even have refined their understanding of the work of the Paraclete through reflection on their experience with the Beloved Disciple. Whatever one makes of the functions of the Paraclete and the Beloved Disciple in relationship to Jesus and the community, the Gospel recognizes the importance of both in mediating the tradition and authority of Jesus at a later time.

Jesus instructs the disciples that love is demonstrated through obedience and that the word and the Spirit are the basis for continued relationship with the risen Lord. Jesus will reveal himself to his own, but the world will not see him. When Judas (not Iscariot) asks how this can be, Jesus explains that he and the Father will make an abiding place *(monēn)* with them. He is not referring either to post-Resurrection appearances or to the Parousia, but to something more vital for the Christian community: his presence and that of the Father with the community of believers through the Spirit. Ironically, the first disciples had asked where Jesus was staying (1:38). Now, the answer is that he was staying with them (14:23). The future eschatology of abiding with Jesus in heaven (14:2) has effectively been transposed into a realized eschatology: Jesus abides with us now.

The Coming of the Paraclete (14:25-31)

The final paragraph of this chapter gathers up the themes of the farewell discourse to this point. Jesus is going away, but his departure is a return to the Father. Satan is called "the ruler of this world" (14:30; cf. 12:31; 16:11), but he has no power over Jesus. We have already been told that Jesus will lay down his life and that he can take it up again (10:17-18).

One of the differences between the East and the West when the church split concerned the origin of the Spirit. John says both that Jesus would send the Spirit (15:26; 16:7) and that the Father would send the Spirit (14:16, 26). The Western church claimed that the Spirit proceeded from the Father and the Son, while the Eastern church maintained that the Spirit proceeded from God alone since there could only be one font of divinity.

John's interpretation of the role of the Spirit is double sided. The Spirit will teach the community all things (there is yet more truth to be revealed), but he will also remind them of what Jesus had said. Whatever may yet be revealed is an extension of what Jesus has already revealed. Such a guideline may have been shaped to help the community discern true prophets from false prophets (cf. 1 John 4:1).

Jesus continues to reveal his legacy to the disciples. He has commanded them to love one another. Now he leaves them his peace (v. 27). This peace *(shalom)* is not the absence of conflict but inner peace in the face of conflict because the Spirit dwells in them. In the next chapter Jesus will add joy to this legacy of love and peace.

JOHN 15

This chapter is composed of four sections of unequal length: (1) the allegory of the vine, (2) commentary on bearing fruit, (3) a warning about persecution, and (4) the role of the Spirit in the experience of persecution.

The Allegory of the Vine (15:1-11)

The concern of the discourse is moving from the departure of Jesus to the abiding of his disciples. The mutual abiding and indwelling of Jesus in the disciples and the disciples in him is now developed further through the image of the vine.

The grapevine and the vineyard often symbolize the fruitfulness of the land in the Old Testament, so it was a short step for the vine to become a symbol for Israel. The Lord is the keeper of the vineyard—Israel. He has cultivated and tended it faithfully, but the vineyard has been unproductive (Isa 5:1-7; 27:2-6) or it has yielded its fruit to false gods (Hos 10:1-2). Israel was a "choice vine," but it became a wild vine (Jer 2:21). Israel, therefore, had to be cut back or pruned through national defeat and exile (Jer 5:10; 6:9; 12:10-11). Fire would consume the fruitless vine (Ezek 15:1-8; 19:10-14).

213

> ### The Vine as a Symbol for Israel
>
> You brought a vine out of Egypt;
>   you drove out the nations and planted it.
> You cleared the ground for it;
>   it took deep root and filled the land.
> The mountains were covered with its shade,
>   the mighty cedars with its branches;
> it sent out its branches to the sea,
>   and its shoots to the River.
> Why then have you broken down its walls,
>   so that all who pass along the way pluck its fruit?
>   (Ps 80:8-12)

The vine was so widely recognized as a symbol for Israel that it is frequently found on coins from the Maccabean period on. A golden vine stood over the entrance to the sanctuary of Herod's Temple (*m. Middoth* 3.8).

In the praise of Wisdom in Sirach 24, Wisdom likens herself to a vine:

"Like the vine I bud forth delights,
   and my blossoms become glorious and abundant fruit.
Come to me, you who desire me,
   and eat your fill of my fruits."

                                               (Sir 24:17-19)

Because the wisdom tradition exerted a formative influence on John's Christology, the use of the image of the vine in that context provides a key to understanding John's use of this image. It is only a short step from the use of the image of the vine to depict Wisdom to its association with the Messiah. For example, 2 Baruch, which was written late in the first century A.D., pictures the Messiah as a vine (2 Bar 39:7; cf. 36–37). Vines and vineyards are also part of the common stock of Jesus' parables in the Synoptics (Mark 12:1-9 and parallels; Matt 20:1-16; Matt 21:28-32).

The striking feature of the symbolism of the vine in John 15 is that it ceases to represent Israel and takes on Christological significance. It represents Jesus himself. Whereas one's salvation had depended on identity with Israel, the people of God, Jesus declares that life depends on abiding in him. He is the source of life. The added emphasis in the words "I am the *true* vine" implies a warning not to accept any other as a substitute. Declaring that Jesus is the true vine also fits the context of conflict with the synagogue that lies so near the surface in the Gospel of John.

The figure of the vine may also have secondary, sacramental meaning. "Blessed art thou, O Lord our God, King of the universe, creator of the fruit of the vine" was the Jewish blessing of the wine at meals. One would expect to find in John 15 the words of institution at the last supper. Instead of offering the cup Jesus offers himself to the disciples: "I am the true vine . . . abide in me." In the Synoptic Gospels, in the same context, Jesus declares that he will not drink again of the fruit of the vine until he drinks it new in the kingdom of God (Mark 14:25). The vine, therefore, was a powerful symbol of the heritage and hope of the people of Israel. Both are fulfilled, John claims, in Jesus.

Bearing Fruit Through Acts of Love and Sacrifice (15:12-17)

What follows is a commentary on the meaning of bearing fruit. It has close parallels to the material in 1 John and serves as an interpretation of the new command and the allegory of the vine. Verse 13 recalls John 10:11—the good shepherd will lay down his life for his sheep. Jesus then says that the disciples are not servants but friends because he has made known to them what the Father is doing. The title "friends" was important in the Johannine community (cf. 3 John 15). Both the term "friends" and the ideal of friendship had a long history in the schools of antiquity. The disciples will bear fruit by their love for one another, even to the point of laying down their lives for the community of friends.

The World Will Hate You (15:18-25)

Talk of laying down one's life was evidently not idle posturing. The disciples, and by extension the Johannine community, would experience the hostility of "the world" firsthand. "The world" is used here in a negative sense for all that is opposed to God (compare the neutral sense in John 3:16 and the negative sense in 1 John 2:15). That sphere of power loves its own, just as the church is to be characterized by love for its own. Because Jesus was persecuted, the disciples should expect to be persecuted also. The Synoptic-like saying, "Servants are not greater than their master"

(15:20; cf. 13:16; Matt 10:24-25), was no doubt drawn from early Christian tradition. Here it is given a distinctively Johannine interpretation in the farewell discourse, reflecting John's persistent dualism and the experience of the Johannine community. The community was setting its own experience in the larger context of the continuing work of the Logos and the world's hostility toward it. Jesus' works have exposed the world's sin (cf. 3:19-21; 9:40-41).

The Paraclete as Advocate (15:26-27)

In this third reference to the work of the Paraclete (cf. 14:16-17, 26), the Paraclete's functions within the persecuted community are described. Jesus offers assurance to the community that although they will be persecuted, he will send the Paraclete who will bear witness to him and enable them to bear witness also. The Greek term for bearing witness *(martyrein)* is here in the process of coming to mean "to bear witness with one's life" (martyrdom).

JOHN 16

This chapter returns to the themes of persecution, the Paraclete, and the "little while" that is coming. Some interpreters identify John 16:4*b*-33 as the third stage or section of the farewell discourse. Numerous echoes of chapter 14 can be detected in this section, if one reads closely.

The Danger of Violence in the Name of Piety (16:1-4a)

These verses offer a brief but clear view of a period in the history of the Johannine community. Those who confess Jesus have been put out of the synagogue, perhaps following a practice that led to the adoption of the Birkath ha-Minim (the twelfth of the eighteen benedictions) at Jamnia.

The Birkath ha-Minim

For the apostates let there be no hope, and let the arrogant government [= Rome] be speedily uprooted in our days. Let the Nazarenes and the Minim [= heretics] be destroyed in a moment and let them be blotted out of the Book of Life and not be inscribed with the righteous. Blessed art thou, O Lord, who humblest the arrogant.[5]

The persecution is clearly religious in nature, for the persecutors think "they are offering worship to God" (v. 2). An ancient commentary on the actions of Phinehas, who put to death an Israelite man and a Moabite woman who had cohabited authorizes the killing of the wicked as an act of service to God (cf. Num 25).

Numbers Rabbah 21 (191) on Numbers 25:13

Did he then offer a sacrifice, since it is said that atonement was made by him? This alone will teach you that everyone who pours out the blood of the godless is like one who offers a sacrifice.[6]

By referring to "the hour" and by having Jesus tell of this coming persecution, the evangelist has drawn a connection between the world's rejection of Jesus and the persecution that the Johannine community suffered during the period of the composition of the Gospel. Understandable as it is that the community would interpret its experience in light of Jesus' death, it laid a dangerous foundation for anti-Semitism in later centuries (see chapter 10 below).

The Work of the Paraclete (16:4b-15)

The farewell discourse reflects on the mystery of revelation, that which was revealed in Jesus and the revelation that came after his departure. In the farewell discourse, Jesus looks ahead and speaks of his departure and the coming of the Paraclete. Because the Paraclete will bring them further understanding and be with them always, it is to their advantage that he is going away. The question of Jesus' departure (16:5) was asked earlier in 13:36 and taken up again in 14:5. One of the functions of the Paraclete will be to convict the world of sin because it does not believe. This statement reflects the fundamental character is sin in Johannine thought: Sin, ultimately, is unbelief. Hence the basic opposition in the plot of this Gospel is between belief and unbelief as responses to the Incarnation.

Truth is time-bound, and truth must be borne. There were some things that Jesus' followers could not understand prior to his death and resurrection. These they would understand later through the work of the Paraclete, who would guide them into all truth. The entire Gospel is a reflection of this later understanding (cf. 2:22; 12:16; 20:9), and by implication the Gospel is presented as the result of the work of the Paraclete through the Beloved Disciple and the Johannine community.

Travail and Joy (16:16-24)

Verse 16 presents a typical Johannine riddle, the riddle of the "little while," which the rest of this paragraph interprets. The image, drawn from the prophets, is that of a woman in labor, whose travail soon turns to joy. Israel's exile was but a temporary travail that would turn to joy, but it requires faith to see that suffering is temporary or purposeful. Faith is enduring the dark night of the soul—which may be the exile, or Jesus' death, or the experience of persecution—in the confidence that because God is still sovereign the experience of travail will only be for "a little while." Jesus' separation from the disciples, from his death until his post-Resurrection appearances, can therefore be an object lesson for the community that its travail also is merely temporary.

Travail as a Prophetic Metaphor

Pains and agony will seize them; they will be in anguish like a woman in labor. (Isa 13:8)

Therefore my loins are filled with anguish; pangs have seized me, like pangs of a woman in labor. (Isa 21:3)

Like woman with child, who writhes and cries out in her pangs when she is near her time, so were we because of you, O LORD. (Isa 26:17)

Writhe and groan, O daughter Zion, like a woman in labor; for now you shall go forth from the city and camp in the open country; you shall go to Babylon. There you shall be rescued, there the LORD will redeem you from the hands of your enemies. (Mic 4:10)

Speaking Plainly (16:25-33)

Jesus concludes his farewell to the disciples by saying that the time is coming when he will speak plainly of the Father. He would not be their intercessor, for the Father himself loves them. In a perfect chiastic turn of phrase, Jesus declares that he has come from the Father (A) and come into the world (B), and now he is leaving the world (B') and going to the Father (A'; 16:28). The disciples say that he is now speaking plainly, but it is clear that they still do not understand. They will all be scattered, and they will be persecuted, but they are to take courage because he has conquered the world. Here—but only here—John employs the motif, so prominent in Revelation, of the Lord as the conqueror who has overcome the hostile world (1 John 2:13-14; 4:4; 5:4-5; Rev 2:7, 11, 17, 26, and more).

The farewell discourse, therefore, reflects on the significance of Jesus' death and departure to the Father, the functions of the Paraclete in their midst, and the assurance of faith through the trials of persecution.

JOHN 17

Theologically, John 17 is one of the most important chapters in the Gospel. The writer captures the inner self of Jesus in this chapter as it frames the farewell discourse between the foot washing and this sublime prayer. The verb tenses here as in other parts of the farewell discourse alternate between the future and the past, as though it were the prayer of the risen Lord looking back on Jesus' public ministry and looking forward to the next generation of believers. In verses 1-5 Jesus prays for himself, in verses 6-19 for the disciples, and in verses 20-26 for future believers.

Jesus' Prayer for Himself (17:1-5)

The reference to lifting up his eyes echoes Jesus' prayer at Lazarus's tomb (11:41). John has moved Jesus' prayer of consecration in preparation for his death from Gethsemane to the end of the farewell discourse. There is no agony here. Jesus is resolutely committed to glorifying the Father. One may also detect interesting parallels with the prologue (John 1:1-18). The giving of power to become children of God (1:12), for example, carries with it the gift of eternal life (17:2).

Verse 3, which succinctly gathers up important Johannine themes, appears to be a parenthesis although it is not unlike the blending of Jesus' and the narrator's voices in John 3:31-36. Eternal life, which is a present reality not merely a future hope, consists essentially in knowing God through Jesus Christ and living in response to that knowledge. Jesus views his life from the point of view of its completion and prays for the restoration of the glory he had as the preexistent Logos.

Jesus' Prayer for the Disciples (17:6-19)

Twice in verse 6 we are told that the disciples were given to Jesus by the Father. After three years, he had only twelve disciples, and he thanks God for them! It is an interesting exercise to note in this chapter the various things that Jesus says the Father has given to him. The disciples are those who have seen that Jesus revealed the Father and have kept "the word" that Jesus gave them.

In this prayer Jesus does not pray for "the world," but only for his followers. Jesus' request for the disciples is that the Father protect them and that they may be one (v. 11). The Father will keep them in Jesus' name, and the unity of the believing community—which is already divided in the Johannine Epistles—will be based on the unity of the believers with Jesus. The scripture referred to in verse 12 is presumably Psalm 41:9, which is quoted in 13:18. Verse 13 recalls the references to joy in 15:11 and 16:24. It is only natural that the world will hate the disciples because they have been given the divine revelation that penetrates and exposes the world's love of darkness. Although they live in the world, the disciples no longer belong to the world (cf. 7:5-7). The world's values and goals are now foreign to them. Still, Jesus does not ask that the disciples be taken out to the world (v. 15). The church should not retreat from the world, but it will need divine protection in order to carry out its mission. The temptation is always to relieve the tension by either compromise with the world or flight from it. Therefore, Jesus commits himself to die glorifying God, so that the disciples may be made holy and sent into the world, just as Jesus was sent. Here, Christology (Jesus' identity and work), ecclesiology (the nature of the believing community), and missiology (the mission of the church in the world) are joined in profound reflection on the meaning of Jesus' death.

Jesus' Prayer for Future Believers (17:20-26)

In the third part of the prayer, Jesus prays for the next generation of believers—which would be the community at the time the Gospel was written—and by extension all future believers. His prayer is that the future believers may all be one. This unity is based on unity with God and reflected in Jesus' unity with the Father. Its purpose is redemptive and missiological: that the world may believe (v. 21). Jesus' legacy to the church is therefore twofold: the Paraclete and the mission to the world. Verses 22–23 are very nearly a repetition of verse 21. Because of their unity the world will know that God loves the disciples and has sent them. Ultimately, therefore, God's love is the basis for the believers' unity with one another and with the Father.

Jesus is in the process of completing the revelatory and redemptive mission of the Logos—to reveal the Father (cf. 1:18) and to take away the sin of the world (1:29, 36). Jesus has revealed the Father to those who have believed in him, and now prays that they too may know the Father's love.

JOHN 18–19

The Johannine narrative, like the Synoptic accounts, contains the arrest in the garden, trials before the Jewish authorities and before Pilate, the crucifixion and burial of Jesus, and the discovery of the empty tomb. It also makes extensive use of Old Testament allusions and quotations. In spite of these similarities, John develops the early Christian tradition in a distinctive way. Much of the delight and significance of the passion material in John is found in its interpretation of Johannine themes; its use of symbolism, irony, and double meanings; its emphasis on Jesus as king; and its interpretation of Jesus' death as his exaltation.

The Arrest (18:1-11)

The Kidron valley lies just to the east of the Temple. John never uses the name Gethsemane, but says that Jesus went to a garden. The Synoptic accounts say that Jesus went to Gethsemane but never say that it was a garden. Christian tradition, therefore, commonly speaks of "the garden of Gethsemane." Judas guides the authorities to Jesus at a time when he could be arrested away from the crowds. Verse 3 says that Judas led a "cohort" of soldiers, which literally would mean six hundred Roman soldiers, and the temple police. They came with lanterns and torches to arrest the "light of the world" (8:12; cf. 1:5). Satan had entered Judas (13:27), who had gone out into the night. Now the serpent enters the garden again.[7]

Judas does not identify Jesus with a kiss, as in the Synoptics. Instead, Jesus takes the initiative, asking the same question he had asked the first disciples, "Whom are you looking for?" (18:4; 1:38; 20:15). When they say, "Jesus of Nazareth," Jesus responds, "I am he" *(egō eimi)*. Jesus' words are repeated three times for emphasis in this brief scene (vv. 5, 6, 8). When Jesus utters these two words, the whole cohort, almost comically, falls back onto the ground. Jesus is not seized by force. He lays down his life (cf. 10:17-18), and he lays down his life for his friends (15:13) because at the moment of his arrest he negotiates their release (v. 8). The disciples, therefore, do not abandon him and flee as in Mark. Jesus' words about the coming events are already being fulfilled (vv. 9; 17:12).

Peter, who could not understand the foot washing and could not accept that Jesus would die (13:6-9, 36-38), now seeks to prevent Jesus' arrest by drawing the sword in his defense. Jesus is betrayed twice in the garden—once by Judas, who turns against him, and once by Peter, who in his zeal tries to defend Jesus by force. Jesus, of course, does not ask that the Father take away the cup of suffering, as in the Synoptic accounts (Mark 14:36), because he is one with the Father (10:30). The Johannine Jesus asks rhetorically, "Am I not to drink the cup that the Father has given me?" (v. 11).

The Trial Before Annas and Caiaphas (18:12-27)

Jesus was taken first to Annas (high priest A.D. 6–15), the father-in-law of Caiaphas (high priest ca. A.D. 18–36). Annas' role at this time is unclear, but one popular way of interpreting John has been to suggest that Annas remained influential through the period of his son-in-law's tenure as high priest.

The "other disciple" who helped Peter get into the courtyard is probably the Beloved Disciple, who is never named but is with Peter whenever Peter is mentioned in the rest of the Gospel (cf. esp. 20:2). We were told three times that Jesus said "I am" *(egō eimi)*, when he was arrested in the previous scene. Now Peter, who had boasted that he would lay down his life for Jesus (13:36-38), says three times "I am not" *(ouk eimi)*, and then turns to warm himself at the charcoal fire. What Peter denies, three times, is that he is Jesus' disciple. John insists on public confession of

Jesus (cf. 1:20; 9:22; 12:42). Peter is a sad example of one who denies his discipleship at the threat of persecution.

As in Mark, the account of the hearing before the high priest is placed after the report that Peter was warming himself at the fire and before his (remaining) denials. In Mark all three denials follow the report of the hearing (cf. Mark 14:54, 66-72). Sandwiching the hearing between the two parts of Peter's denials invites the reader to view what was happening inside in the light of what was happening outside, especially in John where Peter has already denied Jesus once.

The high priest asks Jesus about his disciples and his teachings, perhaps fearing that Jesus was inciting political turmoil (cf. 11:48-50; 12:19). Jesus answers the high priest's question by saying that he has always taught in public places and done nothing in secret, so they could ask those who had heard him. Outside, Peter, one of his disciples, is denying his relationship to Jesus. When one of the police slaps Jesus—the only time we are told that he was slapped—he does not turn the other cheek (Matt 5:39) but demands that justice be done. Because so much of the public ministry of Jesus has taken the form of a legal proceeding—with accusations, responses, and witnesses—little remains to be said at this point in the narrative.

When Peter has denied Jesus for the third time, the cock crows. This may be either the crowing of a rooster before dawn, or it may be the marking of the end of the third watch (from 12:00 P.M. to 3:00 A.M.), which was called "the cockcrow."

The Trial Before Pilate (18:28–19:16)

John artistically develops the trial before Pilate into a dramatic sequence of seven scenes. None of the Synoptics develops the character of Pilate in such detail. Ironically, the Jewish authorities will not enter the Praetorium (the procurator's quarters) because if they did they would be defiled and would not be able to eat the Passover meal that evening. This sets the stage for seven scenes which alternate between Pilate confronting the crowd outside and interrogating Jesus inside. He literally moves back and forth between the two, so that the outcome of the trial—Pilate's response to Jesus—remains in doubt to the end. Will he side with the Jewish authorities or with Jesus?

The Trial Before Pilate

Seven Scenes[8]

Scene 1 (outside): Jewish Authorities Demand Jesus' Death (18:28-32)

Scene 2 (inside): Pilate Questions Jesus About His Kingship (18:33-38a)

Scene 3 (outside): Pilate Pronounces Jesus Innocent (18:38b-40)

Scene 4 (inside): The Soldiers Scourge Jesus (19:1-3)

Scene 5 (outside): Pilate Again Pronounces Jesus Innocent (19:4-7)

Scene 6 (inside): Pilate Questions Jesus About His Origin (19:8-11)

Scene 7 (outside): Pilate Hands Jesus Over for Execution (19:12-16)

Jewish Authorities Demand Jesus' Death (18:28-32). In the first scene, the Jewish authorities bring Jesus from the house of Caiaphas to Pilate early in the morning. Trials at night were prohibited by Jewish law, and John records nothing more than a hearing or interrogation before the Jewish high priest. Only the Roman procurator could legally impose the death penalty. Having decided that Jesus must die, the Jewish authorities bring Jesus to Pilate so that the death penalty can be enacted and so that the blame for it can be placed on the Romans.

The contest of wills between Pilate and the Jewish authorities begins in the first scene. Because they will not enter the praetorium, Pilate is forced to go out to them. Then, when he asks what the charge is, they declare the verdict, that the prisoner is guilty. When he tells them to deal with Jesus according to their law, they raise the stakes by demanding the death penalty. The narrator reminds the reader that Jesus said that he would be "lifted up" (3:14; 8:28; 12:32), so his death by Roman execution—crucifixion—will fulfill his earlier predictions.

Pilate Questions Jesus About His Kingship (18:33-38a). Under Roman law there was no trial by jury, and because Jesus was not a Roman citizen, Pilate had almost unlimited authority to deal with the situation as he saw fit. Normally, the judge would interrogate the accuser, the accused, and any witnesses, and then declare the verdict and penalty (if the accused was found guilty). Having questioned the accusers, Pilate moves inside the praetorium to interrogate Jesus.

Pilate begins the interrogation by asking Jesus whether he is the "King of the Jews." While Pilate questions Jesus about his kingship, a possible basis for a verdict of treason or insurrection, Jesus presses Pilate for a decision about Jesus' identity. Again the issue in this exchange is not Jesus' guilt or innocence, but whether Pilate will recognize who Jesus is and believe in him. In this respect, ironically, it is Pilate who is on trial, not Jesus. Jesus says that his kingdom is not of this world, but he has come to bear witness to the truth. The reader senses the irony and pathos of Pilate's retort, "What is truth?" because in the farewell discourse Jesus declared that he is the way, the truth, and the life (14:6). Now Pilate, looking at Jesus, cynically evades Jesus' appeal by asking "What is truth?" and then walking away. For John, however, "truth" is not academic or propositional; ultimately, truth is personal. Truth is revealed in the Incarnation.

Pilate Pronounces Jesus Innocent (18:38b-40). Outside, Pilate pronounces Jesus innocent. At this point, the trial should be over. Due process has been followed, and the procurator has reached a verdict and declared it publicly. In an apparent effort to appease the crowd and secure the release of Jesus, he refers to an otherwise unknown "custom" of releasing a prisoner at Passover. There is no evidence for this practice outside the Gospels, but it is plausible that Pilate had made it a practice. The evangelist squeezes all the irony he can out of the scene by having Pilate refer to Jesus as "the King of the Jews." The people choose Barabbas, instead, and the evangelist says that Barabbas was an insurrectionist (a *lēstēs*; cf. 10:1, 8), guilty of the crime of which the innocent Jesus was accused. "Barabbas" is Aramaic for "Son of the Father."

The Soldiers Scourge Jesus (19:1-3). Although we are not told that Pilate went inside again, the note in verse 4 that Pilate went out again implies that he had been inside during the previous scene. A flogging normally came after the condemnation of a criminal, not during the trial, much less after the accused had been pronounced innocent. A flogging was such a severe beating that some died from it. John presents the flogging as a futile effort to appease the people who were calling for Jesus' death. The soldiers mock Jesus by placing a crown made of thorns on his head, clothing him in purple (a sign of royalty), and hailing him as the Jewish king.

A Scene of Mockery Recorded by Philo

There was a certain lunatic named Carabas, whose madness was not of the fierce and savage kind, ... but of the easy-going, gentler style. He spent day and night in the streets naked, shunning neither heat nor cold, made game of by the children and the lads who were idling about. The rioters drove the poor fellow into the gymnasium and set him up on high to be seen of all and put on his head a sheet of byblus spread out wide for a diadem, clothed the rest of his body with a rug for a royal robe, while someone who had noticed a piece of the native papyrus thrown away in the road gave it to him for his sceptre. And when as in some theatrical farce he had received the insignia of kingship and had been tricked out as a king, young men carrying rods on their shoulders as spearmen stood on either side of him in imitation of a bodyguard. Then others approached him, some pretending to salute him, others to sue for justice, others to consult him on state affairs.[9] (*Flaccus* 36-38).

Pilate Again Pronounces Jesus Innocent (19:4-7). Pilate now leads Jesus out so that the crowd can see him, beaten and still wearing the purple robe and crown of thorns. For the second time, Pilate pronounces him innocent, and then declares, "Here is the man!"—a declaration that is full of meaning in view of John's emphasis on the Incarnation.

The chief priests and officers reply by shouting "Crucify him! Crucify him!" For the third time Pilate declares that Jesus is innocent. In verse 7, the real offense finally comes out: blasphemy, that is, Jesus offered himself as the Son of God (cf. 5:18; 10:33-36).

Pilate Questions Jesus About His Origin (19:8-11). When Pilate hears the response of the Jewish authorities, his fear may be prompted either by the realization that they will not tolerate Jesus' release or perhaps by his growing recognition of who Jesus is. The question of where Jesus is from is important both politically and theologically. As in the Synoptic accounts, Jesus is silent, fulfilling the suffering servant passage in Isaiah.

Isaiah 53:7-9

He was oppressed, and he was afflicted,
    yet he did not open his mouth;
like a lamb that is led to the slaughter,

> and like a sheep that before its shearers is silent,
> so he did not open his mouth.
> By a perversion of justice he was taken away.
> Who could have imagined his future?
> For he was cut off from the land of the living,
> stricken for the transgression of my people.
> They made his grave with the wicked
> and his tomb with the rich,
> although he had done no violence,
> and there was no deceit in his mouth.

When Pilate appeals to his authority, Jesus reminds Pilate that his authority has been given to him from above (by the Roman emperor, and in a further sense by God). Jesus' authority has already been discussed in John 5:19-29; he has authority from God as the Son of Man. Jesus' claim that the one who delivered him to Pilate has the greater blame may be directed at Judas, at Caiaphas, or at the authorities in general.

Pilate Hands Jesus Over for Execution (19:12-16). In the final scene of this sequence, Pilate tries once again to release Jesus. "The Jews" however cry out this time that if Pilate releases Jesus, he is no "friend of Caesar"—a technical term for a loyal subordinate. Some interpreters argue that the verb in verse 13 is transitive, meaning that Pilate seated Jesus on the judgment seat in an act of further mockery, but the more natural sense of the verse is that Pilate sat on the judgment seat on the platform for his final words on this matter. John notes that it was at about the sixth hour on the day of Preparation, which according to the Jewish reckoning of time would have been noon. According to John, therefore, Jesus was crucified and died on the afternoon of the day when the Passover lambs were slaughtered.

Exodus 12:6

You shall keep it [your lamb] until the fourteenth day of this month; then the whole assembled congregation of Israel shall slaughter it at twilight.

To the Jews Pilate says, "Here is your King!" The chief priests reply, "We have no king but the emperor"—a complete denial of their theocratic heritage.

The Lord as Israel's True King

And the LORD said to Samuel, "Listen, to the voice of the people in all that they say to you; for they have not rejected you, but they have rejected me from being king over them." (1 Sam 8:7)

I will extol you, my God and King, and bless your name forever and ever. (Ps 145:1)

Pilate has won a hollow victory at best, handing Jesus over to be crucified when he knows him to be innocent, though eliciting from the Jewish authorities a pledge of allegiance to Caesar. But did Pilate recognize more of Jesus' identity than he was able to confess?

The Crucifixion and Burial of Jesus (19:16b-42)

Each of the Gospels interprets the death of Jesus by means of the sequence of the scenes around the cross, allusions to the fulfillment of scripture, the words of Jesus and those who speak to him, and reports of the phenomena that accompanied Jesus' death. In light of the significance of these narrative devices, the differences between John's account of Jesus' death and the Synoptic accounts become all the more important.[10]

Elements of the Synoptic Accounts of Jesus' Death That Do Not Appear in John

1. The mockery of Jesus at the cross
2. The penitent thief
3. The darkness, even though John often plays with the symbolism of light and darkness
4. The counting of the hours (except for the comment in 19:14 that it was the sixth hour), though John has spoken repeatedly of the coming of Jesus' hour
5. The rending of the veil, though John tells of the cleansing of the Temple at the beginning of Jesus' ministry
6. The cry of dereliction
7. The earthquake
8. The opening of the tombs, though John has spoken earlier of the opening of the tombs and records the raising of Lazarus

---

9. The confession of the centurion, though John places particular emphasis throughout the Gospel on the recognition of Jesus as "the Son of God"

In spite of the absence of so many features of the Synoptic accounts, John combines traditional elements that appear in the other Gospels with distinctively Johannine developments in an intriguing and vitally important way. As in the Synoptic Gospels, Jesus carries his own cross to "The Place of the Skull" (19:17). They crucify Jesus with two others, and place over him the inscription, "The King of the Jews." The soldiers divide his garments. Mary Magdalene and other women are present. The soldiers offer Jesus vinegar or sour wine. And Jesus' last words are recorded. Witnesses confirm Jesus' death, and the body is then taken down and buried by Joseph of Arimathea. This is only a selection of elements from the Synoptic passion narratives, but the sheer number of parallels between John and the other Gospels at this point—especially given John's independence from the Synoptic tradition elsewhere—shows that John knows of and follows a well-defined tradition of Jesus' death.

John's account of the death of Jesus falls naturally into seven scenes, just as we have found seven scenes in the story of the healing of the blind man (John 9) and in the trial before Pilate.

The Structure of the Johannine Passion Narrative

1. The crucifixion (vv. 16b-18)

2. The inscription (vv. 19-22)

3. The seamless tunic (vv. 23-24)

4. Jesus' mother and the Beloved Disciple (vv. 25-27)

5. Jesus' last words (vv. 28-30)

6. The piercing of Jesus' side (vv. 31-37)

7. The burial (vv. 38-42)

The Crucifixion (19:16b-18)

The crucifixion of Jesus is reported with a minimum of detail. Its significance is interpreted in the scenes that follow. Nevertheless, verses 16-18 contain three elements common to the Synoptic accounts: (1) Jesus carried his own cross, (2) the place of execution was called "The Place of the Skull" (Golgotha), and (3) Jesus was crucified with two others.

The Inscription (19:19-22)

All of the Gospels record the inscription written over Jesus, but only John moves this scene to first place so that it follows immediately after the report of the crucifixion. Only John reports that the inscription was written in three languages, and only John has Pilate declare, "What I have written I have written." The declaration has a special meaning in John because of the way in which it develops motifs from the earlier parts of the Gospel.

The three "lifted up" sayings in John (3:14; 8:28; 12:32) prepare us to understand Jesus' death as an exaltation, a lifting up. It has often been noted that John does not treat the crucifixion of Jesus as a humiliation that is followed by an exaltation, but as the first step in Jesus' exaltation and glorification. The resurrection is compressed into the crucifixion so that they are two stages in one upward motion. Jesus' exaltation on the cross is the first step in his enthronement as "King." When Pilate writes that Jesus is indeed "The King of the Jews," he announces Jesus' vindication. The Jews of the Gospel may reject Jesus' sovereignty, and declare that they have no king but Caesar (19:15), but they cannot depose their king.

What is the significance of having the inscription written in three languages? Interpreters have generally noted that the three languages—Hebrew, Latin, and Greek—represent the three cultures meeting in Judea: Hebrew, the language of the Scriptures; Latin, the language of the Empire; and Greek, the language of Hellenistic culture. These were respectively the languages of religion, the state, and culture. Historical critics have wondered whether soldiers about the business of execution would have had either the learning or the inclination to write the charge in three languages. The significance of this detail, which is unique to John, lies instead in its relationship to John's interpretation of Jesus' death.

In the third of the lifting up sayings (12:32) Jesus declares that if he is lifted up he will draw all people to himself. Now, at his crucifixion, Jesus' true messianic identity is proclaimed to all in the three languages of the area. As at the Pentecost experience in Acts, each heard in his own language. Jesus is the King of the

Jews, but his death is significant for all people. It is the means by which he draws all persons to himself. The exaltation of Jesus, the declaration of his kingship, and the writing of the inscription in three languages demonstrate that through his death Jesus vanquishes "the ruler of this world" and establishes a new sovereignty. All people should now acknowledge him as their king.

Like others in the Gospel, especially the Samaritan woman and the blind man, Pilate seems to come step by step to make at least a partial confession. In 19:5 Pilate says to the crowd, "Here is the man!" After Pilate hears in verse 8 that Jesus claimed to be the Son of God, he asks Jesus the vital Johannine question of his origin: "Where are you from?" (v. 9). Pilate's final declaration, which may or may not be laced with sarcasm, is "Here is your King!" (v. 14). At a minimum, John conscripts Pilate's tongue to make a true confession. On the other hand, we may just as easily infer that Pilate, having declared Jesus innocent, suspects that Jesus' claims are true and voices his true verdict in the written decree, "Jesus, of Nazareth, the King of the Jews."

John's report of the inscription affixed to the cross proves to be rich in overtones that interpret Jesus' death in the Johannine context. The inscription declares Jesus' coronation as King, his messianic identity as King of the Jews, his defeat of "the ruler of this world," and the fulfillment of his promise to draw all people to himself. John has taken an element from the tradition and filled it with new meaning.

The Seamless Tunic (19:23-24)

The casting of lots is another traditional element of the crucifixion scene that is reported in all three of the Synoptic Gospels (Mark 15:24 and parallels). John places this scene after the report of the inscription and expands it from the six to twelve words given to the dividing of the garments in the Synoptics to 67 words in John. In this expanded scene, John reports that the soldiers divided Jesus' garments into four parts, one for each soldier. Because Jesus' tunic was seamless, the soldiers cast lots for the tunic rather than for all his garments. John's story of the garments thereby more precisely fulfills Psalm 22:18, which John quotes in its Septuagintal form (Ps 21:19 LXX) following a formula of fulfillment. The separation of the tunic from the rest of Jesus' garments, with the note that it was seamless and that the soldiers did not want to rend it into pieces, invites the interpreter to probe more deeply into the significance of the seamless tunic in the Johannine context.

One of the first clues the reader is given is that the tunic was woven from the top. The word *anōthen* appears in three other contexts in John. Nicodemus is told that he must be born *anōthen*, "from above" (3:3, 7; cf. 3:31). In Jesus' conversation with Pilate, he rebuffs the procurator's warning by responding that Pilate has no authority except that which is given to him "from above" (19:11). Commentators have noted the *double entendre* here: Pilate's authority was given to him by the Roman emperor, but in a further sense he can send Jesus to his death only because it is given to him by God to do so. Now, at the cross, these significant words, "from above," occur again in the narrator's description of the seamless tunic. It was created in this way, woven from the top through the whole garment. John often uses references to physical details in dramatic ways. What is happening at the cross is all a part of the tapestry of God's redemptive design.

That the tunic is all of one piece, and that the soldiers decide not to rend it, suggests that the seamless tunic is related to John's repeated emphasis on the unity of the church. Jesus declared that there would be one flock, one shepherd (10:16), and that when he was lifted up he would gather all people to himself (12:32). The Johannine narrator takes up the theme in 11:52, commenting that Jesus was about to die in order that he might gather into one the children of God who have been scattered. Jesus and the Father are one (10:30), and Jesus prayed that his disciples might be one, just as he and the Father were one (17:11, 21-23). The net containing the great catch of fish, which may be symbolic of the evangelistic mission of the church, is also untorn (21:11).

Metaphorically, through the description of the seamless tunic, John ties the death of Jesus to the theme of unity. When he draws all people to himself, he draws them into one body, one community. What God weaves, God weaves whole, from above. There is but one vine, one net, one flock, one shepherd, one Son, and one seamless tunic woven from the top.

Jesus' Mother and the Beloved Disciple (19:25-27)

Each of the other Gospels names women who stood by as Jesus hung on the cross. In the other Gospels, the presence of the

232

women as witnesses to Jesus' death is recognized after his death is reported. John moves the scene forward and is the only Gospel to record Jesus' exchange with his mother and the Beloved Disciple. John is also the only Gospel to record the presence of any of the disciples at the cross. Among the women at the cross, Matthew and Mark name Mary, the mother of James and Joseph, but John is the only one who records her presence as Jesus' mother. John seems to list four women at the cross: Jesus' mother, her sister, Mary the wife of Clopas, and Mary Magdalene.

Jesus sees his mother and the Beloved Disciple and says to his mother, "Woman, here is your son" and to the Beloved Disciple, "Here is your mother." The narrator reports that "from that hour" the disciple took her into his home. Through the centuries interpreters have suspected that this scene has a symbolic significance—a suspicion that is supported in part by the observation that neither Jesus' mother nor the Beloved Disciple are named. It has been suggested that the mother and the Beloved Disciple represent a new Adam and Eve, Israel and the Church, or Jewish Christianity and Gentile Christianity. The significance of the scene is to be sought, however, not in symbolic meanings that are anachronistic or extraneous to the Gospel but in symbolism that is tied to themes developed in the Gospel itself. As is often noted, the mother of Jesus appears only once elsewhere in the Gospel, at the wedding at Cana. The scene is in some respects the Johannine counterpart to the Synoptic scene in which Jesus asks who are his mother and his brothers (Mark 3:32-35; Luke 8:19-21). Jesus' sharp response to his mother is not to be glossed over in a misguided effort to rescue Jesus' civility. By his response he distances himself from his mother. Henceforth, flesh and blood relationships will be secondary to those that are born of the spirit and sustained by faith.

The Beloved Disciple appears at all the key moments in the Gospel story: He is on the breast of Jesus at his last meal, he gets Peter into the courtyard during Jesus' trial, he stands by Jesus' mother at the foot of the cross, he runs with Peter to the empty tomb and is the first to believe in the resurrection when he sees the grave wrappings lying there, and he is the first to recognize the risen Lord at the Sea of Galilee. In the closing verses of the Gospel, the risen Lord says that the Beloved Disciple will bear a true witness, and the final editor says that the Beloved Disciple is the one who has written these things and that "we" (the Johannine community) know that his testimony is true. The Beloved Disciple functions as the representative of the Johannine community; he is their founder and their apostolic authority.

Now, at the cross, when Jesus' hour has come, Jesus employs a revelatory formula ("Behold") and performative language. Like a marriage declaration, his pronouncement actually accomplishes or effects the new relationship that it declares. By his declaration, Jesus constitutes a new family, mother and son. From the beginning, the Gospel of John has employed the metaphor of kinship to characterize the believer's new relationship to God. Those who respond to the revelation in Jesus—those who are called, drawn, and chosen by the Father and who believe in Jesus' name—are empowered to become "children of God" (1:12). Moreover, the narrator has explained that Jesus did not die for the nation only, but to gather together all the scattered children of God (11:52). The formation of this new family at the cross provides a nucleus for the community of believers. The Johannine community looked to the Beloved Disciple as their eyewitness, their link with Jesus. Inevitably, the community would have identified with the Beloved Disciple in this scene. Their new status began at the cross. More than a theory of atonement, John has an underlying ecclesiology of the cross.

Jesus' Last Words (19:28-30)

The reader may notice first the repeated emphasis on fulfillment in these verses. The narrator reports that Jesus knew that all things were now completed. Here, having constituted the new family of "his own," and knowing that he has accomplished all that he was to do, Jesus says he thirsts. The narrator comments that Jesus said he was thirsty in order to fulfill the scriptures. The term used here is unusual; it is the same root as that in the first part of verse 28 and in Jesus' last word in verse 30, "It is finished." In fulfillment of John 10:18, Jesus lays down his life—but only after he has completed the work the Father had given him to do. In the Gospel of John, therefore, Jesus' death marks the completion of his mission to make known the Father, take away the sin of the world, bear witness to the truth, and give life abundantly to "his own."

It is generally agreed that the most likely candidates for the scripture passage in view are Psalm 69:21 or 22:15; both are cited elsewhere in the passion narratives. Psalm 69 specifically mentions thirst and opponents giving the just one vinegar to drink. Because the scriptural reference is not quoted, however, it seems doubtful that the significance of Jesus' thirst is to be found primarily in the nuances of the earlier text. Instead, we must once again look for the meaning of Jesus' thirst within the Gospel itself. The Samaritan woman recalls "our father Jacob," who dug the well to satisfy their thirst; John 7:38-39 refers to another obscure passage in scripture and forecasts the giving of the Spirit at the glorification of Jesus. Whether or not one reads John 19:28-29 as an echo of Psalm 69:21, any reader who misses the connection with references to thirst earlier in the Gospel will miss much of the figurative, metaphoric, and ironic sense of John's account of Jesus' death. In John food and drink are symbolic of a higher reality. Similarly, when Peter attempted to prevent the arrest of Jesus, Jesus responded, "Am I not to drink the cup that the Father has given me?" (18:11). Now that he has completed all that he was to do, Jesus is thirsty. He is ready to drink the last swallow from the cup given to him. Only in John does Jesus actually drink the sour wine, and in doing so he symbolically drinks the cup of suffering as he dies.

In John 19:28-29 various elements of scripture are fulfilled: the righteous one thirsts, sour wine is given, hyssop is used, and Jesus gives up the Spirit. The reference to hyssop, of course, signals a fulfillment of the Exodus motif in the Gospel of John. The narrator tells the reader at the beginning that whereas the Law came through Moses, "grace and truth came through Jesus" (1:17). Jesus was announced to the disciples as the one "about whom Moses in the law and also the prophets wrote" (1:45). Jesus would be "lifted up" as Moses had lifted up the bronze serpent in the wilderness (3:14). Moses does not condemn Jesus, but bears witness to him (5:45-46). Like Moses, Jesus feeds the multitude in the wilderness and crosses the sea, demonstrating that he himself is the true bread of life which has come down from above. The motif of Jesus' fulfillment of the role of Moses or the promised "prophet like Moses" (Deut 18:15, 18) culminates at the cross. Jesus also dies at the hour of the slaughter of the Passover lambs; fulfilling the rule for the slaughter of the Passover lambs, his legs are not broken; and he drinks from the hyssop that is offered to him as he dies.

The narrator's report that Jesus bowed his head and "gave up his spirit" (19:30) resonates with the narrator's comment in John 7:39 that the Spirit had not yet been given because Jesus had not yet been glorified. In the farewell discourse Jesus promised his disciples that it was better for them that he depart because when he departed he would send the Paraclete to be with them (16:7). The reader has already been prepared, therefore, to understand that at the death of Jesus the Spirit would come to guide the community of disciples after Jesus' death. The evangelist is subtly reminding the reader of this promise by the way he narrates the death of Jesus. John's theology of the cross, therefore, is artfully developed in the narrative mode of the Gospel.

Five Observations About John's Account of Jesus' Death

1. For all its differences from the other Gospels, the Gospel of John drew from a tradition of Jesus' death that included many of the same elements we find in the Synoptics. At no point in these verses, however, does it appear that John drew directly from the Synoptic Gospels.
2. The fourth evangelist selected and developed certain elements from the tradition in his own way and for his own purposes. John's handling of the tradition, including the development of these four scenes around Johannine themes, illustrates how John has constructed a narrative interpretation of the death of Jesus. The narrative now functions as both a *metaphor* for the meaning of Jesus' death and as the *medium* for drawing John's readers into that metaphor.
3. The distinctive emphases of the Johannine passion narrative stand in clear relief when we trace the development of the Johannine themes that climax in the passion narrative. John's account of Jesus' death fits organically into the rest of the Gospel.
4. John's narrative of Jesus' death highlights its significance for the church, tracing the origin of the new community to the cross: a new kinship is constituted here, one transcending differences in language, subject to the sovereignty of Jesus, undivided by schism, and sustained by "living water" and the Spirit.
5. John's account of Jesus' death reflects an important theological insight: the Church has its origin at the cross (not just at the empty tomb), and therefore what happened at the cross reveals God's design for the Church and should forever define the mission and life of the Church.

The Piercing of Jesus' Side (19:31-37)

Following the death of Jesus, in the Synoptic accounts, the veil in the Temple is rent in two and the centurion confesses that Jesus is the Son of God. John, however, reports a different set of events. Because the next day was the Sabbath—indeed, a special Sabbath that coincided with Passover—the bodies could not be left on the crosses.

The Command to Bury the Dead

When someone is convicted of a crime punishable by death and is executed, and you hang him on a tree, his corpse must not remain all night upon the tree; you shall bury him that same day, for anyone hung on a tree is under God's curse. You must not defile the land that the LORD your God is giving you for possession. (Deut 21:22-23)

The Romans often left the bodies of executed criminals on the crosses or threw them on the garbage heaps. A proper burial for one who had been crucified would have been rare. The soldiers broke the legs of the other two, either to hasten death or to insure that if they were not dead they could not escape after they had been taken down from the crosses. John finds significant fulfillment of scripture in the tradition that Jesus' legs were not broken, but rather his side was pierced and water and blood flowed from him. The flow of water should probably be understood in light of the earlier reference in John 7:37-39—Jesus has died, so the Spirit can now be given. Blood was the life force and communicated sacrificial significance. Jesus was the Passover lamb, slain so that others might live.

The one who saw these things and bore witness to them is almost surely the Beloved Disciple, since these verses so closely parallel the reference to the Beloved Disciple at the end of the Gospel (21:24-25). The meaning of the piercing of Jesus' side rather than breaking his legs can be seen in the fulfillment of references in scripture to the Passover lamb, to God's protection of the righteous, and to the mourning for the victim in Jerusalem.

237

The Fulfillment of Scripture in the Handling of Jesus' Body

"You shall not take any of the [Passover] animal outside the house, and you shall not break any of its bones". (Exod 12:46)
"They shall leave none of it until morning, nor break a bone of it. " (Num 9:12)

"Many are the afflictions of the righteous,
    but the Lord rescues them from them all.
He keeps all their bones;
    not one of them will be broken." (Ps 34:19-20)

"And I will pour out a spirit of compassion and supplication on the house of David and the inhabitants of Jerusalem, so that, when they look on the one whom they have pierced, they shall mourn for him, as one mourns for an only child, and weep bitterly over him, as one weeps over a firstborn." (Zech 12:10)

The Burial (19:38-42)

One of the earliest confessions found in the New Testament mentions the burial of Jesus (1 Cor 15:3-5), and it became part of the early Christian preaching (Acts 13:29). Joseph of Arimathea is named in the Synoptic accounts also, but here he is identified as "a secret believer" (cf. 12:42) for fear of the Jewish authorities. Nicodemus's role in the burial of Jesus is recorded only in John (cf. 3:1; 7:50). Nicodemus, who came to Jesus at night, now shows his attachment to Jesus publicly.

The importance of the details of the burial are that they show that Jesus received a proper burial according to Jewish practice, even a lavish burial appropriate for the kingship motif in John, and that the place of Jesus' burial was known to his followers. Jesus is buried in a new tomb—therefore, in a clean tomb, one where there would be no confusion from the presence of other bodies. The only reference to haste relates to the selection of the site, which was near where Jesus was crucified. Jesus is anointed with a lavish quantity of spices—one hundred Roman pounds, or seventy-five pounds in today's standard. According to John, therefore, there would be no need for the women (who are not mentioned here) to return later to anoint the body.

JOHN 20

John 20 reports the discovery of the empty tomb and the appearances to Mary Magdalene and the disciples on Easter and the Sunday following Easter. The chapter is composed of two major sections (the discovery of the empty tomb and the appearances to the disciples) and a conclusion.

The Structure of John 20

1. The discovery of the empty tomb (vv. 1-18)

    A. Mary Magdalene's report (vv. 1-2)

    B. The disciples at the tomb (vv. 3-10)

    C. The appearance to Mary Magdalene (vv. 11-18)

2. The appearances to the disciples (vv. 19-29)

    A. The appearance to the disciples without Thomas (vv. 19-23)

    B. The appearance to the disciples with Thomas (vv. 24-29)

3. Conclusion: the Gospel's purpose (vv. 30-31)

The Discovery of the Empty Tomb (20:1-18)

Each of the Synoptic Gospels reports that a group of women found Jesus' tomb open and empty. John is distinctive in that Mary Magdalene goes to the tomb alone and finds it empty. This focus on one individual is consistent with John's attention elsewhere to Nathanael, Nicodemus, the woman at the well, Mary and Martha, Lazarus, and others. The setting, "while it was still dark," must carry theological significance in view of John's recurring use of the symbolism of light and darkness, day and night. Mary Magdalene reports her discovery to Peter and the Beloved Disciple in words that become her refrain: "They have taken the Lord out of the tomb, and we do not know where ..." (v. 2).[11] If Nathanael does not know where Jesus is from, and Peter cannot accept that Jesus must die, and Thomas cannot accept his resurrection, Mary Magdalene does not understand where Jesus has gone. In the farewell discourse, Jesus told the disciples that he must go away and they could not come where he was going, that he was leaving the world and going to the Father. Now John uses the tradition of

239

the empty tomb to develop in narrative action this theme from the words of Jesus.

The Beloved Disciple and Peter are paired in this scene, just as they are at the Last Supper, at the great catch of fish (John 21), and possibly in the courtyard at Jesus' trial. In general, the Gospel tradition is that the women discovered the tomb empty, and Jesus later appeared to the disciples. These separate lines of tradition have been linked in both directions, however. In Matthew, Jesus appears to the women as they leave the tomb (Matt 28:2-9), and in Luke 24:12 Peter runs to the empty tomb. John reports that the disciples ran to the tomb, and the Lord subsequently appeared to Mary Magdalene at the tomb. This means that, in John, the Beloved Disciple (who reclined on Jesus' breast at the Last Supper, stood by the cross, received Jesus' mother, and witnessed the water and the blood flowing from Jesus' side) is also the first disciple to see the empty tomb and the only one who believes as a result of what he sees there. The first appearance, moreover, is not to Peter, or any of the Twelve, but to a woman.

Peter—who elsewhere in John refuses to let Jesus wash his feet, pledges to lay down his life for Jesus, and lashes out with his sword when Jesus is arrested—does not stand at the door but enters into the tomb. The narrator reports that both disciples saw the grave wrappings lying there and then describes what the disciples saw: the cloth that had been around Jesus' head was folded and lying separately. The significance of these details may be either the fact that the grave wrappings were lying there or the position in which they were left. The position could indicate that Jesus had taken them off and left them neatly folded, or perhaps that the body was simply gone and the wrappings had collapsed where they were. In any case, the presence of the grave wrappings suggests that the body had not been stolen, and the reader may recall that Lazarus had emerged from the tomb still bound by the wrappings (11:44).

The Beloved Disciple sees and believes. He is the only character in the New Testament who believes in the resurrection merely because of the physical evidence at the tomb. Typically, Easter faith arises in response to an encounter with the risen Lord. The narrator again points to the significance of the study of scripture after the event. Only later did the church understand the meaning of events the disciples had witnessed—after they had studied the scriptures, reflected on what Jesus had said, and been enlightened by the Paraclete (cf. 2:22; 12:16; 20:9).

After the disciples left, Mary Magdalene stood outside the tomb weeping. When she looked into the tomb, she saw two angels sitting where the body had been. In the Synoptic accounts the young man (Mark), angel (Matt), or angels (Luke) serve the function of interpreting the significance of the empty tomb. They announce the central theme of the kerygma of the early church: "Do not be alarmed; you are looking for Jesus of Nazareth, who was crucified. He has been raised; he is not here. Look, there is the place they laid him. But go, tell his disciples and Peter that he is going ahead of you to Galilee; there you will see him, just as he told you" (Mark 16:6-7). The angels in John announce nothing; they merely ask Mary why she is weeping so that she can repeat her refrain: "They have taken away my Lord, and I do not know where they have laid him" (v. 13; cf. 20:2). Jesus then appears to her, but she does not recognize him, setting up another recognition scene (see the discussion of recognition scenes in chapter 4 above).

Jesus asks two questions: the same question the angels asked ("Why are you weeping?") and the same question he had asked the first disciples and the band that came to arrest him (1:38; 18:4—"Whom are you looking for?"). This time Mary offers a variation of her refrain. Supposing that Jesus was the gardener (cf. 15:1), Mary asks if he has taken away the body: "Tell me where" (v. 15). She does not understand the meaning of Jesus' departure. The risen Lord responds by calling her by name, fulfilling Jesus' earlier declaration that the good shepherd calls his sheep by name (10:3, 16; cf. "Lazarus" 11:43; "Simon son of John" 21:15). Mary responds by calling Jesus "Rabbouni" (Teacher) and embracing him, a response which may indicate that she was reclaiming her former relationship to Jesus, her Teacher. She still does not understand that Jesus' death and resurrection, his exaltation, mean his departure to the Father. The misunderstanding prompts Jesus to declare this facet of the resurrection unequivocally: "I am ascending to my Father and your Father, to my God and your God" (v. 17). As in all the post-Resurrection appearance accounts, there is a commissioning. Jesus sends Mary as the messenger to his disciples. Significantly, Jesus says, "go to my brothers," but Mary goes to the disciples, not to his flesh and blood brothers (cf. 7:5-7). As a result of the completion of Jesus' mission at the cross and the formation of a new family of faith, the disciples have now become his "brothers," "children of God" (cf. 1:12; 11:52).

The Appearances to the Disciples (20:19-29)

The appearances of the risen Lord in the other Gospels may be grouped according to location. John is distinctive in that it is the only Gospel to record appearances in both Jerusalem and Galilee.

The Appearances Recorded in the Four Gospels		
Gospel	*Person or Group*	*Location*
Mark 16:6-7 (predicted)	The disciples and Peter	Galilee
Matthew 28:8-9	The women	At the tomb
Matthew 28:16-20	The disciples	Galilee
Luke 24:13-35	Two disciples	Emmaus
Luke 24:36-49	The disciples	Jerusalem
John 20:11-18	Mary Magdalene	At the tomb
John 20:19-23	The disciples (without Thomas)	Jerusalem
John 20:24-29	The disciples (with Thomas)	Jerusalem
John 21:1-23	Seven disciples	Galilee

The early morning and evening of the first day of the week were the customary times for Christians to gather for worship since Sunday was a working day.[12] The disciples' fear of the Jewish authorities may have resonated with the fear of persecution in the Johannine community. The risen Lord greets the disciples with the common Jewish greeting, "Shalom," but in this context it also conveys fulfillment of Jesus' promise of peace in the farewell discourse (14:27-28; 16:33). Jesus had said that he would come to the disciples (14:18), that they would see him (14:19), and that their sorrow would turn to joy (15:11; 16:20-24). His hands and his side proved that the one they were seeing was the one who had died on the cross.

This appearance centers around Jesus' consolation of the disciples, and his commissioning of them for their mission in the world. Jesus sends the disciples, just as he had been sent (v. 21). Jesus then breathes the Holy Spirit into the disciples, fulfilling his promise to send the Paraclete to them. His act of empowering the disciples for their mission is almost a reenactment of the creation scene in Genesis 2:7. Jesus also authorizes the disciples; they will either bring forgiveness to those to whom they are sent or they will bind them to their sin. This act of commissioning is a constitution of the believing community, defining its role and consecrating it for its mission. All the focus is on Jesus' words, so the scene ends abruptly.

Because Thomas had not been with the other disciples, he declared that he could not believe that Jesus had risen from the dead unless he saw for himself Jesus' hands and side. A week later, apparently again on a Sunday (thereby validating the Christian practice of worship on the first day of the week), Jesus appeared again to the disciples. After greeting them again, "Peace be with you," he invited Thomas to do exactly what he had said he would need to do in order to believe. There is no inconsistency between Jesus' admonition to Mary, "Do not hold on to me" (20:17) and his invitation for Thomas to touch him. In both cases he was inviting each one to do what he or she needed to do to take the next step in faith and understanding. Mary needed to recognize that Jesus was going to the Father; Thomas needed to believe that the one who had died was alive again (cf. 11:16).

The narrator does not say that Thomas actually touched the risen Lord. Instead, he reports Thomas's confession, "My Lord and my God." The New Testament is reluctant to call Jesus "God," perhaps in an effort to avoid the charge that the church violated the cardinal tenet of monotheism and worshiped two gods. Nevertheless, Thomas's confession is the highest confession offered in the Gospel. It is the complement to the announcement that "the Word became flesh ... and we have seen his glory" (1:14; cf. 1:1-2, 18; Rom 9:5).[13] With Thomas's confession the series of recognition scenes reaches a high point, if not a conclusion: Jesus' full identity has been recognized.

Jesus responds with a final beatitude, a blessing on those who would come later and believe without having seen. In this regard, Thomas personifies the doubt of the disciples (see Matt 28:17 and the longer ending of Mark). Throughout the Gospel, John has analyzed the relationship between seeing and believing, allowing a role for the signs, but calling readers toward a faith that is not based on signs. Thomas serves as a response to those readers who might demand a sign. Signs have been given, and even Thomas believed, but signs should never be a prerequisite for faith. Those, like the second generation of the Johannine community (cf. 17:20), who believe without having seen have attained a higher level of faith.

The Gospel's Purpose (20:30-31)

The last two verses of John 20 appear to provide a suitable ending for the Gospel: Jesus has appeared to the disciples and commissioned them, the Holy Spirit has been given, Thomas has offered the Gospel's highest confession, and Jesus has pronounced a blessing on future believers (including, potentially, the Gospel's readers). Verses 30-31 report the Gospel's purpose, to lead the reader to believe. Because there is a textual variant regarding the tense of the verb "believe" (either aorist or present), scholars have debated whether the nuance is that the reader may begin to believe or continue to believe. Seen in a larger context, the Gospel as a whole appears to have been written primarily for the believing community, to provide encouragement and clarification, but perhaps also to provide ready material for telling the church's story for those who do not believe. John clarifies the reasons for unbelief and explores various misunderstandings and stages of faith (see above chapter 5). It also reflects a rhetorical strategy that leads the reader to embrace the narrator's affirmation of Jesus as the Christ (see above chapter 4). And to those who believe, it promises life, life in the Johannine sense—true, abundant life that begins now and transcends death.

JOHN 21

Many interpreters believe the Gospel originally ended with John 20 and that John 21 was an early addition to the Gospel. This judgment is based primarily on the apparent ending created by John 20:30-31. No early manuscripts of the Gospel end with chapter 20 (in contrast to the early manuscripts of Mark

244

that end with Mark 16:8), and the material in John 21 is thoroughly Johannine (again in contrast to the non-Markan character of Mark 16:9-20). The Gospel of John was apparently composed in several stages over an extended period of time (see chapter 2 above), and John 21 was probably added late in the Gospel's composition history by a member of the Johannine school drawing on Johannine tradition. John 21 serves a vital function because it preserves the tradition of an appearance in Galilee, records the restoration of Peter, and clarifies the role of Peter and the Beloved Disciple.

The Miraculous Catch of Fish (21:1-14)

Counting the appearances to the disciples, John 21:14 notes that this is the third appearance of the risen Lord. It is possible, even probable, that the account of an appearance in Galilee, while the disciples were fishing, originally circulated independent of other appearances as the first appearance. There is nothing in the appearance itself that indicates that Jesus has appeared previously to the disciples, and the parallels with Luke 5:1-10 show that the story of the miraculous catch of fish was known outside the Johannine community.

Raymond E. Brown lists the common features of the two accounts of the catch of fish:

Ten Points Common to Luke 5 and John 21

1. The disciples fished all night with no results.

2. Jesus challenged them to let down their nets again.

3. The disciples enclosed an enormous catch.

4. "The effect on the nets is mentioned."

5. Peter reacts.

6. "Jesus is called Lord."

7. "Other fishermen take part in the catch but say nothing."

8. The theme of following Jesus is present.

9. "The catch of fish symbolizes a successful Christian missionary endeavor."

10. The same words appear at various points in the two stories.[14]

What are we to make of these parallel accounts? Do the traditions reach back to one event or two? If one event lies behind both accounts, was it originally the call of Peter to discipleship or a post-Resurrection appearance? The tradition has apparently gone through an extended process of development, but the similarities are sufficient to point to a common tradition lying behind both Luke 5 and John 21. Luke's geographical scheme (in which all the appearances take place in or around Jerusalem and the disciples are told to remain there until they receive the Holy Spirit) means that there was no place for a Galilean appearance in Luke; this favors the view that Peter's call to discipleship is secondary in his setting of the story. Because the angelic interpreters at the tomb in Mark instruct the women to tell "his disciples and Peter" to go to Galilee, Mark may have known of a tradition very much like John 21, and if the ending of Mark has been lost, that ending may have been very similar to John 21.

Peter's announcement that he is going fishing may be either an invitation to the others to join him for a night of fishing, or it may be a declaration that he is returning to his old occupation. Six others join him: Thomas, Nathanael, the sons of Zebedee, and two others. We presume that "the sons of Zebedee" are James and John, but this is the only time they appear in the Gospel, and they are not named. As we will see, one of these six is the Beloved Disciple, but it is impossible to tell whether he is John the son of Zebedee or one of the others.

Fishing at night may be good fishing, but given John's symbolism of light and darkness the result is predictable: that night they catch nothing. Early the next morning the Lord appears on the shore and says, "Children, you have no fish, have you?" The term of endearment, "children," is important in view of John's development of the theme of believers as the "children of God" (1:12). The disciples follow Jesus' instructions, cast the net on the right side, and enclose such a large catch that they are not able to haul it in. The Beloved Disciple, typically, is the first to perceive that the stranger on the shore is Jesus, and he tells Peter. The scene is reminiscent of Peter motioning to the Beloved Disciple at the table (13:23-24), the "other disciple" securing Peter's entry into the courtyard (18:16), and the Beloved Disciple and Peter at the empty tomb (20:3-10). Peter, typically (13:8, 37; 18:10-11; 20:6), is the first to act. He tucks in his garment, jumps in the lake, and swims to shore, leaving the other disciples to bring in the boat and the net full of fish.

On the shore they find a scene full of symbolic overtones: a charcoal fire and meal of fish and bread. The only other time "charcoal fire" appears in the New Testament is in the account of Peter's denials in the courtyard (18:18), and the bread and fish are reminders of the feeding of the multitude in Galilee (6:9, 11). The abundance of the catch is consistent with the abundance of wine at the wedding at Cana and the abundance of food at the feeding of the five thousand. When Peter returns to the boat, we are given a description with symbolic overtones that paint a picture of the early church: the apostle Peter, dragging a net full of fish from the boat to the risen Lord, a charcoal fire, and a meal of bread and fish.

The number 153 has intrigued interpreters for centuries. It has been suggested that it is a fisherman's memory of the actual size of the catch, the sum of the numbers from 1 to 17, a sign of the Trinity, an instance of *gematria* (numerical symbolism), or what was believed to be the total number of species of fish in the sea. Luke emphasizes the size of the catch by adding that the nets were breaking, but John has a different point in mind. The untorn net, like the seamless garment, contributes to the theme of unity. Jesus said that there would be one flock and one shepherd (10:16) and prayed that the disciples might be one (17:21-23). Now the apostle drags the untorn net full of fish to the risen Lord, who says, "Let's eat." The same verb (*helkyein*), "to draw" or "to drag," occurs in 12:32 where Jesus declares that if he is lifted up he will draw all people to himself. The wording of verse 13, "Jesus came and took the bread and gave it to them, and did the same with the fish," has eucharistic overtones and is a vivid reminder of the feeding of the five thousand (cf. Luke 24:41-43). The great catch of fish, therefore, is an epiphany that pictures the missionary task of the church.

Peter the Shepherd, the Beloved Disciple
the True Witness (21:15-23)

This section is a continuation of the previous scene with only a shift in focus. The time is after the shore breakfast, dialogue rather than action carries the scene, and its concern is the future role of Peter. Early tradition maintained that the first appearance was to Peter (1 Cor 15:3-5; Mark 16:7; Luke 24:34), and this scene serves to restore Peter following his betrayal of Jesus in the courtyard. Jesus asks Peter three times if he loves him, three times Peter affirms his love for Jesus, and three times Jesus commissions Peter to feed his sheep. The variations in the language have given rise to debates over the nuances of this exchange.

Terms Used in John 21:15-17		
Jesus' Questions	*Peter's Responses*	*Commissioning Statements*
1. Do you love *(agapas)* me more than these?	Yes, Lord; you know that I love *(philō)* you.	Feed my lambs.
2. Do you love *(agapas)* me?	Yes, Lord; you know that I love *(philō)* you.	Tend my sheep.
3. Do you love *(phileis)* me?	Lord, you know everything; you know that I love *(phileis)* you.	Feed my sheep.

When Jesus asks Peter if he loves him "more than *these*," the point of the question is probably to see if Peter will claim that he loves Jesus more than the other disciples do (cf. 13:36-38), but it may be to ask if Peter loves Jesus more than he loves the boats and nets. In the first two questions, Jesus uses *agapas* and Peter answers using *philō*. The third time, Jesus changes to the verb Peter has been using. Is this change significant, and is Peter hurt because Jesus asked him the question three times (perhaps in reference to the three statements of denial earlier), or because Jesus has changed from *agapas* to *phileis*? It is probably best not to place too much emphasis on the different words for love, as though Jesus were asking Peter for a level or quality of love Peter would not affirm. John uses these words for love interchangeably elsewhere in the Gospel.

Synonymous Uses of *agapein* and *philein* in John[15]		
Relationship	*agapein*	*philein*
Father—Son	3:35	5:20
Father—the disciple	14:23	16:27
Jesus—Lazarus	11:5	11:3
Jesus—Beloved Disciple	13:23	20:2

Peter is called to follow Jesus and feed his sheep. This commissioning undoubtedly involves a pastoral role, but it is not different from Jesus' call to every disciple. Ironically, Peter will be a good shepherd in a further sense. Probably by the time John 21 was written Peter had already died a martyr's death during the persecution under Nero (in the 60s). Jesus described his own role as that of a good shepherd who would lay down his life for his sheep (10:11, 17-18). When Peter had boasted that he would die for Jesus (13:36-38), Jesus had to tell him that he was not ready to do so, but the Johannine narrator knows that Peter would indeed glorify God through his death.

Early References to Peter's Death[16]

1 Clement 5.4 (*ca.* A.D. 96)	"Peter, who because of unrighteous jealousy suffered not one or two but many trials, and having thus given his testimony went to the glorious place which was his due."
Tertullian, *Scorpiace* 15 (*ca.* A.D. 211)	"Another fastened Peter with a belt when Peter was bound to the cross."
Eusebius, *Eccl. Hist.* 2.25.5	"Peter likewise was crucified."
Eusebius, *Eccl. Hist.* 3.1.2	(apparently quoting Origen): "... and at the end he [Peter] came to Rome and was crucified head downwards, for so he had demanded to suffer."

The Beloved Disciple would have a different role. He would not die a martyr's death but would live a long life, bearing a true witness. In retrospect, John 21 offers a variety of roles for Jesus' followers: fishing (the mission task), shepherding (the pastoral task), and faithful witness (through death or in life). Peter turns and sees the Beloved Disciple already doing what he has just been instructed to do: follow Jesus. When Peter asks about his fate, he is told that his only concern should be his own faithfulness to Jesus. Rumor spread that the Beloved Disciple would not die but would remain until Jesus came, but the writer (presumably the redactor) must explain that Jesus had not said that the Beloved Disciple would not die. The need to correct this misunderstanding may have arisen because the Beloved Disciple either had died by the time John 21 was written or was near death.

The Authority of the Gospel (21:24-25)

At the end of the Gospel, the editor, who evidently added John 21 and other parts of the Gospel to achieve its final form, identifies the Beloved Disciple as the author of the original edition of the Gospel and the one whose testimony is preserved in the Gospel. He also certifies that the Johannine community ("we") knows that his witness is true. The Gospel is therefore offered as the work of an eyewitness who was with Jesus at all the crucial moments of his ministry, one for whom Jesus had a special love, and the product of memory, reflection, study of scripture, and enlightenment by the Holy Spirit. Jesus did many other things (cf. 20:30), but these have been written with the expressed purpose of leading the reader to gain "life" by recognizing that Jesus was the Logos incarnate.

CHAPTER 9

INTERPRETING THE LETTERS

Although they are commonly treated as a group and referred to under the term "the Johannine Epistles," these three letters are quite distinct. Nevertheless, they were probably written around A.D. 100 by the same person, an elder (2 John 1; 3 John 1) of the community in which the Gospel of John was written. This community was the hub of a network of related house churches, some of which were located in other towns in the area.

First John was written to defend the church against a group that had separated itself from the Johannine community and that at least threatened to draw still others away from the community (for a more complete description of the historical setting, see chapter 3 above). In form, 1 John is not a true letter. It neither begins nor ends like a letter. It is also anonymous; the author does not identify himself by name or title. First John gives the appearance, therefore, of being a homily delivered to the community to clarify its heritage, its core beliefs, and the dangers of its opponents' false teachings. First John begins with an echo of the prologue of the Fourth Gospel. It declares the understanding of the author's group on questions such as sin among believers, the Incarnation, the love command, the role of the Spirit, and eschatological expectations. At each point it distinguishes the group's beliefs from those of its rivals, at least by implication, and rejects the latter as not just mistaken but demonic.

Second and 3 John are short letters written in classic letter form. Second John addresses a church closely related to the elder and the Johannine community. In content it resembles 1 John, repeating some of the same concerns without elaboration. Vocabulary, style, and content all suggest that the two epistles were written at about the same time by the same person. The elder was concerned that those who had divided the "mother church" might also pose a danger to this "sister church." He counsels that the church should not even greet those who do not share its confession.

Third John is not directly concerned with the doctrinal threats alluded to in the other two letters. Instead, it is a personal letter addressed to Gaius concerning the problems caused by Diotrephes, who refused to receive emissaries sent by the elder. This short letter offers tantalizing insights into the problems and organization of the early church. Perhaps in an effort to prevent dissension and false teachings from reaching his church, Diotrephes asserted his leadership, refused to receive those who came from the elder, and even excluded from the church those who did offer them hospitality. In response, the elder praised Gaius for his hospitality to "the brothers," criticized Diotrephes for his defiance, and commended Demetrius, one of the faithful. Unfortunately, these three do not appear anywhere else in the New Testament.

We will treat the three letters in their canonical sequence, but various theories have been offered regarding their historical sequence and their relationship to the Gospel of John.[1] Because the Gospel of John was composed over an extended period of time (see chapter 2 above), one may ask whether the letters were written early in this process, during the later stages of the composition of the Gospel, or after its completion. The vocabulary and concerns of the letters find their closest parallels in the Gospel in the farewell discourse and in the sections that were probably added or revised late in the Gospel's composition history. Whether the final editor of the Gospel and the elder who wrote the letters were one and the same person or two different members of the Johannine community is an interesting question that has not yet been settled. Raymond Brown, in his encyclopedic commentary has shown that the letters presuppose at least the same tradition as the Gospel and that the elder and those who had left the community both drew on this tradition but interpreted it in different ways. The elder insists on the reality of the Incarnation ("the Word became flesh"), the importance of Jesus' death, the danger of sin among believers, and the importance of the love command. In the process, Brown shows that the teachings of the Gospel are consistent with emerging orthodoxy, even though the earliest known champions of the Johannine writings in the second century were Gnostics (see chapter 2 above). In fact, the Johannine letters may have played an important role in leading the church to accept the Gospel as orthodox. At various places in our survey we will highlight the points of contact and the relationship between the Gospel and the letters.

1 JOHN

While the letter structure of 2 and 3 John is conventional and clear, that of 1 John is more open and ambiguous, with the result that various structures have been proposed. The individual paragraphs are fairly distinct, but commentators have divided it into two, three, four, and more major sections depending on whether one is guided primarily by recurring thematic statements, transitional markers, chiastic patterns, parallels to the structure of the Fourth Gospel, or differences between Christological and ethical material. Each proposed structure, consequently, is a "reading strategy" that organizes the text in such a way that certain themes stand out more clearly. The structure followed here is an amalgam of structures adopted by others that sets the letter in the historical context sketched above. Its aim is to facilitate reading the letter in the context of the Christological and ethical concerns that had divided the Johannine community.

A Structure for the Reading of 1 John

Prologue: The Word of Life (1:1-4)

I. A Community Faithful to the Confession That God Is Light (1:5–2:27)

    A. The Dangers of Denying Sin (1:5–2:2)

    B. Love as the Command of the New Covenant (2:3-11)

    C. The Danger of the World's Temptations (2:12-27)

II. A Community Faithful to the Confession That God Is Righteous (2:28–4:6)

    A. Doing Right and Avoiding Sin as the Mark of God's Children (2:28–3:10)

    B. Love as the Command of the New Covenant (3:11-24)

    C. The Danger of the Spirit of Deceit (4:1-6)

III. A Community Faithful to the Confession That God Is Love (4:7–5:12)

    A. Love Comes from God and Is Rooted in Faith (4:7-21)

    B. Faith in the Son of God Is the Root of Love (5:1-12)

Epilogue: Assurances to the Faithful Community (5:13-21)

Prologue: The Word of Life (1:1-4)

The opening sentence of the letter is a grammatical minefield composed of five relative clauses:

"What was from the beginning,
what we have heard,
what we have seen with our eyes,
what we have looked at and touched with our hands ...
what we have seen and heard...."

These clauses are interrupted by an intrusion (v. 2), which restates the meaning of the phrase "concerning the word of life." The main clause is "we declare to you," and a statement of purpose finishes the sentence: "so that you also may have fellowship with us." Deliberate echoes of both Genesis and the new genesis described in the prologue to the Gospel of John reverberate in the opening words of 1 John. The author traces the message of the letter to what "was from *the beginning*." This term will be used later for the earliest days of the Johannine church and the proclamation of the gospel (2:7, 24; 3:11; 2 John 5-6).

God is neither silent nor invisible, the elder claims. They have heard God in the words of Jesus and seen God in the face of Jesus. The taproot of the Christian community reaches deep into the mystery of the Incarnation. The elder emphasizes the sensory perception of revelation: "heard" (vv. 1, 3), "seen" (vv. 1, 2, 3), "looked at" (v. 1), "touched" (v. 1). In part at least the eschatological hope of seeing God has already been realized (see 3:2). The parenthesis in verse 2 relates the essence and quality of life promised by the gospel to the character of life that they had witnessed in Jesus of Nazareth. The gospel draws others to that life. The two verbs for reception in verse 2 (*revealed* and *seen*) are balanced by two verbs for transmission (*testify* and *declare*).

The last clause of this extended first sentence contains the first statement of the purpose for writing this letter: "so that you also may have fellowship with us." In Johannine dualism, one has fellowship with either truth or falsehood, light or darkness. On the other hand, 1 John is probably not a missionary tract for unbelievers but a communication with those who belong to the church but are in danger of turning from it. Some have already crossed that line (2:19). For the elder, the fellowship of his community is "with the Father and with his Son Jesus Christ." The implication is that apart from fellowship with the earthly community of faith there is no fellowship with God. The pluralism of the church today makes it difficult for us to grasp the exclusiveness of the spirit of 1 John. This exclusiveness raises the difficult issue of the proper limits of toleration and diversity. On the one hand, there can be no truly Christian fellowship with that which is opposed to Christ's redemptive work, but on the other, there can be no truly Christian fellowship that is not as inclusive as God's love.

Where fellowship is only partial, joy can never be complete. Jesus left his joy to his followers (John 15:11; 16:20-24; 17:13), but that joy can never be complete so long as his redemptive work is still unfinished. The prologue to 1 John, therefore, reaches from "the beginning" through the present ("we declare") to the consummation of God's purposes, when partnership and joy can both be complete.

A Community Faithful to the Confession That God Is Light (1:5–2:27)

As we have seen, the letter may be divided into three major parts, the first of which develops the Christological and ethical significance of declaring that God is light. There are three subsections to each of the first two parts of the letter, and some parallels in theme can be seen in the three subsections of these major parts.

Thematic Parallels in 1 John 1:5–2:22 and 2:29–4:6		
1:5–2:2	The Dangers of Denying Sin and the Importance of Doing Right	2:29–3:10
2:3-11	Love as the Command of the New Covenant	3:11-24
2:12-27	The Danger of the World's Temptations	4:1-6

The Dangers of Denying Sin (1:5–2:2). Following the opening paragraph, the author turns to one of the major divisive issues. Some believers were denying that they were guilty of sin. They apparently thought that through their belief in Jesus they had become enlightened and were free from sin. If sin was at root unbelief (see John 16:8-9), then because they believed they could not be guilty of sin. While holding to the same tradition, the elder argues that those who reason this way are badly deceived.

Verse 5 begins the first major section of the epistle. The phrase "this is the message" recurs in 3:11, and Raymond E. Brown regards it as a key to the structure of the epistle.[2] The inference drawn from the affirmation that God is light was that since there is no darkness in God, there can be no darkness in his followers. But this state of sinlessness, the elder argued, does not follow automatically from believing in Jesus. First John 1:5–2:2 is organized around a series of six conditional sentences. Each concerns the place of sin in the life of the believer. Three express conditions that are misguided and destructive (1:6, 8, 10), and three

256

offer constructive alternatives (1:7, 9; 2:1b-2). The three statements regarding the consequences of denying the reality of sin
can serve as an outline for this section, with verse 5 standing as
an introduction and 2:1-2 functioning as a conclusion. Since the
three disapproved conditions each begin with the phrase, "if we
say ...," it is reasonable to assume that some in the community
were actually making these assertions and others were in danger
of accepting these views. The three rejected conditions have a
similar form and develop progressively in their seriousness.

The Form of 1 John 1:6-10		
1:6	a	If we say that we have fellowship with him
	b	while we are walking in darkness,
	c	we lie
	d	and do not do what is true.
1:8	a	If we say we have no sin,
	b	
	c	we deceive ourselves
	d	and the truth is not in us.
1:10	a	If we say that we have not sinned,
	b	
	c	we make him a liar,
	d	and his word is not in us.

Similar patterns can be found in 1:7, 9, and 2:1-2. The logic of
this progression is clear. We cannot live in God's fellowship if our
lives are darkened by sin. Moreover, we cannot deny the reality of
sin, even among believers, but if we confess our sin, God is sure
to forgive us.

Whereas Christology dominates the Gospel of John, 1 John is
theocentric: it explores the nature of God's character. Light is universally regarded as a quality of the divine character, and it
appears frequently in the Jewish and Greek background materials and in the Gospel of John. In the Logos there was life which
was "the light of all people" (John 1:4), but the road to perfection
is more difficult than some members of the community thought.
Verse 6 pinpoints the problem of contradiction between the
claims one may make and one's way of life. The Johannine Christians claimed fellowship with God. No higher claim can be made

for one's life, for it implies that one has come to know the character of God (John 17:3) and that the character of God has become the transforming reality for one's life. In turn, living under the reality of God's grace makes community possible. The reference to Jesus' death in the latter part of verse 7 may come as a surprise. The significance of Jesus' death may have been unclear for the Johannine community both because John places so much emphasis on the Incarnation and Jesus' role as Revealer and because his death is portrayed not as a sacrifice but as an enthronement and exaltation to the Father. If there is substance to the suspicion that some Johannine Christians denied that the Logos actually became flesh or that the Logos could have died, then the elder may be reclaiming a neglected part of the earlier tradition and drawing the community closer to the views of Jesus' death that we find elsewhere in early Christianity.

The first sentence of the second chapter restates the elder's reason for writing. In 1:4 he had said that he was writing so that their joy might be fulfilled; here he claims to write so that they might not sin. He too shares the ideal of sinlessness, but he knows that sin is a reality in the life of believers. Confession is the means to freedom from sin because we have an advocate or intercessor (Greek, *Paraclete*) before the Father. The Greek word *hilasmos* occurs only here and in 4:10 in the New Testament. It is drawn from the cultic act of offering a sacrifice to remove the offense of sin. The primary emphasis in this context is not the anger of God but the role of Jesus in covering or removing sin. As C. H. Dodd aptly commented, "Our forgiveness rests upon the justice and faithfulness of God, not upon the possibility of averting His anger."[3]

Love as the Command of the New Covenant (2:3-11). Even more basic than recognizing the reality of sin in one's life is the question of whether one knows God or not. Having dealt with the dangers of denying sin, the elder turns to the hypocrisy of claiming to know God when one's life gives no evidence of such knowledge.

Those who claimed to be sinless could quite naturally also claim to have an intimate knowledge of God, which they probably also viewed as conveying salvation. Such at least was the common assumption of Hellenistic thought, the mystery cults, and later Gnostic groups. The Gospel of John also describes the goal of religious experience as the knowledge of God: "And this is eternal life, that they know thee the only true God, and Jesus Christ whom thou hast sent" (John 17:3, RSV). What tests could one apply to verify or deny such knowledge of God? To these the elder now directs the attention of his readers.

Jeremiah looked forward to a new covenant which he described in phrases so parallel to this section of 1 John that we can hardly escape the conclusion that the elder had the words of Jeremiah 31 in mind.

Jeremiah 31:33-34

I will put my law within them, and I will write it on their hearts; and I will be their God, and they shall be my people. No longer shall they teach one another, or say to each other, "Know the LORD," for they shall all know me, from the least of them to the greatest, says the LORD; for I will forgive their iniquity, and I will remember their sin no more.

Those who claim to know God must therefore have his laws inscribed on their hearts. Keeping God's commands is evidence that one knows God; and equally true, if one does not keep God's commands, that person cannot claim to know God.

Like the previous section, 1 John 2:3-11 contains three allusions to the claims of the elder's opponents. Rather than following the earlier patterns of relating these claims in conditional sentences, the author reports them using the formula, "whoever says ..."

2:4 Whoever says, "I have come to know him ..."
2:6 Whoever says, "I abide in him ..."
2:9 Whoever says, "I am in the light ..."

The three claims are not in themselves false or objectionable. The elder might well make each of these claims for himself and those who follow his teachings. His point is that those who make such claims must show by their lives that they are speaking the truth. By implication we may gather that his opponents made precisely these claims but did not maintain a pattern of life consistent with their claims.

Only two specific commandments are given in John: "Believe in

God, believe also in me" (John 14:1), and "as I have loved you, you also should love one another" (John 13:34; 15:12). These commandments are repeated in 1 John 3:23: "And this is his commandment, that we should believe in the name of his Son Jesus Christ and love one another, just as he has commanded us." These commands defined the center of the Johannine community's life, but they left the concrete expressions of belief and love, the perimeter of the community, undefined. The lack of more specific commands freed the community from legalism but threatened its life by the absence of structure and limits. Without such commands, the elder appealed to the only pattern for Christian living for which he could claim authority: Live as he lived. Imitate Jesus.

This imperative is based on the significant Johannine concept of *abiding* in him. The experience of abiding in him, and he in the one who abides (cf. John 14:23), changes the whole character of one's life. Adverbs seldom carry theological significance, but in the Johannine writings *just as* draws comparisons that trace the course of revelation and lay bare the lines of authority: just as it is written; just as Jesus said or did; and just as the Father did for the Son, so Jesus did for the disciples or the disciples should do for others. These analogies display the basis of authority for the Johannine Christians. The authority of Scripture was retained, but to it was added the authority of Jesus' words, the events of his life, and the pattern of the Father's relationship to him and his relationship to the disciples.

The appeal in verse 6 is to the pattern of Jesus' life. What the elder has in mind, above all, is the love Jesus showed for his own, and which he commanded for them. This is no new command but one they had from "the beginning." God's love—revealed and conveyed by Jesus, extended through the new commandment, and realized in the community—is both the force driving out darkness and the evidence that the new age has come.

We do not know how much may have been intended by the claim of the opponents to be in the light. They may have been claiming direct communion with God or Christ, a higher quality of spiritual enlightenment, or simply partnership with the Johannine community. By their refusal to love other members of the community, however, they show that they are still in the darkness (cf. John 13:30). On the other hand, love within the community is genuine evidence of knowledge of God and fellowship with Christ.

The Danger of the World's Temptations (2:12-28). Having responded to the false claims of the opponents, the elder now encourages the community of the faithful by assuring them that the benefits of the covenant are theirs and warning them against the world's temptations. In verses 12-14 the writer breaks out in two stanzas of assurance that are almost poetic in structure. Patterns of three predominate. Verses 12-13 contain three statements, each beginning "I write to you..." (NEB). Verse 14 repeats the pattern in a different tense, "I have written..." (NEB). In both stanzas three groups are mentioned: children, fathers, and young men. The most vexing problem posed by these verses is the identity of these three groups. Are the references literal or figurative? Is the writer addressing three different age groups, or the community and its leaders? The latter is more likely because the words are appropriate for all believers: "your sins are forgiven" (v. 12) and "you know the Father" (v. 14). These are clear echoes of the provisions of the new covenant in Jeremiah 31:34, "they shall all know me ... for I will forgive their iniquity, and remember their sin no more." To the young men, the writer assures victory. As deep as the dualism of the Johannine literature is, it is not an absolute dualism; God in Christ has triumphed over the powers of darkness. The assurance of victory, therefore, is a recurring theme of these writings.

Verses 15-17 expose the opposition, origin, and ends of two conflicting loves, the love of the Father and the love of the world. On first reading, 1 John 2:15 seems to be irreconcilable with John 3:16, but "the world" in John 3:16 encompasses all human life while in 1 John 2:15 it represents all that is opposed to Christ (cf. John 17:9). The two loves cannot be reconciled. One comes from the Father, the other from the world. In Johannine thought, one does not escape one's origins: to be *from* the world means always *to belong to* the world. The only hope of escape is a new beginning, a new birth *from above* (John 3:3).

First John as a whole can be interpreted as a warning against deception. The elder was locked in conflict with another group, which apparently emerged from the Johannine community but taught a different doctrine. In this section more than any other the elder writes specifically about the opposing movement which had divided the community. The terms "the last hour" and "antichrist" appear only in the Johannine letters in the New Testament, but both terms have contacts with early Christian apocalyptic thought. Sketching the opponents in the darkest colors possible and raising the sense of crisis, the elder coins new terms related to traditional apocalyptic language. Those who have left the community are "antichrists," and their appearance shows that the terrors of the last days have already begun. Verse 19 confirms that a part of the community had separated from it, but does not tell us why or how. Other passages (for example, 4:1-2) suggest that the issue was primarily Christological. Inevitably, some who remained did not see the issues so clearly and were on the verge of leaving the community to join the other group. The elder writes, therefore, as a leader of the community, to set forth the differences sharply and encourage unity among those who remained. Resisting the corrupting influence of the world (vv. 15-17) meant specifically resisting the group that had left the community.

In the Gospel, Judas and the Galilean defectors "went out" from the disciples who remained with Jesus (John 6:66-67; 13:30-31). In contrast, the community of the faithful has received an "anointing" (v. 20), which is probably an assurance that they have been anointed with the Holy Spirit. One who denies Christ, or refuses to confess the reality of the Incarnation (see 4:1-2), is a liar, and he is from "the Liar," the devil. On the other hand, those who confess Christ have the anointing of the Spirit, which means that they have no need of someone to teach them (and hence possibly teach them falsely). In his appeal for the Johannine community to remain true to Christ by remaining faithful to the tradition they had received, the elder shows that his authority is limited. The community was very egalitarian because they all had the anointing of the Spirit. Only the Spirit is able to guide the community to know the truth.

A Community Faithful to the Confession
That God Is Righteous (2:28–4:6)

The second major section of 1 John follows from the confession, "He is righteous" in 2:29. Verse 28 is sometimes taken as the conclusion to the preceding section since it has links with both what precedes and with the material that follows. Some parallels in structure can be detected between the first and second part of the letter. Each contains a warning about the incom-

262

patibility of sin and righteousness, an exhortation to obey the love command, and a warning about the error of those who have left the community.

Doing Right and Avoiding Sin as the Mark of God's Children (2:28–3:10). This paragraph is dynamically linked with the preceding sections. It extends the discussion of the division of light and darkness, the separation of the community from the world, and the opposition between the community and those who have departed from it. That separation now leads to a clear distinction between "the children of God" and "the children of the devil." These expressions are drawn from traditional Johannine language, but they are here redefined to interpret the danger the community faces from its opponents.

The elder reassures the faithful that they are "children of God" (cf. John 1:12; 11:52) and reminds them of the hope they share. The first evidence that God claims them as children is the love that God has already given them. The believers are already children of God even if the world does not regard them as such. In fact, rejection by the world is further confirmation of their status. Because of the Father's love, the address "beloved" is all the more appropriate (see 2:7; 3:21; 4:1, 7, 11).

The words "now" and "not yet" show that God's work is not complete. They are already God's children, and that will not change, but what they will be has not yet been revealed. The confidence of those who know God and abide in Christ is that when he appears, they shall see that they are like him (cf. 1 Cor 13:12; Matt 5:8).

Having written of "everyone who does right" (2:29), the elder turns his attention to "everyone who commits sin" (3:4). Sin exposes the inner nature of those it claims. Jesus' death cleanses us from sin (1:7); he is our expiation (2:2). The implications follow: If Christ came to remove sin and was sinless himself, then those who have been born of God and abide in Christ cannot continue in sin. Sin and righteousness are incompatible. Those who live a life of sin are from the devil (3:8). The world is under the devil's power (John 12:31; 14:30; 16:11), so a new birth is required for those who become children of God.

1 John 3:9 is one of the most problematic verses in the epistle. How are the various statements about sin in 1 John to be explained?

The Elder's Claims About Sin

1:8   If we say that we have no sin, we deceive ourselves, and the truth is not in us.

1:10   If we say that we have not sinned, we make him a liar, and his word is not in us.

3:6   No one who abides in him sins; no one who sins has either seen him or known him.

3:8   Everyone who commits sin is a child of the devil.

3:9   Those who have been born of God do not sin, because God's seed abides in them; they cannot sin, because they have been born of God.

5:18   We know that those who are born of God do not sin.

Commentators have spared no ingenuity in attempting to resolve the tension between those passages in 1 John that recognize the reality of sin in the life of the believer (1:8, 10) and those that claim there can be no sin in a believer's life (3:6, 8-9; 5:18). Solutions that postulate multiple authors, editors, sources, or opponents do not solve the problem of how the finished product was meant to be understood. Moreover, it is doubtful that the difference in verb tenses can be made to resolve the difficulty (perfect in 1:10, aorist in 2:1, and present in 3:6, 9; 5:18—but present also in 1:8). The present tense often implies continued action, so it has been suggested that the verses may be harmonized by a strict interpretation of their grammar: believers cannot continue to sin but must recognize that they do sin. At a minimum, however, the author would have to be charged with depending too heavily on a subtle difference in grammar to make such a significant distinction. At issue again is probably the difference between the elder and those who left the community. Because both share the heritage of the Johannine tradition, with its sharp dualism and its perception of sin as arising from unbelief, both also hold to the view that those who have been born of God no longer belong to this world and are no longer under the power of evil. As God's children they have been delivered from sin. The elder recognizes the continuing presence of sin in the lives of believers and the danger of assuming that the believer no longer needs to be concerned about sin. The opponents apparently exaggerated and distorted the community's emphasis on realized eschatology by claiming that believers were already free from sin. On the other hand, those who abide in Christ and have the Spirit abiding in them will lead lives characterized by righteousness rather than sin.

Love as the Command of the New Covenant (3:11-24). The phrase, "This is the message you have heard from the beginning," echoes 1 John 1:5 and introduces a new section of the letter. Verses 13-18 interpret the specific requirements of the love command. Verses 19-22 give assurance that those who live by God's commands do not need to fear God's judgment, and verses 23-24 conclude the section by repeating the words "and this is his commandment." The interpretation of the love command that follows continues the exposition that began in 2:7-11.

The Johannine love command is more limited than the commands to love elsewhere in the New Testament (contrast Matt 5:44, 46; Luke 6:27, 32; 10:25-27). For the elder, love for his enemies would have constituted love for the world (2:15) since his opponents belonged to the world (4:5). On the positive side, he emphasizes the importance of exemplary love within the Christian community. To set off that love as sharply as possible, the elder appeals to its antithesis: Cain, who murdered his brother. Cain was "from the evil one," the devil. The elder's point is graphic: those who *hate* their fellow Christians are following the path of their elder brother, Cain.

The change of address in verses 13 to "brothers and sisters" is appropriate following the reference to Cain and his brother. In the sharp dualistic categories of the Johannine community, there is no middle ground. One either loves or one is a murderer. If one is a member of the community, one hates the world, and the world hates the community. But those who know Christ and practice love have already "passed from death to life." Echoes of the Gospel, especially the farewell discourse, are evident throughout this paragraph.

Echoes of the Gospel in 1 John 3:11-17		
1 John 3		*The Gospel of John*
3:11	"that we should love one another"	13:34; 15:12
3:12	"a murderer"	8:44
3:12	"his own deeds were evil"	3:19

3:13	"the world hates you"	7:7; 15:18-25
3:14	"we have passed from death to life"	5:24
3:16	"We know love by this, that he laid down his life for us"	15:13

Verses 16-18 return to the meaning of the love command, which was introduced in verses 11 and 14. Verse 16 states the general principle that we ought to love one another as Christ loved us, but it magnifies the principle by relating it to Christ's giving his life for his own. Verse 17 draws specific implications. It consists of a series of three conditions followed by a devastating question: "But if any one has the world's goods and sees his brother in need, yet closes his heart against him, how does God's love abide in him?" (RSV). *Agape* demands that those who are full give to those who are hungry and that those who "cannot find anything to wear" give to those who would be glad to have something to wear. Verse 18 concludes the paragraph with an exhortation to show love through what one does, not just what one says.

Verses 19 to 22 have been interpreted variously by the commentators. Is the author responding to the charges of the defectors, who charged that the members of the Johannine community were not really righteous because they were still worried about sinning (see 1:8, 10)? Is the elder assuring his readers that they can have confidence before God even if they know they are not blameless (R. E. Brown)?[4] Is he urging them to be sinless by warning that God's judgment upon them will be even more severe than their judgment on themselves (K. Grayston)?[5] Or is he saying that we can have confidence because God, who know all things, can be more objective and merciful than we (I. H. Marshall)?[6] The tone seems to be one of assurance, and the elder has already insisted that there is forgiveness for those who confess their sins. The reassuring interpretation is to be preferred, therefore, over the severe or mediating positions.

The conclusion to this section in verses 23-24 sums up the elder's understanding of what it means to be a Christian as well as any verse in the letter. It is a definitive statement of "the message you have heard from the beginning" (3:11). The command is twofold, and both parts are drawn from the Gospel: "believe in the name of his Son,

Jesus Christ" (John 1:12; 3:16; 14:1; 20:31), and love one another
(John 13:34; 15:12). This twofold command is the Johannine version
of the great commandment to love God and to love your neighbor as
yourself (Deut 6:4; Lev 19:18; Mark 12:28-31). These commands are
the conditions of the covenant. Those who keep them (see 2:3) can
be assured that they abide in God and God abides in them. That
assurance is sufficient to overcome either self-doubt or the accusations of others. One's sense of guilt is overcome not by being unconcerned about righteousness or by imagining oneself to be innocent
but by believing in Christ and by loving one's brother and sister.

The Danger of the Spirit of Deceit (4:1-6). In the last line of chapter
3 a new term appears for the first time in the epistle, "spirit." Jesus
had promised the coming of the Paraclete, the Holy Spirit (John
14:16-17). Very likely, both the Johannine Christians and those who
had gone out from them claimed that God had given them the Spirit.
Prophets played a significant role in the life of the early church,
speaking directly for God and providing direction for the church.
Gradually a more official structure of pastors and deacons replaced
the early charismatic leadership of the church. The Johannine community had not yet developed an official leadership, as we can see
from the problems in 3 John. The elder can only appeal to his
authority as one who represents the tradition of the community.

The problem the community faced is one that plagues religious
communities in every age: What distinguishes the true prophetic
voices from the false ones? First John 4:1-6 encourages the community to test the spirits because there were many false voices. It offers
two criteria for distinguishing true from false prophets: the content of
their message and their reception by the world. Those who confess
Jesus Christ who has come in flesh are from God; those who do not
are from the antichrist. Those who listen to the community belong to
God; those who listen to its opponents belong to the world. There are
two spirits, therefore: the spirit of truth and the spirit of deception.

The command not to believe in every spirit but to test the spirits should be interpreted literally against the prevailing worldview
of the first century, according to which the world was populated
by various kinds of angels, demons, and unclean spirits. The verb
"to test" is drawn from the testing of coins to distinguish those that
are genuine from the counterfeit. Unfortunately, there are attractive counterfeits from whom the faithful need protection because
naive piety is often blinded by sparkle and oblivious to substance.

Deuteronomy 13:1-5 legislated the criterion of content: even if the prophet's sign or wonder comes to pass, if he calls for worship of another god, do not listen to him. What constitutes a true confession? First John 4:2 adds a phrase to the confession toward which the Gospel of John leads its readers. It was no longer enough to believe that Jesus was the Christ, the Son of God (John 20:31). Both the affirmation that Jesus was the Christ and the affirmation that the Christ came in flesh are essential. Holding either one without the other is not only insufficient but exposes one as an antichrist and false prophet. Those who had gone out from the community apparently affirmed the divinity of Jesus but denied or diminished the significance of his humanity. The elder insists on the importance of the Incarnation.

Those who had separated from the community may have been more numerous or more prosperous than those who remained with the elder, but he assures them that they have "conquered" the antichrists. Perhaps contrary to appearances, the faithful were assured of victory because the spirit within them was stronger than the spirit of the antichrist. The language of victory, of course, also plays an important role in the book of Revelation.

Verse 5 introduces the second criterion, reception. The world receives those who belong to it, just as the children of God receive God's word. The full extent of the dualism of 1 John is now clear and may be sketched in the following diagram.

The Dualism of 1 John

	God
the antichrist, the devil	Christ
the spirit of deception	the Spirit of Truth
the children of the devil	the children of God
the world	the Johannine community
antichrists, false prophets	the brothers, beloved
the defectors who went out into the world	those faithful to the elder
they	you

There is no middle ground, and no room for compromise. Nevertheless, the dualism is not complete, as in some philosophical systems, because there is no cosmic counterpart to God. The logic is clear, but as we can see from 1 John itself, it was probably ineffective in dealing with the schism of the community. The enduring significance of this section is its clear-eyed recognition that there are people who claim inspiration but pose a serious threat to the church. Where there are conflicting voices two tests may be applied: What are they saying, and who is listening to them? More specifically, are the religious leaders affirming the historic confessions of the church, or are they advocating departures from the church's doctrines?

A Community Faithful to the Confession
That God Is Love (4:7–5:12)

The Johannine double command in 3:23 requires that we believe in the name of Jesus Christ and that we love one another. Keeping that command is possible because the one who gave the command also gave his Spirit. The previous verses (4:1-6) clarify the criteria by which his Spirit can be discerned, so the elder now returns to the new command of community love. Major sections of 1 John are marked by "God is . . . " statements: "God is light" (1:5), "[God] is righteous" (2:29), and now "God is love" (4:8). The two parts of this section explore the relationship between faith and love. First John 4:7-21 is the third and most profound treatment of love in 1 John. First John 5:1-12 then gathers up the main themes of the letter and relates them to the nature of faith.

Love Comes from God and Is Rooted in Faith (4:7-21). This moving interpretation of the nature of perfect love unfolds in three movements: (1) the source of perfect love (4:7-10), the experience of perfect love (4:11-16a), and the confidence of perfect love (4:16b-21). The opening word of verse 7 is significant: those who are commanded to love are themselves "beloved." Continuing the concern of the previous paragraph, the elder adds that love is another criterion that distinguishes those who know God from those who do not. God is the source of perfect love because love is essential to the very character of God. All who practice love for others show thereby that they have come to know something of God's character and are living in response to God as God's children. Knowledge of God, therefore, is not manifested in some esoteric lore but in a quality of character and life that can come only from God. The revelation of God's love was accomplished through the sending of God's Son. Verses 9 and 10 appear to offer a commentary and reflections on John 3:16. The main terms of John 3:16 appear here: God, loved, the world, sent, only Son, and life. Love is realized not by human effort but by divine disclosure. The elder does not say that God loved "the world" (cf. 2:15), but rather, "God sent his only Son *into the world* so that *we* might live through him." That life so transforms the lives of the faithful that the elder can say that they have "passed over from death to life" (3:14).

The end of verse 10 links the death of Jesus to the revelation of God's love. It was not just the Incarnation that revealed the Father's love; that love was also revealed by Jesus' atoning death. The elder may have needed to drive this point home for the community because they may have emphasized the coming of Jesus, neglecting the importance of his death. The prologue to the Gospel, after all, extols the significance of the Incarnation but says nothing about the atonement.

The elder's thought moves from the command to love to that which enables us to do so. Having dealt with the second part of the double command stated in 3:23, he returns in verses 13-16*a* to the first part, "believe in the name of his Son Jesus Christ." Belief is the response to God's love that enables the community to practice love for one another. This section continues the commentary on John 3:16. The outline of the verse can be seen in the emphasis on "God loved" in 4:11, gave and "sent" in 4:13-14, "the Son" in 4:15, and "believe" in 4:16*a*. The experience of God's love, perfected (or completed) in us, therefore, is the meaning of eternal life.

The third section (4:16*b*-21) makes three points. First, the mutual indwelling of the believer in God and God in the believer brings God's love to completion (v. 16*b*). Second, the experience of God's perfect love produces a fearless confidence on the day of judgment (vv. 17-18), and third, anyone who claims to love God and yet does not love others is a liar (vv. 19-21). The elder's point is that his opponents, who do not love the Johannine Christians, have shown thereby that they do not love God either. We cannot claim a personal faith that involves only our relationship to God. God's love will not tolerate such limits. Only those who give themselves for the well-being of others can claim to love God. The elder thought only of the imperative to love one's fellow Christians, but ultimately God's love will not tolerate that limitation either, as other New Testament witnesses verify. The greatest gift that we can give in return for the love God has shown in the sending of the Son is to love one another in his name.

Faith in the Son of God Is the Root of Love (5:1-12). The last section of the body of the letter brings together the primary themes of the letter: belief in Christ and obedience to the love command.

The Structure of 1 John 5:1-12

I. Faith, Love Leading to Victory (5:1-4)
    5:1 Everyone who believes that Jesus is the Christ
    5:4 This is the victory
II. Faith, The Testimony of Three Witnesses (5:5-9)
    5:5 ... the one who believes that Jesus is the Son of God
    5:9 This is the testimony
III. Faith, God's Testimony Expressed in Life (5:10-12)
    5:10 Those who believe in the Son of God
    5:11 This is the life

Verse 1 reintroduces the theme of faith (or believing), which serves as a unifying theme for this section. Of the nine occurrences of the verb "to believe" in 1 John, five are in this section. The first unit (5:1-4) relates believing to the imperative of love, which was the theme of the preceding section. Who is the child in verse 1, Christ or the believer? Probably the latter. The elder is building toward the same conclusion he has drawn before: the faithful can tell who has been born of God by seeing who shows love for fellow believers. One who lives in fellowship with God will inevitably love others who share in this fellowship. Verse 2 is almost the Johannine equivalent of the Jewish *Shema,* the command to love God (Deut 6:4-9), and the command to love one's neighbor (Lev 19:18). Professions of love for God are genuine, however, only when they are accompanied by obedience to God's commands. The statement that God's commands are not heavy, burdensome, or difficult runs deep in the biblical tradition (Deut 30:11; Matt 11:30). The paragraph ends with the assurance of victory. All who belong to God will share in God's victory over the world.

The content of victorious faith is preeminently Christological. It affirms that *Jesus* is the Son of God. Emphasis on his earthly life may be implied. The nuances of "water" and "blood" in verse 6 have been vigorously debated. Do they refer to Jesus' birth, baptism, and death? Or to Baptism and the Lord's Supper? The context of the letter makes it likely that the elder was emphasizing the reality of the Incarnation and the importance of Jesus' death for salvation. The Word did not just appear to become flesh in Christ, and his death was not merely his return to the Father. In John's account of Jesus' death, all three of the witnesses cited in 1 John 5:6-8 are mentioned: water, blood, and the Spirit. The three witnesses fulfill the biblical requirement that testimony must be validated by at least two witnesses (Deut 19:15).

A famous insertion, the so-called Johannine Comma, occurs at the end of verse 7. In the Latin manuscript tradition the words "in heaven: Father, Word, and Holy Spirit; and these three are one; and there are three who testify on earth" were inserted beginning in the fourth-century manuscripts that come from North Africa and Spain. The Johannine Comma does not appear in any Greek manuscript before A.D. 1400, however, and is now recognized as a gloss motivated by the trinitarian debates of the fourth and fifth centuries.

God's testimony, fundamentally, is the life and death of Jesus. Those who believe in the Son of God have been born of God (5:1), conquer the world (5:5), and have God's testimony in their hearts (5:10). That testimony is interior and self-authenticating. One who rejects Jesus has therefore rejected God's testimony, in effect declaring the testimony false and the witness a liar.

The body of 1 John begins with the words "this is the message" (1:5), and it ends with the formula "this is the testimony" (5:11). That testimony is that God has given us eternal life. It is a testimony to the character and purpose of all God's creative and redemptive works. The body of 1 John ends with the promise of life, just as the Gospel of John does (cf. John 20:30-31; 1 John 5:13). Genuine faith is therefore validated by love, which is ultimately victorious, by testimony to the saving significance of Jesus' death, and by life lived in fellowship with other believers and with God. Eternal life is the fulfillment of God's own being, God's love for us, and God's redemptive work. Faith, therefore, is self-authenticating, but only for believers because these are truths the world cannot grasp.

Epilogue: Assurances to the Faithful Community (5:13-21)

The concluding verses call the readers to the certainties of their faith. Attention to the essentials of true faith in the previous section now allows the elder to take stock of the verities assured by faith. The theme of certainty is set from the beginning. Verse 13, which resembles closely the conclusion of the Gospel (20:30-31), begins, "I write these things to you ... so that you may *know*." Verse 14 speaks of the confidence we have, and verse 15 reasons, "If we know ... [then] we know ..." The verb "know" then becomes the unifying theme of verses 18-20. Verses 16 and 17 are a caveat or clarification regarding intercession for forgiveness. Certainty about their beliefs will be the community's best defense against false teachings.

The community can have confidence in prayer. When the elder speaks of confidence (2:28; 3:21-22; 4:17), it is always confidence before God. Confident prayer, however, can only come from those who know God as their Father and know themselves as God's children. Apart from God's faithfulness there could be no certainty at all.

Having introduced the topic of prayer in verses 14 and 15, the elder turns to the delicate matter of prayer for the forgiveness of sins. For the Johannine Christians this was a difficult subject because of their insistence on the ideal of perfection (3:6). The elder has maintained, however, that if they will confess their sin, God, who is faithful and just, will forgive them (1:9). Therefore, if any Christian sees a brother or sister committing a sin "not unto death" (KJV), he or she should ask forgiveness for that person. Ultimately only God can give life, but through intercessory prayer the Christian can have a role in restoring an erring brother or sister.

The more difficult issue is the distinction between sin "unto death" and sin "not unto death." Distinctions among sins were already common in the first century (Lev 4:1-3; Num 15:22-31; Deut 17:12). The distinction in 1 John 5:16 is probably drawn from the community context. The language is characteristically Johannine. "Death" refers to a spiritual condition—separation from the life that is only available in Christ. Sin is refusal to

273

believe in Jesus (John 16:8-9). Those who refuse to believe are without excuse (John 15:22) and will die in their sin (John 8:21, 24). The sin "unto death" is therefore refusal to believe in Jesus as the Christ come in flesh (1 John 4:2). Those who held to a different Christology and had left the community were cut off from Christ, the giver of life. Their sin had brought them to death, so the elder admonishes the faithful not to pray for such persons. In imposing this restriction, which many find objectionable, the elder was being consistent with the tradition of the Fourth Gospel. Jesus would not pray for the world (John 17:9), so the elder advises the faithful that they are not to pray for those who belong to the world (cf. 4:5). The primary distinction in verses 16 and 17 is therefore not between types of sin but between persons for whom one should pray. Pray for fellow Christians who have fallen into sin. Do not pray for those who have refused to believe in Christ. The elder's dualism has led to a restriction that most interpreters have felt must be qualified by more moderate, compassionate, and optimistic pronouncements elsewhere in the New Testament.

C. H. Dodd on the Elder's Admonition
Not to Pray for the Opponents

Upon the ground of the general teaching of the Gospel, and of the New Testament as a whole, we may take leave to accept the affirmation [about prayer] and to ignore the qualification. We cannot think that it can ever be contrary to the will of Him who came to call sinners to repentance that we should pray for even the worst of sinners (who may after all be—ourselves).[7]

Verse 17 treads between two unacceptable attitudes toward sin: one which holds that minor sins are of no consequence and one which holds that there can be no forgiveness for sin. Although sin can be forgiven, the elder is concerned that it never be taken lightly.

The closing verses of the epistle offer three assurances, continuing the theme announced in 5:13. The structure of the conclusion is marked by the repetition of "we know" at the beginning of verses 18, 19, and 20. First, the faithful are assured that the children of God do not sin, because the Son of God protects them. Second, the community is assured that it belongs to God. Third, they are assured that they have the discernment of truth. Assurance, protection, and confession that Jesus is the Son of God are the vital themes of these verses. Finally, because they know the only true God through Jesus Christ, the community is warned to guard itself from the idols that were so common in first-century religion. Anything less than or contrary to the saving knowledge of God in Christ Jesus is merely idolatry.

2 JOHN

Second John is closely related to 1 John and may have been written shortly after the longer letter. The sequence of the letters could be reversed, but the similarities between them are more easily explained as echoes than as expansions. While 1 John was a communication to the Johannine community, 2 John is a true letter, written in contemporary Hellenistic letter form to a sister church in a nearby town.

The Form of 2 John[8]

I. Prescript (vv. 1-3)

A. Address (vv. 1-2)

B. Greetings (v. 3)

II. Body (vv. 4-11)

A. Petition (vv. 4-6)

B. Warning (vv. 7-11)

III. Closing (vv. 12-13)

A. Desire for a personal visit (v. 12)

B. Greetings (v. 13)

The members of that church are warned about the teachings of those who had gone out from the Johannine community. They have departed from the received teachings. They are deceivers and antichrists, and are not even to be greeted. The elder hopes to visit the sister church soon and will tell them more about the situation then.

Greetings (2 John 1-3)

The salutation follows the traditional letter form: A to B, greetings. In 2 John, however, the sender is identified by title rather than by name, the recipient is identified by a metaphorical reference ("an elect sister and her children"), and the greeting is delayed until after an elaborate description of the elder's relationship to the recipients. The elder was probably a member of the community who could claim the authority of its tradition by virtue of his association with those who had preceded him, perhaps even the Beloved Disciple.

Although commentators have occasionally suggested that "the elect lady" was an individual Christian woman, it is now generally agreed that this title refers to a sister church. Her "children" then are fellow Johannine Christians. The elder loves the elect lady's children "in truth" because as fellow Johannine Christians who share the same tradition and the same beliefs they too are "children of God." Coming to know the truth is tantamount to conversion and salvation in Johannine terms. Verse 3 does not express a wish or prayer, as do greetings in other New Testament letters. It is a further assurance of God's blessings to all who belong to the truth. They have grace, mercy, and peace (cf. 1 Tim 1:2 and 2 Tim 1:2). In the greeting, therefore, the elder establishes the basis for his communication to the church: his love for them in truth.

Petition: Love Those Who Walk in Truth (2 John 4-6)

Probably written on a single sheet of papyrus, 2 John follows the conventions of a Hellenistic letter as closely as any other in the New Testament. Following the greeting a thanksgiving was customary. The cause for the elder's rejoicing is not the receipt of a letter from the other church but finding that its members are "walking in the truth." The petition follows immediately after the commendation: "But now, dear lady, I ask you . . ." (v. 5). However, the elder is not asking as though he were writing some new requirement for them. Instead, he is calling them back to a command that they have had "from the beginning" (1 John 2:7-8, 24). The "new command" has become an old one. The Johannine community took the command to love one another as the center—and almost exclusive content—of its community ethic. The elder does not seem to be pleading that a ruptured relationship between the two churches be repaired. On the contrary, he writes as one whose admonitions will be heeded, and he writes to prevent the kind of trouble the defecting group has caused within his own community.

Warning: Do Not Receive Those Who Spread Deception
(2 John 7-11)

The exhortation to unity is followed by a warning against those who are alienated from the community and who will seek to destroy its faith. Verses 7 and 8 state a general warning against such deceivers. Verses 9-11 instruct the church regarding how it may expect to encounter this threat and how it is to respond.

The elect lady is warned, "Many deceivers have gone out into the world." Every word rings with echoes from the Johannine materials (cf. John 6:60; 13:30; 1 John 2:15, 18-19; 4:1). The deceivers do not confess that Jesus Christ is coming, or has come, in flesh. Some interpreters take the first and more literal sense, contending that the error is denial of the return or parousia of the Lord. The similarity between verse 7 and 1 John 4:2, however, has led most to interpret 2 John in the light of the more detailed description of the false teaching in 1 John. Accordingly, the problem is not denial of the parousia (as in 2 Pet 3:3-4) but denial of the Incarnation. The warning seems to concern those who had recently gone out from the Johannine community. Believing in Jesus, the elder claims, means offering the proper confession, affirming not just that Jesus was the Christ (John 20:31) but that he came in flesh, with the attendant recognition of the significance of his ministry and death.

Verse 8 heightens the urgency of the situation. The danger is that the faithful might lose what they had worked for and fail to receive their reward. Most commentators understand these terms as a reference to their faith and their eternal life: the believers have worked for their faith (John 6:27, 29), and eternal life is their reward (John 20:31; 1 John 2:25). Alternatively, the elder may be referring to the growth of the church and the joy that accompanies their fellowship (1 John 1:4).

Verse 9 can be read as a repressive condemnation of any new ideas, but the elder does not intend such a general condemnation. After all, the bold theological developments of the Gospel of John are authorized as the work of the Paraclete. The deceivers neither

277

practice the love command nor hold the confession of Jesus Christ come in flesh. On the other hand, the faithful abide in the teachings of Christ by being faithful to the tradition that has been received by the community. Based on this distinction, the elder advises the sister church that if travelers come who do not convey this teaching, they should not receive them into the house or even greet them. The danger is that those who have gone out from the community may now attempt to spread their teachings in the Johannine churches in neighboring towns. The "house" would be a house church. The refusal of hospitality is obviously an extreme measure, and 3 John shows that it was not altogether effective.

Closing: The Fulfillment of Joy (2 John 12-13)

It was common for letters to close with a review of why the letter was written, the promise of a visit, and a farewell or statement of greetings. Just as the Gospel closes with the statement that Jesus did many other signs (John 20:30; 21:25), so the elder declares that he has many other things to say to them. Some interpreters suggest that the elder was not able to make the promised visit and wrote 1 John instead. On the other hand, the differences in the situation portrayed in the letters make it difficult to consider that the two letters were written to the same audience. The specific problem addressed in 2 John, itinerant teachers who will come bearing a false teaching, is not addressed at all in 1 John.

Truth and love are the cardinal virtues of this family of faith. The ideals of 2 John stand as an enduring challenge for the church, even if one would choose other practical measures than the one it recommends for attaining those ideals.

3 JOHN

Several superlatives distinguish 3 John: it is the shortest letter in the New Testament, the only book of the New Testament that does not mention Jesus or Christ, and the only Johannine writing to mention "the church." Third John is also one of the most enigmatic New Testament writings. Because of the similarities with 2 John, it is commonly assumed that 3 John was written by the same author, "the elder." Third John is addressed to an individual, Gaius, whom the elder praises for his hospitality to itinerant Johannine Christians. The elder solicits Gaius's support against

278

Diotrephes, who high-handedly rejected the elder's emissaries and refused to acknowledge the elder's authority. The elder also commends Demetrius to Gaius as one who is faithful. In conclusion, the elder promises a visit and extends a greeting from "the friends."

The Form of 3 John[9]

I. Prescript (vv. 1-4)

  A. Address (v. 1)

  B. Greetings (vv. 2-4)

II. Body (vv. 5-12)

  A. Petition (vv. 5-8)—praising Gaius for his hospitality

  B. Warning (vv. 9-11)—criticism of Diotrephes for his lack of hospitality

  C. Commendation (vv. 11-12)—of Demetrius for his faithfulness

III. Closing (vv. 13-15)

  A. Desire for a personal visit (vv. 13-14)

  B. Greetings (v. 15)

Beyond these essential facts, the situation assumed in 3 John is difficult to describe with any confidence. Questions abound. Who are each of the three individuals named in the letter, and what was their relationship to one another and to the elder? Answers will be suggested below, but readers should recognize that interpreters are divided on these issues.

Greetings to a Beloved Brother (3 John 1-4)

The letter begins with the same opening as 2 John: "The elder to..., whom I love in truth." The elder is presumably known to Gaius, since he does not need to identify himself by name. This Gaius should probably not be identified with any other New Testament figure with the same name (Acts 19:29; 20:4; Rom 16:23; 1 Cor 1:14). As a fellow Johannine Christian, Gaius is "beloved." To love in truth means to love within the experience and knowledge of God's love revealed by Jesus.

The common Johannine address, "beloved," begins new paragraphs in verses 2, 5, and 11. The traditional wish for good health is followed by an expression of hope that Gaius is "having a good journey" (author translation). Just as in 2 John, the elder expresses great joy that his brother is walking in truth. The "friends" who brought this report are presumably other Johannine Christians who have been traveling among the Johannine churches. They had apparently been well treated by Gaius and returned with the report that he was walking in truth because he practiced love for "the friends." Doctrine is not an issue. Even though there is no evidence of prior contact between the elder and Gaius, he includes Gaius among his own, from whom he expects compliance. With subtle tact, the elder insures that he will have Gaius's continuing cooperation.

Praise for Gaius's Hospitality (3 John 5-8)

The petition section opens with further praise for Gaius. The picture conveyed is that Gaius had been receiving faithful Johannine Christians who traveled to his city, even though he was not closely tied to the network of hospitality practiced within the Johannine churches. There is no evidence that Gaius was the head of a house church. He had simply distinguished himself by his willingness to provide hospitality for fellow Christians. Hospitality was a sign of love (v. 6), which confirmed that Gaius lived in the truth (v. 3). Since verse 3 said that the friends had come with a report regarding Gaius, we may assume that they had testified regarding Gaius before the elder's church. The main purpose of the letter is delicately stated in the commendation in verse 6. Gaius has done well and will continue to do well by receiving itinerant Johannine Christians.

The reference to pagans or nonbelievers in verse 7 cannot mean Gentiles here, since the three names that appear in 3 John are all Gentile names. The issue of division between Jewish and Gentile believers is not a problem here and has not been mentioned anywhere in the Johannine epistles. "The world" will not receive the believers because they bear Jesus' name, so the itinerant friends are totally dependent on the hospitality of fellow believers. The importance of hospitality is further illustrated by the irony that at the same time the elder wrote 3 John, he also wrote 2 John urging the "elect sister" not to extend hospitality to any who did not share their Christology.

Criticism of Diotrephes' Defiance (3 John 9-10)

The reason why the elder appealed to Gaius for hospitality now emerges. He had already written to the church, but his initiatives were blocked by Diotrephes. Various theories have been advanced to explain the relationship between the elder and Diotrephes. Dodd suggested that Diotrephes was either the "first monarchical bishop" in the area or had "usurped quasi-episcopal functions."[10] Käsemann reversed conventional interpretations by contending that Diotrephes was a representative of the orthodox church who had rejected the elder because of his Gnostic heresies.[11] Diotrephes' office is no clearer than that of the elder, however. The restraint of 3 John and the notable absence of the strident language of 1 and 2 John suggest that the differences between the elder and Diotrephes were not doctrinal. When the elder declares that he had written something to the church, it is also unlikely that he is referring to either 1 or 2 John. Those epistles dealt with the problem created by those who had left the church over doctrinal differences; here the elder's concern is hospitality and cooperation for emissaries traveling among the Johannine churches. The elder's complaints regarding Diotrephes are detailed in verses 9 and 10.

Diotrephes

1. "likes to put himself first"
2. does not acknowledge the elder's authority
3. is spreading false charges against the elder and those loyal to him
4. refuses to welcome "the friends"
5. prevents others from doing so and expels them from the church

---

Diotrephes may not have held an appointed or elected office; in that case, he simply assumed authority. Gaius may or may not have been a member of the church controlled by Diotrephes. Ironically, by not receiving the itinerant friends, Diotrephes adopted the same tactic the elder advised in 2 John. If Diotrephes had been aligned with those who held a false Christology, the elder would have branded him a deceiver. Diotrephes may therefore have simply desired to protect the community from dissension, but was unable to distinguish the false teachers from others and hence refused hospitality for all itinerants. Again, Diotrephes may have been able to cast out church members by his own decree, or he may have led the church to do so. By casting members out, Diotrephes disrupted the fellowship *(koinonia)*, violated the promise of Jesus in John 6:37 (anyone "who comes to me I will not cast out" RSV), and practiced instead the policy of the synagogue which had excluded those who confessed Jesus as Messiah (John 9:22, 34-35). From these verses we can see that 3 John reflects the struggles of a community of churches attempting to work out cooperative relationships and yet defend themselves against unacceptable teachings.

Praise for Demetrius's Truthfulness (3 John 11-12)

The last point of the letter is to commend Demetrius to Gaius. The command to imitate is common in Hellenistic ethical materials and in Paul's letters, but does not occur elsewhere in the Johannine writings. All we are told about Demetrius is that (1) everyone testifies for him, (2) the truth itself testifies for him, and (3) "we" testify for him. This threefold testimony forms a strong commendation for Demetrius. Was Demetrius a member of Diotrephes' church who had been excluded from the church for defying Diotrephes? Alternatively, and perhaps more likely, Demetrius was one of the traveling friends who needed hospitality but had not stayed with Gaius before. He may even have been the bearer of the letter. The "we" of verse 12 is probably a reference to the Johannine community that remained loyal to the elder (cf. John 19:35; 21:24). Now Gaius is reminded that he too should acknowledge the elder's authority and receive Demetrius as a brother.

Peace for "the Friends" (3 John 13-15)

The closing verses of 3 John closely parallel the ending of 2 John. The elder had many other things to say but preferred not to put them on paper, hoping soon to be able to speak to Gaius face to face. Verse 15 extends greetings and uses the distinctive term "friends" for members of the Johannine community (see John 15:13-15). Reading the closing verses of each letter in English, one sees their similarities but may miss the fact that in expression they differ in virtually every phrase.

Third John is the counterpart to 2 John. Second John warns a sister church to guard the truth, especially their belief in the Incarnation. Third John appeals for support for faithful friends traveling to spread the gospel. The appeal was necessary because Diotrephes was refusing to extend hospitality to the friends sent by the elder. Deceivers and friends were apparently using the same methods both for propagating their beliefs and for excluding those with whom they disagreed. The difference between deceivers and friends, according to all three epistles, is that the faithful believers hold to the truth that has been conveyed to them, they obey Jesus' commands, and they practice love for one another. By doing so, they show that they are "children of God."

PART THREE

RESPONDING
TO THE
JOHANNINE
WRITINGS

CHAPTER 10

THE GOSPEL OF JOHN AS A DOCUMENT OF FAITH

The Gospel of John has always been one of the most influential documents of the Christian faith. It has spoken to people of different cultures and ages, transcending cultural barriers while communicating the essence of the Christian gospel. The increasing pluralization of our culture, however, and the heightened ethical sensitivities that accompany these changes force us to examine a question seldom discussed in either the university or the church: Can the Gospel of John continue to function for Christians as a document of faith in the increasing pluralism of American culture? What problems or resources does it present to believers who live in a pluralistic culture?

The question is framed deliberately. It concerns the function of the Gospel of John for Christians. A *document of faith* is a text that shapes the character and content of one's religious beliefs. Traditionally, Christians (and Protestants in particular) have confessed that the scriptures are the sole sufficient guide in matters of faith and practice. In other words, we say that the scriptures are our authority when it comes to defining what we believe and how we are going to live. The question, therefore, juxtaposes the authority of the Gospel of John with the increasing pluralism of American culture. As the culture in which we live becomes increasingly pluralistic, religious communities are forced to confront issues posed by the beliefs, experiences, values, and religious traditions of individuals from widely different social, ethnic, racial, and religious backgrounds. To rephrase the question, to what kind of practice of faith does the Gospel of John lead believers, and is this practice acceptable as a response to the challenges of a pluralistic culture? Before we attempt to fashion a response, let us briefly remind ourselves of two challenges to the use of the Gospel of John as a document of faith in earlier eras.

THE THEOLOGICAL CHALLENGE

In the second century, questions were raised about the *theological orthodoxy* of the Gospel. The Gospel of John first appeared as a document of faith among second-century Gnostics. One Gnostic school in Rome took the name of Valentinus, who lived between A.D. 100 and 175 and founded a school with the purpose of raising Christian theology "to the level of pagan philosophical studies."[1] We cannot be sure that Valentinus knew the Gospel of John, but it is clear that his followers used it. Ptolemy, one of Valentinus's early students, wrote a commentary on the prologue of John, and Heracleon, another Valentinian, wrote the first commentary on the Gospel about A.D. 170. Sketchy as the evidence is, it shows that while the Johannine writings were used only tentatively by the Church Fathers before Irenaeus (about 180), the Gospel was treated as an authoritative writing by the Valentinian school in Rome.[2]

Several sources between A.D. 150 and 180 confirm that John was widely known, but the status of the fourfold Gospel was still fluid: Marcion accepted only an edited version of Luke, the Valentinians added the Gospel of Truth, and Tatian wove the four Gospels into one continuous account.

When others began to use the Gospel of John, Gaius, a presbyter and noted orthodox scholar at Rome, rejected the Gospel and denied that it was written by an apostle. Gaius was an opponent of the Montanists, an enthusiastic group in Asia Minor who based their claims regarding the Spirit on John. While his basic concerns seem to have been theological, Gaius sought to discredit John by carefully noting its historical discrepancies and the places where it contradicted the synoptic Gospels. Gaius is significant because he shows that the authority of John was not so firmly established that it could not be challenged by one of the leaders of the church. The form of his argument is also telling: he sought to discredit the Gospel of John by showing that it contradicted the synoptic Gospels, which by implication served as the standard by which a gospel could be judged.[3]

Moreover, if the Muratorian Canon is to be traced to Rome during this same period (A.D. 180–200), it can be seen as a defense of the authority of the Gospel of John in a social context in which it had been called into question. Specifically, it reports that the other disciples urged John to write his Gospel. Together they fasted for three days, and it was revealed to Andrew that all of the disciples were to go over the Gospel, but John should write everything down in his own name.[4]

Irenaeus, more than any other figure, mounted a defense of the Gospel of John as an orthodox gospel and fashioned a powerful anti-gnostic theological synthesis. He was also the first writer to offer a defense of the apostolic authorship of the Gospel of John, the first to claim that it was written in Ephesus, and the first to report that the apostle John lived to an old age in Ephesus. A major element in Irenaeus's defense of the Gospel was his appeal to a chain of tradition reaching back to the apostle John (see above, chapter 2). Irenaeus reports that he had heard Polycarp, the bishop of Smyrna, who was martyred about A.D. 156. Irenaeus claims that Polycarp was "instructed by the apostles" and that Irenaeus himself, in his youth, had heard Polycarp. Even so, the credibility of Irenaeus's testimony has been sharply debated.[5]

Given the uncertainty of the evidence, exaggerated claims—either that John was used only by the Valentinians and Montanists before Irenaeus or that the authority of the Gospel was clearly established before Irenaeus—are out of place. Nevertheless, with Irenaeus the battle for the fourfold Gospel was won. The authority of the Gospel of John as scripture was never again in question.

THE HISTORICAL CHALLENGE

The second challenge to the use of the Gospel of John as a document of faith was signaled by the publication in 1820 of a work by Karl Gottlieb Bretschneider and its influence on David Friedrich Strauss's *The Life of Jesus Critically Examined* (first published in 1835). This time the issue concerned primarily the Johannine discourses and their implications for the messianic consciousness of Jesus. In the Johannine discourses, Jesus speaks not about the kingdom of God but about his own identity as the Son of God and his role as the revealer of the Father. More broadly, the question was to what extent the Gospel of John gives us a reliable portrait of Jesus. Is it the historical memory of the apostle John or the theological construction of a later writer? The challenge to John's historical accuracy was again tied to comparisons between the Synoptics and John.

Karl Gottlieb Bretschneider (1820)

It is accordingly quite impossible that both the Jesus of the [first] three Gospels and that of the Fourth can at the same time be historically true, since there is the greatest difference between them, not only in the manner of discourse but also in the argumentation and the behavior of the two; it is also quite incredible that the first evangelists invented Jesus' practices, teachings, and method of instruction; but it is quite believable that the author of the Fourth Gospel could have created his Jesus.[6]

Prior to Strauss, the Gospel of John had been the favorite of post-Enlightenment German theologians, including Friedrich Schleiermacher, who constructed his argument that Jesus is the ideal archetype from the Gospel of John. For Schleiermacher, Jesus was the model of human consciousness in his awareness of being dependent on God. Although Strauss waffled on his judgments regarding the Gospel of John in the third edition of his work, he mounted arguments against the credibility of the Fourth Gospel that profoundly shaped subsequent scholarship. Repeatedly, Strauss subjects the Johannine materials to detailed comparisons with the Synoptic accounts. Whereas in the Synoptics Jesus speaks in aphorisms and parables, in John he offers extended discourses which employ an entirely different style and vocabulary. The discourses of Jesus in John resemble the idiom of the evangelist (or the elder of the Johannine epistles), not the style of the parabler of the synoptic gospels.[7] The synoptic sayings are brief, pithy, and memorable, but it is inconceivable that anyone should have remembered the long and repetitious Johannine discourses word for word.[8] Strauss concludes, "We therefore hold it to be established, that the discourses of Jesus in John's gospel are mainly free compositions of the Evangelist."[9]

The challenges of Bretschneider and Strauss did not lead to a reconsideration of the Gospel's canonical status, but they set the stage for a century and a half of debate over whether John should be read as history or theology. Although the debate is by no means settled, today most interpreters recognize that John is both history and theology: the fourth evangelist used historical traditions while composing the Gospel with considerable freedom and creativity.

THE ETHICAL CHALLENGE

For many contemporary believers, however, the battles of the past no longer seem relevant. Generations of theologians have shown that whatever the circumstances of the composition or early use of the Gospel of John, its thought complements and extends the theology and Christology of the rest of the New Testament. Indeed, many would say that it forms the pinnacle of theological reflection in the New Testament. Neither do the challenges to the Gospel's historical reliability form the center of concern for many today. In place of the theological and historical challenges of earlier eras, a series of new concerns has arisen. These concerns are not primarily theological or historical but ethical: (1) Is the Gospel of John anti-Jewish? (2) Does the Gospel have anything to say to the marginalized and the oppressed? and (3) How should we interpret the theological exclusivism of the Gospel in a pluralistic culture? We will treat each of these questions individually.

Anti-Judaism in the Gospel of John

My own early responses to the charges that John is anti-Jewish or anti-Semitic were probably not unlike those of many others for whom the Gospel is a treasured book of scripture. I readily turned to counterarguments that John does not teach hatred of Jews: (1) it reflects a historical period in which there was tension within the synagogue and Jews and Christians were not clearly distinct; (2) Jesus and the disciples were all Jews, and the first Christians were Jews; and (3) the Gospel of John opposes not Jewishness but the response of unbelief. In John, therefore, the Jews are simply representatives of unbelief. I still believe these points are correct, but they no longer constitute an adequate response.

Jewish friends and scholars have persuaded me that such responses to the issue do not take sufficiently seriously the Gospel's role in fostering anti-Jewish sentiment in Christian communities. We may be able to demonstrate historically or exegetically that the Gospel of John does not condemn Jews as a people, but what are we to do with the statements that vilify the Jews, or to be precise the *Ioudaioi,* in John?

The Gospel of John contains some of the most hostile, anti-Jewish statements in the Christian scriptures. So sharp is the contrast between Jesus' exhortations to his followers to love one another and the hostile references to "the Jews," that Kaufmann Kohler, an eminent Jewish scholar at the turn of the century, commented that John is "a gospel of Christian love and Jew hatred."[10]

A Sample of the Anti-Jewish Statements in John[11]

"But I know that you [Jews] do not have the love of God in you." (5:42)

"Then Jesus said to the Jews who had believed in him, ... 'You look for an opportunity to kill me, because there is no place in you for my word. I declare what I have seen in the Father's presence; as for you, you should do what you have heard from the Father ... You are from your father the devil, and you choose to do your father's desires. He was a murderer from the beginning and does not stand in the truth, because there is no truth in him. When he lies, he speaks according to his own nature, for he is a liar and the father of lies.... Whoever is from God hears the words of God. The reason you do not hear them is that you are not from God.'" (8:31, 37-38, 44-47)

In the farewell discourse, Jesus warns the disciples: "They [the Jews] will put you out of the synagogues. Indeed, an hour is coming when those who kill you will think that by doing so they are offering worship to God. And they will do this because they have not known the Father or me." (16:2-3).

The effect of these and other passages, when they are read as part of the scriptures of the church, has often been to incite anti-Jewish feelings in Christian communities. In eastern Europe in particular Jews feared the celebration of Easter because they knew that it frequently led to pogroms or organized massacres of Jews.

It is now widely accepted that the Gospel of John reflects a period of sharp controversy with the synagogue during the time the Gospel was written. John has therefore interpreted Jesus' debates with the religious authorities in the light of the experience of his own community. In this process, references to scribes, chief priests, and in places even the Pharisees have given way to a polemic against "the Jews."[12] Even if the Greek term *hoi Ioudaioi* once denoted Judeans or the Jewish authorities, the Gospel of John generalized and stereotyped those who rejected Jesus by its use of this term and elevated the bitterness and hostility of the polemic to a new level.[13] Perhaps even more important, the Fourth Gospel is the first document to draw a connection between the authorities who condemned Jesus and the Jews known to the Christian community at a later time. By means of this transfer of hostility, effected by merging events in the ministry of Jesus with the conflict with the synagogue in the time of the evangelist, the Gospel allowed and perhaps even encouraged Christians to read the Gospel in an anti-Semitic fashion.

Christians after the Holocaust—and indeed in a time of resurgence of "ethnic cleansing"—can no longer ignore the role of anti-Jewish statements in John and elsewhere in the New Testament in inciting or justifying prejudice and violence against Jews. We may argue that in its historical context the Gospel of John cannot have been anti-Semitic. Nevertheless, since the influential work of Rosemary Radford Ruether,[14] Christian scholars have begun to recognize that the Gospel rejects Judaism, contends that its festivals and observances have been replaced, and uses the generalizing term *hoi Ioudaioi* to identify those who rejected God's revelation and persecuted Jesus and his followers. We must therefore reckon with the legacy of the Gospel and its effects on those of us who read it as Scripture. Is it possible for Christians who are sensitive to these issues to interpret the Gospel in a way that does not foster antipathy and violence toward Jews, or should the Gospel be set aside as a document of faith?

Constructive proposals have taken various forms. Christian

interpreters may begin to sensitize others to the dangers of John's anti-Jewish references and the difficulties of translating the term *hoi Ioudaioi* in John. Some have called for limiting the use of certain passages in John by excluding them from the common lectionary used by many churches. Others have proposed altering the translations of the Gospel on the logic that if it did not originally condemn Jews as Jews then modern translations should not support or even allow for such an interpretation of the Gospel.[15] Most would agree, however, that if translations are altered, it should be because the text demands it, not because translators are seeking to change or diminish the anti-Jewish tone of the Gospel.

The Greek term *hoi Ioudaioi* can mean "the Jews," as it is usually translated, but it can also mean "the Judeans." In the Gospel of John the group designated by this term appears to be variously Judeans (as opposed to Galileans or Samaritans), the Judean leaders (where it is used interchangeably with "the Pharisees"), or—less frequently—Jews as opposed to Gentiles. The meaning of the term *Ioudaioi*, which is used 71 times in the Gospel, must therefore be determined by the context of each occurrence. There are places in John where the term can hardly mean "the Jews." A different translation would actually convey the sense of the text more accurately. For example, although the crowd in Jerusalem at the festival of Booths must have been predominantly Jewish, they still fear the *Ioudaioi*. By translating *hoi Ioudaioi* as "the Jews" in this context, the NRSV and other translations produce a reading that makes little sense.

John 7:11-13, NRSV

The Jews *[hoi Ioudaioi]* were looking for him at the festival and saying, "Where is he?" And there was considerable complaining about him among the crowds. While some were saying, "He is a good man," others were saying, "No, he is deceiving the crowd." Yet no one would speak openly about him for fear of the Jews *[hoi Ioudaioi]*.

Here it is clear that *hoi Ioudaioi* refers to a more limited group opposed to Jesus, either certain Judean Jews or the religious authorities. The same difficulties appear elsewhere in the Gospel.

Improving translations by rendering each reference to *hoi*

Ioudaioi contextually may contribute to eradicating anti-Jewish readings of John, but if the Gospel is to continue to have a viable place in shaping Christian faith and practice, biblical scholars and Christian theologians are going to have to continue aggressively promoting awareness of John's anti-Judaism. John's circumscribed love command—that you love one another, that is, fellow Christians—is no longer adequate. To paraphrase Matthew rather ironically, "Do not the Gentiles do the same?" (Matt 5:47). The anti-Judaism of the Gospel of John must be repudiated, and hard questions must be addressed regarding its theological exclusivism, but more on this shortly.[16]

The Marginalized and the Oppressed in the Gospel of John

The second major challenge to the Gospel of John is whether it has anything to say to the marginalized and the oppressed. Various groups have raised this question. What does the Gospel say to women who are striving for a place in the church as well as a voice in society at large? What does it offer the African American who is searching for a story and a heritage for those whose ancestors were violently displaced and forced into slavery—and who themselves have been oppressed by racism? What does the Fourth Gospel offer to Hispanics, to Asian Americans, and—lest we forget—to the Native Americans we displaced from their lands?

Unfortunately, biblical scholarship at least until recently has been dominated almost exclusively by white, male Europeans and Euro-Americans. The voices of those who have been culturally marginalized have scarcely been heard. The methods of critical biblical scholarship were developed and defined by European scholars, and the concerns they brought to the text were defined by their own academic, ecclesiastical, and cultural contexts. Women, African Americans, and Third World readers rightly point out that the authority of the Bible has been wielded in the interests of the status quo, the powerful, and the educated. As a result, even our Bible dictionaries, encyclopedias, and commentaries are not free from hermeneutical bias.

The interpreter must exercise a "hermeneutics of suspicion": Whose interests are being served by this or that interpretation, and whose voice is being suppressed? What do we communicate when we treat the blind man in John 9 and scarcely note that he was a beggar, or when we interpret John 4 and pay little attention to the social location of a Samaritan woman? On the other hand, the patriarchal bias of the biblical stories is often taken as normative for society today.

Along the margins, however, we are beginning to hear the call for a reading of the Bible that grows out of the struggle of various groups for freedom, economic equality, and the integrity of their own voice.

Itumeleng J. Mosala, a Black South African

"The particularity of the black struggle in its different forms and phases must provide the epistemological lenses with which the Bible is read. Only such a position seems to us to represent a theoretical break with dominant biblical hermeneutics. Anything less is a tinkering with what in fact must be destroyed."[17]

Elsa Tamez, a Latin American Woman

"It is precisely the Gospel's spirit of justice and freedom that neutralizes antifemale texts. A reading of the Bible that attempts to be faithful to the word of the Lord will achieve that goal best when it is done in a way that reflects the liberating meaning of the Gospel, even when sometimes fidelity to the Gospel forces the reader to distance herself or himself from the text. Therefore, a time has come to acknowledge that those biblical texts that reflect patriarchal culture and proclaim women's inferiority and their submission to men are not normative.... The rationale behind this statement is essentially the same as that offered by the Scriptures: the proclamation of the gospel of Jesus calls us to life and announces the coming of the kingdom of justice."[18]

Gustavo Gutierrez, on the Struggles of the Poor

"Prophetic language makes it possible to draw near to a God who has a predilection for the poor precisely because divine love refuses to be confined by the categories of human justice. God has a preferential love for the poor not because they are necessarily better than others, morally or religiously, but simply because they are poor and living in an inhuman situation that is contrary to God's will."[19]

The examples could be multiplied, but these eloquent voices suffice. The influence of the perspective, the culture, and the social location of the interpreter is being recognized. No text, and no interpretation, is ever completely unbiased or neutral. Some interests are advocated, privileged, or defended, while others are denied or subjugated. The implications of this shift in critical theory are just beginning to be considered. If no interpretation can claim to be neutral, and if the quest for scholarly objectivity and detachment has often functioned as an excuse for failure to recognize the ethical, political, or social implications of our work, then the challenge of increased pluralism for interpreters of the Gospel is to be deliberate about the ethics of our interpretations. The quest for objectivity and detachment should now be replaced by a quest for an ethics of interpretation that arises out of the highest ideals of the Bible and the Christian tradition, an ethics that is adequate to guide the interpretive community as it seeks to live out these ideals in a pluralistic culture.

As a step in this direction, interpreters are beginning to take seriously what may be called the "p" codes within the text: power, privilege, property, poverty, and persecution. Who is privileged and who is oppressed, and how are each treated in the text? The issues of power and social stratification—land, education, social class, religious obligation, and work—often guide us to readings of the text that respond to its ethical implications. In what ways does the text undermine prevailing power relationships: male—female, master—servant, rich—poor, patron—client, citizen—alien? Whose interests are protected or advanced by our reading of the text? Does it protect the status quo or empower the dispossessed?

This challenge calls us to examine our interpretations as well as the texts we seek to interpret. What do they have to say to the poor and the marginalized? Do they perpetuate the interests of the privileged or liberate the oppressed? And where must they be read with a hermeneutics of suspicion, looking in the gaps and silences for what is not said?

Various interpreters are already leading the way. Three small books illustrate that John need not be read from the perspective of the empowered. Richard J. Cassidy states his thesis clearly at the outset: "In depicting Jesus' identity and mission within his Gospel, the evangelist John was concerned to present elements and themes that were especially significant for Christian readers facing Roman imperial claims and for any who faced Roman persecution."[20] Such a perspective allows Cassidy to read the Gospel's claims for the sovereignty of Jesus, the Roman trial, the farewell discourses, and John 20–21 in light of how they would have been understood by persecuted communities under Roman rule.

David Rensberger notes that John seems to be the least likely of the Gospels to support a theology of liberation because of its overriding focus on Christology. Nevertheless, Rensberger cautiously notes that although John does not offer a political program, and the situation of its first readers was different in significant respects from that of oppressed communities today, the Gospel of John is "the product of an oppressed community."[21] John 15:18, 20*b;* 16:2*b* show that the Johannine Christians at least saw themselves as oppressed: "If the world hates you, be aware that it hated me before it hated you.... If they persecuted me, they will persecute you.... Indeed, an hour is coming when those who kill you will think that by doing so they are offering worship to God."[22]

Rensberger then interprets Nicodemus as one faced with the decision whether to identify publicly with the oppressed, marginal Christian community: "The choice that faced Nicodemus was whether or not to side, no longer in private but openly, with a specific oppressed group in his society—indeed, with those whom the members of his own rank and class, the people whose company he truly preferred, were oppressing.... In essence, Nicodemus is to be found wherever one whose life is secure must face those whose life is insecure, or who struggle in the cause of God, and decide to say, 'I am one of them.' "[23] When read in this light, John's passion narrative and ethic of love also speak prophetically to contemporary readers who are sensitive to the situation of the oppressed.[24]

In a little book entitled *Jesus and the Marginalized in John's Gospel,* Robert J. Karris calls attention to the neglect of this subject in Johannine studies.[25] Successive chapters deal with the poor, those who are ignorant of the Law, the physically afflicted, geographically marginalized people, and women in John's Gospel. Those in John 7:49 who do not know the law are interpreted on the basis of rabbinic materials as "people of the land" who may not necessarily have been poor but who were marginalized by the religious authorities because they did not know the Law. The lame man in John 5:1-15 and the blind beggar in John 9 are treated as representatives of the "people of the land" who were also physically afflicted. The Galilean *basilikos* in John 4:46-54 and the Samaritans represent those who were geographically marginalized. In a helpful excursus, Karris argues that a military context is absent in John 4:46-54, leading to the conclusion that in this context *basilikos* designates a "Jewish royal official, directly subject to 'King' Herod Antipas."[26] As a Galilean, he was held in low regard by the Judean rabbis. Because of their marginalized status in antiquity, women often exerted influence through religious communities and activities. Gathering up these threads in the concluding chapter, Karris contends—building on the widely held thesis that the Johannine community was experiencing conflict with the Jewish authorities—that the Jewish authorities opposed the community because it gathered in the poor, Galileans and Samaritans, the physically afflicted, those ignorant of the Law, and women. The result of such compromising of the traditional standards of election was that the Johannine Christians were drummed out of the synagogue. The Gospel consequently encourages believers to remember that the Messiah to the marginalized was himself marginalized.[27]

In sum, Cassidy, Rensberger, and Karris have each contributed to sensitizing readers of the Gospel to its concern for the persecuted and those marginalized in various ways by society and religion. When read in this light, the Gospel challenges contemporary believers to oppose prevailing structures and social patterns that oppress the marginalized.

Theological Exclusivism in the Gospel of John

The third sign of the emerging challenge to the use of John as a document of faith is expressed in the question: How should we interpret the theological exclusivism of the Gospel in a pluralistic culture?

The Gospel of John is not alone in the New Testament in asserting that salvation is attained only through confession of Jesus as Lord, but the Gospel's pronouncements are a central item on the agenda of current interfaith dialogues. While the following passages articulate the core of faith for some, they pose an insurmountable obstacle to faith for others.

Theologically Exclusive Claims in John

"I am the way, and the truth, and the life. No one comes to the Father except through me." (John 14:6)

"No one can come to me unless drawn by the Father who sent me.... Everyone who has heard and learned from the Father comes to me.... Unless you eat the flesh of the Son of Man and drink his blood, you have no life in you." (John 6:44, 45, 53)

"Whoever does not abide in me is thrown away like a branch and withers; such branches are gathered, thrown into the fire, and burned." (John 15:6)

These verses raise problematic issues of exclusivism. Does the Gospel of John offer the Christian reader any basis for dialogue with persons from other religious traditions, or does it demand that there is no hope of salvation apart from confession of the Lordship of Jesus?

Global questions are sometimes best approached through the struggles of a particular individual. I have learned a great deal about the issues of exclusivism and pluralism from a Japanese Christian. Dickson Kazuo Yagi has written of his struggle to shape what he terms a "yellow theology."[28] Yagi is a third generation Japanese-American convert from a Shingon Buddhist home. For more than twenty years he has taught Christian theology and world religions at Seinan Gakuin University in Japan. His grandfather prayed daily for the family before his Buddha altar. On his death bed, the grandfather asked Yagi if he would pray for the family. At first the grandfather wanted to pass on his altar, but he realized that his grandchildren would know little of the Japanese language and nothing of Buddhism. So, he asked Yagi to pray for the family, saying "Of course, you are not a Buddhist, but a Christian minister. Yet surely the Buddhas would understand the cultural problem and accept your Christian prayers."[29] And so Yagi asks, "Will the God of Abraham, Isaac, Jacob, and Jesus Christ also understand ... the collision of the absoluteness of the Christian Cross and the cultural relativity of our multi-religious modern world"?[30]

The difficulty, he observes, is that Christianity is a gospel with two centers: faith (epitomized by Paul) and love (epitomized by

John). A gospel with two centers results in two questions that cannot be answered.

Dickson Kazuo Yagi

"The first is what can we say about those who believe in Jesus Christ but do not love? The second is what can we say about those who do not believe in Jesus Christ and yet love their neighbor? Because there are two centers to the gospel, not one, these two questions are unanswerable. Just as Christians who do not love are solidly rejected by one center, non-Christians who do love are affirmed by the other center."[31]

Yellow theology rejects a gospel with only one center. The most serious problem faced by Christianity in Asia is ancestor worship. As a response to the abuse of indulgences, the Reformation cut all ties to the dead, committing them to the hands of God. But because the dead are honored daily in Asian homes, the Asian Christian can hardly abandon hope for those who die without confessing Christ. After all, only .08 percent of the population is Christian.[32] Questioned about his hope of seeing his grandfather after death, the Japanese Christian responded, "If I got to heaven, though, and could not find him, I would immediately go to be with him wherever he was—be it hell or purgatory. Why should I go to heaven to be with white folks while my people are burning in hell?"[33] Yagi therefore calls on whites and blacks in the West to recognize the "gravitational pull" of this issue on Asian Christians as they fashion a yellow theology that expresses an authentic biblical faith. One of the avenues to such a theology that Yagi considers is that of the Cosmic Christ in John 1:9. According to John 1:9, Christ is the true light that enlightens every man.

The Gospel's opening gambit is to describe the work of the Logos by drawing from the Wisdom tradition.[34] As Wisdom, the Logos was the creative agent. Wisdom manifests God's design and power in all the creation. As John N. Jonsson observes in "Wisdom: The Threshold of God in Human Existence": "The universal phenomenon of wisdom, impregnated within the human consciousness across the world, highlights how pathetically inappropriate all our exclusivist religious belief systems are in the light of the stern realities and anomalies of our contemporary pluralistic world."[35] The exclusivist claims of the Fourth Gospel, such as those cited above, must therefore be understood in the context of the opening claim that the revelation that came through Jesus Christ is the same as that which is universally present in the Logos.

John N. Jonsson

"Wisdom belongs to the diversity of human pluralism, necessitating a pluralism in theological expression in the prolongation of the mystery of the incarnation, i.e. God becoming a human being absorbed into the cultures of all people of the world. Here there is a paradox in faith between the particularity of the Jesus of Nazareth and the universality of the cosmic Christ, the 'logos' of God."[36]

Because the Gospel presents Jesus as the Incarnation who made known the work of the Logos from the creation and through all time, it undercuts the triumphalism of claims that Christendom has a monopoly on the revelation of God. The further implication is that what one says about the nature of revelation has direct implications for salvation through the work of the Logos. Just as the Logos brought a saving knowledge of God to Abraham, Moses, and Isaiah, so the Logos continues to speak to persons through other religious traditions as part of God's effort to draw all people to a knowledge of God. The cosmic understanding of wisdom personalized in Yahweh, the one God, is the antecedent on which John's Logos Christology rests. One of the cruxes in the interpretation of the prologue of John is whether verses 9-13 refer to the work of the preexistent Logos or to the period of the Incarnation. Obviously, if this section describes the former, it further clarifies that the work of the preexistent Logos was not only creative but redemptive. Accordingly, John's Logos Christology allows Christians to affirm that adherents of other religious traditions may come to know God through the work of the Cosmic Christ.

If Christian theologians have hesitated to draw the implications of these biblical perspectives on revelation, it is due in part to understandings of salvation that are too narrow, inflexible, and legalistic. Permit me a personal reference. After a full career as a missionary and later professor of missions and world religions, my father's last published statement was a brief expository article in which he dealt with the problem of exclusivism by interpreting Acts 4:12. He translated the verse quite literally, as follows: "and there is not in any other one salvation. For neither is there another (kind) of name under heaven given among men in whom it is necessary for us to be saved."[37] His comment calls for a reconsideration of the meaning of language about "being saved."

Hugo H. Culpepper

"The understanding of this last word, 'saved,' is crucial to the exposition of this verse. If we follow the popular understanding of salvation as being something objective which we can 'have' or 'not have,' i.e. as being an objective status, we miss the mark. It becomes legalistic, juridical, judicial. It has nothing of the personal, of what we are in ourselves, or of the relational, of how we relate to God and other human beings. If God is the ultimate reality, our vocation is to be such as is in harmony with him."[38]

His concluding affirmation is a reflection of his own understanding of the work of Christ as the Logos: "If there is a God beyond all gods, surely he uses every culture, all the differing religious traditions, even all history in seeking to get through to as many people as possible and bring them voluntarily into relationship with himself!"[39]

Yagi's quest for a yellow theology, John Jonsson's reflections on the significance of Wisdom, and my father's reflections on persons of faith from other religious traditions have sensitized me to both the difficulties and the values of taking the Gospel of John as a document of faith—both for Asian Christians and for American Christians in our increasingly pluralistic society.

A HERMENEUTICS OF ETHICAL ACCOUNTABILITY

The question we began with was: Can the Gospel of John continue to function for Christians as a document of faith in the increasing pluralism of American culture? In large measure the answer to that question depends on how we interpret the Gospel. Whereas previous challenges to the use of the Gospel as a document of faith were based on theological and historical concerns, we are witnessing the emergence of a third challenge based on what we might characterize as ethical concerns. I would readily admit that there were social and ethical differences between interpreters in both the second century and the nineteenth century. The questions that face us now, however, are clearly more ethically defined than previous challenges: How should those of us who derive our religious teachings from the Gospel of John respond to Jews who are concerned that the Gospel is anti-Jewish, to those who have been marginalized and oppressed by the church and by Christians in society, and to persons of other religious traditions? These questions concern the very character of religious faith.

They also raise new sensitivities and concerns for those who interpret the Gospel. The position toward which I have been moving assumes that the role of the Gospel of John as a document of faith will depend on the hermeneutics of the ecclesiastical and scholarly reading communities: it depends on how we interpret the Gospel. One could argue that the two challenges we have discussed from earlier eras contributed to the definition of new methods of interpretation—the first to the allegorical method and the second to historical criticism. Our quest then is for critical methods—now much more self-consciously hermeneutical—that will be adequate to the challenge of reading the Gospel in an increasingly pluralistic culture.

The following principles may be useful in our common search for more ethically sensitive responses to the Gospel of John:

1. For the sake of clarity, it is important to question interpretations that claim to be objective, neutral, or nonpartisan and to seek to be clear about the assumptions, commitments, and interests that guide our own work as interpreters.

2. One of the issues to be discussed is whether the biblical texts are themselves inherently liberationist or oppressive and how to treat those texts that are oppressive.[40] Interpretation always calls for the interpreter to identify the elements of the text that shape his or her interpretation and show how those facets of the text undermine antithetical or incongruous elements of the text. Part of the solution, therefore, may be for interpreters to allow the

voices of the oppressed and excluded to raise new sensitivities and concerns.

3. Because the challenge we face is in many respects an ethical one, our reading of the Gospel must be informed not only by theological tradition and historical criticism but also by concern for the effects and ethical implications of our interpretation. Only by asking whether our interpretation of the Gospel serves to put an end to violence against Jews and other ethnic minorities, to give voice and power to the marginalized and oppressed, and to bring understanding and acceptance between persons of different religious traditions can we expect that our interpretation will be relevant to the challenges of our culture.

Sensitized to the challenges of our pluralistic culture—indeed, of our world—the interpreter may find that another part of the solution comes from the Gospel itself. That is, he or she may be able to identify facets of the text that resonate with our quest for what we may call *a hermeneutics of ethical accountability*. For example, the Fourth Gospel's declaration of God's boundless love for the world undermines its polemic against "the Jews." Its concern that the community of faith may be one undermines social and ethnic barriers between believers, and its affirmation that the work of the Logos cannot be confined to the period of the Incarnation opens the way for affirming the experiences and heritages of persons of faith in other religious traditions.

Christian interpreters still have much to do. Accountability requires us to seek interpretations that are both faithful to the text and ethically responsible. Only by asking whether our interpretation of the Gospel serves to put an end to violence against Jews and other ethnic minorities, to empower the marginalized and oppressed, and to bring understanding between persons of different religious traditions can we expect that our interpretations will stand the test of accountability when they are read with a "hermeneutics of suspicion."

NOTES

1. INTRODUCTION TO THE JOHANNINE LITERATURE

1. I am indebted to Norman Petersen for this way of interpreting the difference between the story lines of John and the Synoptics.

2. Ernst Käsemann, *The Testament of Jesus: A Study of the Gospel of John in the Light of Chapter 17*, trans. Gerhard Krodel (Philadelphia: Fortress, 1968), 27, 66, 75.

3. D. Moody Smith, *John Among the Gospels: The Relationship in Twentieth-Century Research* (Minneapolis: Fortress, 1992), 6.

4. Percival Gardner-Smith, *Saint John and the Synoptic Gospels* (Cambridge: Cambridge University Press, 1938).

2. THE COMPOSITION OF THE JOHANNINE WRITINGS

1. For a full discussion of these verses, see R. Alan Culpepper, *John, the Son of Zebedee: The Life of a Legend* (Columbia: University of South Carolina Press, 1994), 56-72.

2. See ibid., 72-85.

3. B. F. Westcott, *The Gospel According to St. John* (1882; reprint, Grand Rapids: Wm. B. Eerdmans, 1971), v-xxv.

4. John A. T. Robinson, "The New Look on the Fourth Gospel" (a paper delivered to the Oxford Conference on 'The Four Gospels' in 1957), *Studia Evangelica, Texte und Untersuchungen* 73 (Berlin, 1959), 338-50; reprinted in *Twelve New Testament Studies*, Studies in Biblical Theology 34 (London: SCM, 1962), 94-106.

5. Julius Wellhausen, *Das Evangelium Johannes* (Berlin: G. Reimer, 1908), 5.

6. Eduard Schwartz, "Aporien im vierten Evangelium," *Nachrichten der Gesellschaft der Wissenschaften in Göttingen* (1908): 115-48, 149-88, 497-560.

7. Emanuel Hirsch, *Das vierte Evangelium in seiner ursprunglichen Gestalt verdeutscht und erklärt* (Tübingen: J. C. B. Mohr, 1936).

8. D. Moody Smith, *The Composition and Order of the Fourth Gospel: Bultmann's Literary Theory* (New Haven: Yale University Press, 1965).

9. Eugen Ruckstuhl, *Die literarische Einheit des Johannesevangeliums* (Fribourg: Paulusverlag, 1951); idem, "Johannine Language and Style: The Question of Their Unity," in *L'Evanglie de Jean: Sources, rédaction, théologie,* ed. M. de Jonge, Bibliotheca ephemeridum theologicarum lovaniensium, 44 (Louvain: Louvain University Press, 1977), 125-47; and Eduard Schweizer, *Ego Eimi: Die religionsgeschichtliche Herkunft und theologische Bedeutung der johanneischen Bildreden, zugleich ein Beitrag zur Quellenfrage des vierten Evangeliums,* FRLANT, n.s. 38 (Göttingen: Vandenhoeck & Ruprecht, 1965).

10. Robert T. Fortna, *The Gospel of Signs: A Reconstruction of the Narrative Source Underlying the Fourth Gospel,* SNTS Monograph Series, 11 (Cambridge: Cambridge University Press, 1970); idem, *The Fourth Gospel and Its Predecessor: From Narrative Source to Present Gospel* (Philadelphia: Fortress, 1988). See also Urban C. von Wahlde, *The Earliest Version of John's Gospel* (Wilmington, DE: Michael Glazier, 1989).

11. Raymond E. Brown, T*he Gospel According to John (I-XII),* Anchor Bible, vol. 29 (Garden City, NY: Doubleday, 1966), xxxiv-xxxix.

3. THE GOSPEL AND LETTERS AS THE LITERATURE OF A COMMUNITY

1. J. Louis Martyn, *History and Theology in the Fourth Gospel,* rev. ed. (Nashville: Abingdon, 1979).

2. Emil Schürer, *The History of the Jewish People in the Age of Jesus Christ (175 B.C.–A.D. 135),* rev. and ed. Geza Vermes, Fergus Millar, and Matthew Black (Edinburgh: T. & T. Clark, 1979), 2:461.

3. See further John Ashton, "The Identity and Function of the *Ioudaioi* in the Fourth Gospel," *Novum Testamentum* 27 (1985): 40-75; R. Alan Culpepper, "The Jews in the Gospel of John," *Review and Expositor* 84 (1987): 273-88; Malcolm Lowe, "Who Were the *Ioudaioi?*" *Novum Testamentum* 18 (1976): 101-30.

4. See Raymond E. Brown, *Community of the Beloved Disciple: The Life, Loves, and Hates of an Individual Church in New Testament Times* (New York: Paulist, 1979), 59-91. He sees six groups reflected in John: the world, the Jews, the adherents of John the Baptist, the crypto-Christians, the Jewish Christian churches of inadequate faith, and the Christians of apostolic churches.

5. For the view that the Letters were w.0ritten before the Gospel, see: Kenneth Grayston, *The Johannine Epistles,* New Century Bible Commentary (Grand Rapids: Wm. B. Eerdmans, 1984), 12-14; Georg Strecker, "Die Anfänge der johanneischen Schule," *New Testament Studies* 32 (1986): 31-47. For the view that the letters were written after the Gospel see: Raymond E. Brown, *The Epistles of John,* Anchor Bible 30 (Garden City, NY: Doubleday, 1982), 32-35.

6. For a fascinating reconstruction of this period of the Johannine community's history, see Raymond E. Brown, *The Community of the*

Beloved Disciple (New York: Paulist, 1978), 93-144, to which I am indebted for much of the following material.

7. The following section is excerpted and adapted from R. Alan Culpepper, "John," in *The Books of the Bible*, Bernhard W. Anderson, Editor. Vol. II, pp. 203-228. Copyright © 1989 Charles Scribner's Sons, an imprint of Simon & Schuster Macmillian.

8. Oscar Cullmann, *The Johannine Circle*, trans. John Bowden (Philadelphia: Westminster, 1976), 39-53.

9. Helmut Koester, *History and Literature of Early Christianity* (Philadelphia: Fortress, 1982), 2: 178-98.

10. See James H. Charlesworth and R. Alan Culpepper, "The Odes of Solomon and the Gospel of John," *Catholic Biblical Quarterly* 25 (1973): 298-322.

11. Brown, *Community of the Beloved Disciple*, 43-47.

12. J. Louis Martyn, *History and Theology in the Fourth Gospel*, 50-55; see above, pp. 43-44.

13. See R. Alan Culpepper, "The *amen, amen* Sayings in the Gospel of John," in P*erspectives on John: Method and Interpretation in the Fourth Gospel*, ed. Robert B. Sloan and Mikeal C. Parsons, NABPR Special Studies Series, 11 (Lewiston: Edwin Mellen Press, 1993), 57-101.

14. See R. Alan Culpepper, *The Johannine School*, SBL Dissertation Series, 26 (Missoula: Scholars Press, 1975), 267-70.

4. THE GOSPEL AS LITERATURE

Portions of this chapter were originally published in "The Plot of John's Story," *Interpretation* 49 (1995): 347-58.

1. F. R. M. Hitchcock, "Is the Fourth Gospel a Drama?" *Theology* 7 (1923): 307-17, reprinted in Mark W. G. Stibbe, ed., *The Gospel of John as Literature: An Anthology of Twentieth-Century Perspectives* (Leiden: E. J. Brill, 1993), 15-24.

2. Mark W. G. Stibbe, *John's Gospel* (London and New York: Routledge, 1994), 35-36.

3. Mark W. G. Stibbe, *John as Storyteller: Narrative Criticism and the Fourth Gospel*, SNTS Monograph Series 73 (Cambridge: Cambridge University Press, 1992), 147.

4. C. W. Votaw, "The Gospels and Contemporary Biographies," *American Journal of Theology* 19 (1915): 45-73 and 217-49; reprinted as *The Gospels and Contemporary Biographies in the Graeco-Roman World*, Facet Books (Philadelphia: Fortress, 1970); Philip L. Shuler, *A Genre for the Gospels: The Biographical Character of Matthew* (Philadelphia: Fortress, 1982); David E. Aune, *The New Testament in Its Literary Environment*, Library of Early Christianity (Philadelphia: Westminster 1987), see 46-76; Charles H. Talbert, *What Is a Gospel: The Genre of the Canonical Gospels* (Philadelphia: Fortress, 1977); idem "Once Again: Gospel Genre," *Semeia* 43 (1988): 53-73; Richard A. Burridge, *What Are the Gospels: A Comparison with Graeco-Roman Biography*, SNTS Monograph Series 70 (Cambridge: Cambridge University Press, 1992).

5. Talbert, "Once Again: Gospel Genre," 55.
6. Ibid.
7. Ibid., 56-57.
8. Ibid., 59.
9. Burridge, *What Are the Gospels,* 65.
10. Ibid., 80-81.
11. According to ibid., 225.
12. Ibid., 226.
13. Ibid., 227.
14. Ibid.
15. Ibid., 229.
16. Ibid., 230.
17. Ibid., 232.
18. Ibid., 233.
19. Ibid., 234.
20. Ibid., 236.
21. Ibid., 237.
22. Fernando F. Segovia, "The Journey(s) of the Word of God: A Reading of the Plot of the Fourth Gospel," *Semeia* 53 (1991): 23.
23. Ibid., 33. See also Charles H. Talbert, *Reading John: A Literary and Theological Commentary on the Fourth Gospel and the Johannine Epistles* (New York: Crossroad, 1992), esp. 91, 165, 177-178. Talbert interprets John as the biography of a holy man; in a series of seven episodes it demonstrates that Jesus, the holy man, supersedes traditional Jewish worship.
24. In his focus on the journeys of Jesus, Segovia builds on the work of Matthias Rissi, "Der Aufbau des vierten Evangeliums," *NTS* 29 (1983): 48-54; and Jeffrey L. Staley, *The Print's First Kiss: A Rhetorical Investigation of the Implied Reader in the Fourth Gospel,* SBL Dissertation Series 82 (Atlanta: Scholars Press, 1988), esp. pp. 50-73.
25. For a comprehensive survey of analyses of the structure of the Gospel based on a wide range of criteria see: George Mlakuzhyil, *The Christocentric Literary Structure of the Fourth Gospel* (Rome: Pontifical Biblical Institute, 1987).
26. Stibbe, *John's Gospel,* 53.
27. Ibid., 45.
28. Ibid., 47.
29. Ibid., 48.
30. Rudolf Bultmann, *Theology of the New Testament,* trans. Kendrick Grobel (New York: Charles Scribner's Sons, 1955), 2:40.
31. Rudolf Bultmann, *The Gospel of John: A Commentary,* trans. G. R. Beasley-Murray, et al. (Philadelphia: Westminster, 1971), 66.
32. Bultmann, *Theology of the New Testament,* 2:42.
33. Ibid., 2:46.
34. For this insight I am indebted to Norman Petersen.
35. D. A. Russell and M. Winterbottom, eds., *Ancient Literary Criticism: The Principal Texts in New Translations* (Oxford: Clarendon, 1972).
36. Whitney J. Oates and Eugene O'Neill, Jr., ed., *The Complete Greek*

Drama (New York: Random House, 1938), 2:1075. See Bennett Uchegbulam Enyioha, "Nonrecognition as a Motif in the Post-Resurrection Appearance Narratives" (Ph.D. dissertation, Southern Baptist Theological Seminary, 1985), 94.

37. Euripides, "The Bacchantes" (lines 1277-1297), in *Aeschylus, Sophocles, Euripedes, Aristophanes,* Great Books of the Western World, vol. 5 (Chicago: Encyclopedia Britannica, 1952), 350-51. Cf. Mark W. G. Stibbe, *John as Storyteller: Narrative Criticism and the Fourth Gospel,* SNTS Monograph Series 73 (Cambridge: Cambridge University Press, 1992), 132-47.

38. See Geoffrey Nuttall, *The Moment of Recognition: Luke as Story-Teller,* Ethel M. Wood Lecture, 1978 (London: University of London, Athlone Press, 1978).

39. Although each of us is arguing a different case, it should be noted that there are parallels between the understanding of John that I am developing here and the work of John Painter on the quest stories in John and the thesis of Mark W. G. Stibbe regarding "the elusive Christ." See John Painter, *The Quest for the Messiah,* 2nd ed. (Nashville: Abingdon, 1993); and Mark W. G. Stibbe, "The Elusive Christ: A New Reading of the Fourth Gospel," in *The Gospel of John as Literature: An Anthology of Twentieth-Century Perspectives,* ed. Mark G. Stibbe (Leiden: E. J. Brill, 1993), 231-47.

40. See Meir Sternberg, *Expositional Modes and Temporal Ordering in Fiction* (Baltimore and London: Johns Hopkins University Press, 1978), 98-99; and Culpepper, *Anatomy of the Fourth Gospel* (Philadelphia: Fortress, 1983), 18-19.

41. See R. Alan Culpepper, "John 5:1-18—A Sample of Narrative Critical Commentary," in *The Gospel of John as Literature: An Anthology of Twentieth-Century Perspectives,* ed. Mark W. G. Stibbe (Leiden: E. J. Brill, 1993), 193-207.

42. See Fernando F. Segovia, *The Farewell of the Word: The Johannine Call to Abide* (Minneapolis: Fortress, 1991), 5-20; and Talbert, *Reading John,* 200-201.

43. See R. Alan Culpepper, "The Johannine *Hypodeigma:* A Reading of John 13," *Semeia* 53 (1991): 133-52.

44. Paul S. Minear, " 'We Don't Know Where ...' John 20:2," *Interpretation* 30 (1976): 125-39.

45. See the insightful work of Sandra Schneiders, "John 20:11-18: The Encounter of the Easter Jesus with Mary Magdalene—A Transformative Feminist Reading," in *"What Is John?" Readers and Readings of the Fourth Gospel,* ed. Fernando F. Segovia (Atlanta: Scholars Press, 1996), 155-68. She finds three parts to this scene marked by the three participles, weeping (v. 11), turning (v. 16), and telling (v. 18).

5. THE THEOLOGY OF THE JOHANNINE WRITINGS

This chapter substantially reproduces an essay originally published as "The Theology of the Gospel of John," *Review and Expositor* 85 (1988): 417-32.

1. See Elaine H. Pagels, *The Johannine Gospel in Gnostic Exegesis: Heracleon's Commentary on John*, SBL Monograph Series (Atlanta: Scholars Press, 1973).
2. Eusebius, *Ecclesiastical History* 6.14.7.
3. Jaroslav Pelikan, *Jesus Through the Centuries: His Place in the History of Culture* (New Haven: Yale University Press, 1985), 58.
4. See Gail R. O'Day, *Revelation in the Fourth Gospel: Narrative Mode and Theological Claim* (Philadelphia: Fortress, 1986): "Throughout the Fourth Gospel, what is said cannot be experienced apart from how it is said!" (96). The text "enables the reader to participate in the narrative and thus to experience for himself or herself the way in which Jesus makes God known in the Fourth Gospel" (104).
5. See James H. Charlesworth, "A Critical Comparison of the Dualism in 1QS 3:13–4:26 and the 'Dualism' Contained in the Gospel of John," in *John and Qumran*, ed. James H. Charlesworth (London: Geoffrey Chapman, 1972), 76-106.
6. See N. H. Cassem, "A Grammatical and Contextual Inventory of the Use of *kosmos* in the Johannine Corpus with Some Implications for a Johannine Cosmic Theology," *New Testament Studies* 19 (1972): 81-91.
7. See Timothy L. Owings, "The Concept of Sin in the Fourth Gospel" (Ph.D. dissertation, Southern Baptist Theological Seminary, 1983).
8. See further John Painter, "Johannine Symbols: A Case Study in Epistemology," *Journal of Theology for South Africa* 27 (1979): 26-41; R. Alan Culpepper, *Anatomy of the Fourth Gospel* (Philadelphia: Fortress, 1983), 190-92; Judith M. Lieu, "Blindness in the Johannine Tradition," *New Testament Studies* 34 (1988): 83-95.
9. John Painter, *John: Witness and Theologian*, 3rd ed. (Mitcham, Australia: Beacon Hill Books, 1986), 73.
10. Some of the material in this section is adapted from my essay "John," *The Books of the Bible*, ed. Bernhard W. Anderson (New York: Charles Scribner's Sons, 1989), 2:224. For a list of all the titles used of Jesus in the Gospel of John see George R. Beasley-Murray, *John*, Word Biblical Commentary 36 (Waco: Word Books, 1987), lxxxi.
11. James D. G. Dunn, "Let John Be John," in *Das Evangelium und die Evangelien*, ed. Peter Stuhlmacher, Wissenschaftliche Untersuchungen zum Neuen Testament 28 (Tübingen: J. C. B. Mohr, 1983), 330-37; Michael E. Willett, *Wisdom Christology in the Fourth Gospel* (San Francisco: Mellen Research Univeristy Press, 1992); Martin Scott, *Sophia and the Johannine Jesus*, JSNT Supplement Series 71 (Sheffield: Sheffield Academic Press, 1992).
12. Paraphrase of *Epigrammata Sacra. Aquae in Vinum Versae*, trans. Richard Crashaw (1612?–1649), cf. *The Oxford Dictionary of Quotations*, 3rd ed. (Oxford University Press, 1979), 169.
13. Rudolf Bultmann, *Theology of the New Testament*, trans. Kendrick Grobel (New York: Charles Scribner's Sons, 1955), 2:62.
14. Nils Dahl, "The Neglected Factor in New Testament Theology," *Reflection* 73 (1975): 5-8; cf. John R. Donahue, "A Neglected Factor in the

Theology of Mark," *Journal of Biblical Literature* 101 (1983): 563-94; Culpepper, *Anatomy of the Fourth Gospel*, 112-15; Paul W. Meyer, "'The Father': The Presentation of God in the Fourth Gospel," in *Exploring the Gospel of John*, ed. R. Alan Culpepper and C. Clifton Black (Louisville: Westminster/John Knox, 1996), 255-73.

15. Dale Moody, "'God's Only Son': The Translation of John iii 16 in the RSV," *Journal of Biblical Literature* 72 (1953): 213-19.

16. C. H. Dodd, *Historical Tradition in the Fourth Gospel* (Cambridge: Cambridge University Press, 1963), 386 n. 2.

17. See further Rudolf Schnackenburg, "The 'Son of Man' in the Fourth Gospel," in *The Gospel According to St. John*, trans. Kevin Smyth (New York: Herder and Herder, 1968), 1:529-42.

18. Bultmann, *Theology of the New Testament*, 2:21.

19. For a more detailed discussion, see Culpepper, *Anatomy of the Fourth Gospel*, 145-48.

20. See Paul S. Minear, *Images of the Church in the New Testament* (Philadelphia: Westminster, 1960); and E. Frank Tupper, "A Baptist Vision of the Church," *Review and Expositor* 84 (1987): 617-32.

21. See R. Alan Culpepper, "The Pivot of John's Prologue," *New Testament Studies* 27 (1980), esp. 17-30.

22. See D. Moody Smith, *The Composition and Order of the Fourth Gospel: Bultmann's Literary Theory* (New Haven: Yale University Press, 1965), 213-17.

23. See Raymond E. Brown, *The Gospel According to John (XIII–XXI)*, Anchor Bible, vol. 29a (Garden City, NY: Doubleday, 1970), 1074-76.

24. These two paragraphs are taken from my essay on John in *The Books of the Bible*, 2:227. See this essay for further discussion of the life setting, narrative style, and principal themes of the Gospel of John.

25. For further material on the Paraclete, see Brown, *The Gospel According to John (XIII–XXI)*, 1135-44; Eskil Franck, *Revelation Taught: The Paraclete in the Gospel of John*, Coniectanea Biblica, New Testament Series 14 (Lund: CWK Gleerup, 1985).

26. For further reading in Johannine Theology, see D. Moody Smith, *The Theology of the Gospel of John*, New Testament Theology (Cambridge: Cambridge University Press, 1995).

6. INTERPRETING THE FOURTH GOSPEL: JOHN 1–4

1. Ernst Käsemann, "The Structure and Purpose of the Prologue to John's Gospel," *New Testament Questions of Today* (London: SCM Press, 1969), 144-46.

2. Rudolf Bultmann, *The Gospel of John: A Commentary*, trans. George R. Beasley-Murray, et al. (Philadelphia: Westminster, 1971), 60-64.

3. Raymond E. Brown, *The Gospel According to John (I–XII)*, Anchor Bible, vol. 29 (Garden City, NY: Doubleday, 1966), 28-29.

4. M. E. Boismard, *St. John's Prologue*, trans. Carisbrooke Dominicans (London: Blackfriars Publications, 1957), 79-80.

5. R. Alan Culpepper, "The Pivot of John's Prologue," *New Testament Studies* 27 (1980): 1-31.

6. Bultmann, *The Gospel of John*, 13.

7. The following section on John 1:43-51 is abridged and adapted from R. Alan Culpepper, "A Literary Model," in *Hermeneutics for Preaching*, ed. Raymond Bailey (Nashville: Broadman, 1992), 77-104.

8. See the discussion of *Ioudaioi* on pp. 45, 291-95.

9. Craig R. Koester, "Messianic Exegesis and the Call of Nathanael (John 1:45-51)," *Journal for the Study of the New Testament* 39 (1990): 30-31.

10. See R. Alan Culpepper, *Anatomy of the Fourth Gospel: A Study in Literary Design* (Philadelphia: Fortress, 1983), esp. chapters 4 and 5.

11. See R. Alan Culpepper, "The *Amen, Amen* Sayings in the Gospel of John," in *Perspectives on John: Method and Interpretation in the Fourth Gospel*, ed. Robert B. Sloan and Mikeal C. Parsons (Lewiston, NY: Edwin Mellen Press, 1993), 57-101.

12. See the discussion of J. Louis Martyn above, pp. 43-44, 57.

13. Paraphrase of *Epigrammata Sacra. Aquae in Vinum Versae*, trans. Richard Crashaw (1612?-1649), cf. *The Oxford Dictionary of Quotations*, 3rd ed. (Oxford University Press, 1979), 169.

14. See R. Alan Culpepper, "John 5.1-18—A Sample of Narrative Critical Commentary," in *The Gospel of John as Literature*, ed. Mark W. G. Stibbe (Leiden: E. J. Brill, 1993), esp. 198-99.

15. For further discussion of John's water symbolism, see Culpepper, *Anatomy of the Fourth Gospel*, 192-95; Craig R. Koester, *Symbolism in the Fourth Gospel: Meaning, Mystery, Community* (Minneapolis: Fortress Press, 1995), 77-82, 155-84.

16. See the interpretation of Nicodemus in the latter sense in David Rensberger, *Johannine Faith and Liberating Community* (Philadelphia: Westminster Press, 1988), esp. 37-41, 54-57, 113-116.

17. A. D. Nuttall, *Overheard by God: Fiction and Prayer in Herbert, Milton, Dante, and Saint John* (New York: Methuen, 1980), 131.

18. Robert Alter, *The Art of Biblical Narrative* (New York: Basic Books, Inc., 1981), 47-62.

19. See Culpepper, *Anatomy of the Fourth Gospel*, 219.

20. Florentino García Martínez, *The Dead Sea Scrolls Translated: The Qumran Texts in English*, trans. Wilfred G. E. Watson (Leiden: E. J. Brill, 1994), 35, 36, 46, 345-46.

7. INTERPRETING THE FOURTH GOSPEL: JOHN 5–12

1. See R. Alan Culpepper, "John 5.1-18—A Sample of Narrative Critical Commentary," in *The Gospel of John as Literature: An Anthology of Twentieth-Century Perspectives*, ed. Mark W. G. Stibbe (Leiden: E. J. Brill, 1993), esp. 198-200.

2. Raymond E. Brown, *The Gospel According to John (I–XII)*, Anchor Bible, vol. 29 (Garden City, NY: Doubleday, 1966), 207. Brown notes that

Tertullian (ca. A.D. 200) and Chrysostom (ca. A.D. 400) seem to have known of this verse.

3. See A. E. Harvey, *Jesus on Trial: A Study in the Fourth Gospel* (Atlanta: John Knox Press, 1976), esp. 67-81.

4. C. H. Dodd, *Historical Tradition in the Fourth Gospel* (Cambridge: Cambridge University Press,1963), 386, n. 2; also, Dodd, *More New Testament Studies* (Grand Rapids: Wm. B. Eerdmans, 1968), 30-40; R. Alan Culpepper, "The *Amen, Amen* Sayings in the Gospel of John," in *Perspectives on John: Method and Interpretation in the Fourth Gospel,* ed. Robert B. Sloan and Mikeal C. Parsons (Lewiston: Edwin Mellen, 1993), 67-71.

5. Rudolf Bultmann, *The Gospel of John: A Commentary,* trans. George R. Beasley-Murray et al. (Philadelphia: Westminster, 1971), 209-10.

6. Brown, *The Gospel According to John (I–XII),* 238.

7. See John Painter, *The Quest for the Messiah,* 2nd ed. (Nashville: Abingdon, 1993), esp. 6-10; Mark W. G. Stibbe, "The Elusive Christ: A New Reading of the Fourth Gospel," in *The Gospel of John as Literature: An Anthology of Twentieth-Century Perspectives* (Leiden: E. J. Brill, 1993), 231-47.

8. Rudolf Bultmann, *Theology of the New Testament,* trans. Kendrick Grobel (New York: Charles Scribner's Sons, 1955), 2:21.

9. Ibid., 23.

10. For this structure I am indebted to Barnabas Lindars, *The Gospel of John,* New Century Bible (London: Oliphants, 1972), 286.

11. Brown, *The Gospel According to John (I–XII),* 318.

12. Herbert Danby, trans., *The Mishnah* (Oxford: Oxford University Press, 1954), 179.

13. For the textual history of this story, see Bruce M. Metzger, *A Textual Commentary on the Greek New Testament* (New York: United Bible Societies, 1975), 219-21.

14. See Gail R. O'Day, "John 7:53–8:11: A Study in Misreading," *Journal of Biblical Literature* 111 (1992): 631-40.

15. Ibid., 636-37.

16. Danby, *The Mishnah,* 179-80.

17. See above, chapter 3.

18. The best discussion of the options for interpreting this riddle is Adele Reinhartz, *The Word in the World: The Cosmological Tale in the Fourth Gospel,* SBL Monograph Series 45 (Atlanta: Scholars Press, 1992). See also Johannes Beutler and Robert T. Fortna, eds., *The Shepherd Discourse of John 10 and Its Context,* SNTS Monograph Series 67 (Cambridge: Cambridge University Press, 1991); and J. Louis Martyn, "Glimpses into the History of the Johannine Community," in *The Gospel of John in Christian History* (New York: Paulist, 1978), esp. 115-21.

19. See above, chapter 4.

20. Miguel de Unamuno, *Tragic Sense of Life,* trans. J. E. Crawford Flitch (New York: Dover, 1954), 330.

21. Ibid., 263.

22. See R. Alan Culpepper, *John, the Son of Zebedee: The Life of a Legend* (Columbia: University of South Carolina Press, 1994), esp. 76-77.

8. INTERPRETING THE FOURTH GOSPEL: JOHN 13–21

1. For further discussion of the layers of tradition in the farewell discourse, see Raymond E. Brown, *The Gospel According to John (I–XII)*, Anchor Bible, vol. 29 (Garden City, NY: Doubleday, 1970), 581-603; and John Painter, *The Quest for the Messiah*, 2nd ed. (Nashville: Abingdon, 1993), 417-35.

2. The following exposition of John 13 is a very abridged form of R. Alan Culpepper, "The Johannine *Hypodeigma:* A Reading of John 13," *Semeia* 53 (1991): 133-52. For more detail, see the full essay.

3. C. K. Barrett, *The Gospel According to St. John*, 2nd ed. (Philadelphia: Westminster, 1978), 439.

4. Barnabas Lindars, *The Gospel of John*, New Century Bible (London: Oliphants, 1972), 448.

5. George R. Beasley-Murray, *John*, Word Biblical Commentary 36 (Dallas: Word, 1987), 277.

6. Ibid., 278.

7. For this insight I am indebted to Paul Duke.

8. R. H. Strachan, *The Fourth Gospel: Its Significance and Environment*, 3rd ed. (London: SCM Press, 1941), 310; cf. Brown, *The Gospel According to John (XIII–XXI)*, Anchor Bible, vol. 29a (Garden City, NY: Doubleday, 1970), 859.

9. *Philo*, trans. F. H. Colson, Loeb Classical Library (Cambridge, MA.: Harvard University Press, 1941), 323.

10. Material in the following section is an abridged version of a lecture given at the 1997 annual meeting of the New Testament Society of South Africa. For the full text, see R. Alan Culpepper, "The Theology of the Johannine Passion Narrative (John 19:16b-30)," *Neotestamentica* 31 (1997): 25-41.

11. See Paul S. Minear, " 'We Don't Know Where …' John 20:2," *Interpretation* 30 (1976): 125-39.

12. See Pliny's letter to Trajan in Henry Bettenson, ed., *Documents of the Early Church*, 2nd ed. (New York: Oxford University Press, 1963), 3.

13. See Raymond E. Brown, "Does the New Testament Call Jesus God?" in *Jesus God and Man* (New York: Macmillan, 1967), 1-38.

14. Raymond E. Brown, *The Gospel According to John (XIII–XXI)*, 1090.

15. Brown, *The Gospel According to John (I–XII)*, 498.

16. Brown, *The Gospel According to John (XIII–XXI)*, 1108; Kirsopp Lake, trans. *The Apostolic Fathers*, Loeb Classical Library (Cambridge, MA: Harvard University Press, 1912), 17; A. Cleveland Coxe, ed., *The Ante-Nicene Fathers*, vol. 3: *Latin Christianity: Its Founder, Tertullian* (rpt. Grand Rapids: Eerdmans, 1986), 648; Kirsopp Lake, trans., *Eusebius: The Ecclesiastical History*, Loeb Classical Library (Cambridge, MA: Harvard University Press, 1926), 181, 191.

9. INTERPRETING THE LETTERS

This chapter reproduces and abridges material originally published in *1 John, 2 John, 3 John,* Knox Preaching Guides (Atlanta: John Knox, 1985).

1. For a survey of current views, see R. Alan Culpepper, "1-2-3 John," in *The General Letters,* Proclamation Commentaries, rev. ed., ed. Gerhard Krodel (Minneapolis: Fortress Press, 1995), 110-18.

2. Raymond E. Brown, *The Epistles of John,* Anchor Bible, vol. 30 (Garden City, NY: Doubleday, 1982), 125-29.

3. C. H. Dodd, *The Johannine Epistles,* Moffatt Commentaries (London: Hodder and Stoughton, 1946), 26.

4. Brown, *The Epistles of John,* 478.

5. Kenneth Grayston, *The Johannine Epistles,* New Century Bible Commentary (Grand Rapids: Wm. B. Eerdmans, 1984), 115-16.

6. I. Howard Marshall, *The Epistles of John,* New International Commentary on the New Testament (Grand Rapids: Eerdmans, 1978), 198.

7. Dodd, *The Johannine Epistles,* 137.

8. R. Alan Culpepper, "1-2-3 John," in *The General Letters,* ed. Gerhard Krodel (Minneapolis: Fortress, 1995), 122; cf. Duane F. Watson, "A Rhetorical Analysis of 2 John According to Greco-Roman Convention," *New Testament Studies* 35 (1989): 104-30.

9. Culpepper, "1-2-3 John," 125; cf. Duane F. Watson, "A Rhetorical Analysis of 3 John: A Study in Epistolary Rhetoric," *Catholic Biblical Quarterly* 51 (1989): 479-501.

10. Dodd, *The Johannine Epistles,* 162.

11. Ernst Käsemann, "Ketzer und Zeuge: Zum johanneischen Verfasserproblem," *Zeitschrift für Theologie und Kirche* 48 (1951): 292-311.

10. THE GOSPEL OF JOHN AS A DOCUMENT OF FAITH

This chapter substantially reproduces an essay originally published as "The Gospel of John as a Document of Faith in a Pluralistic Culture," *"What is John?" Readers and Readings of the Fourth Gospel,* ed. Fernando F. Segovia, Symposium Series (Atlanta: Scholars Press, 1996), 107-27.

1. Bentley Layton, *The Gnostic Scriptures* (Garden City, NY: Doubleday, 1987), 267.

2. See R. Alan Culpepper, *John, the Son of Zebedee: The Life of a Legend* (Columbia, SC: University of South Carolina Press, 1994), esp. 114-19.

3. Ibid., 120-22. The place of Gaius in this history has been significantly clarified by Joseph Daniel Smith, "Gaius and the Controversy over the Johannine Literature" (Ph.D. diss., Yale University, 1979).

4. Culpepper, *John, the Son of Zebedee,* 128-29.

5. Ibid., 123-28.

6. Karl Gottlieb Bretschneider, quoted by W. G. Kümmel, *The New Testament: The History of the Investigation of Its Problems,* trans. S. McLean Gilmour and Howard C. Kee (Nashville: Abingdon, 1972), 85-86.

7. David Friedrich Strauss, *The Life of Jesus Critically Examined*, ed. Peter C. Hodgson and trans. George Eliot, Lives of Jesus Series (Philadelphia: Fortress, 1972), 384.

8. Ibid., 381-82. On p. 647, Strauss adds "it is scarcely conceivable how John could accurately remember these long discourses."

9. Ibid., 386. Strauss adds: "but we have admitted that he has culled several sayings of Jesus from an authentic tradition."

10. Kaufmann Kohler, "New Testament," *Jewish Encyclopedia* (1905): 9:251.

11. See Michael J. Cook, "The Gospel of John and the Jews," *Review and Expositor* 84 (Spring 1987): 260-61. In light of our earlier discussion of Strauss's arguments and their influence, it is interesting to note that later in this article Cook observes that the Johannine dialogues "convey no impression of verisimilitude" (p. 266). One may compare Strauss's comment: "Hence, I confess, I understand not what is the meaning of verisimilitude in the mind of those who ascribe it to the discourses of Jesus in the Gospel of John" (*The Life of Jesus*, 381). Cook also poses the question whether John should be considered primarily a historian, a polemicist, or a theologian. Discrepancies between John and the Synoptics are again marshaled against the view that John was primarily a historian. While maintaining that John is "assuredly anti-Jewish" Cook recognizes that "anti-Judaism is hardly foremost on John's agenda" (p. 267). He therefore contends that John should be understood primarily as a theologian. Long established issues have, therefore, been given a new focus by the increased sensitivity of both Jewish and Christian scholars to the need to find effective ways of blunting the effects of John's anti-Jewish pronouncements.

12. Robert T. Fortna, "Theological Use of Locale in the Fourth Gospel," in *Gospel Studies in Honor of Sherman E. Johnson*, ed. M. H. Shepherd, Jr. and E. C. Hobbs, Anglican Theological Review Supplementary Series 3 (Evanston, IL, 1974): 90.

13. Reginald Fuller, "The 'Jews' in the Fourth Gospel," *Dialog* 16 (1977): 35.

14. Rosemary Ruether, "Theological Anti-Semitism in the New Testament," *Christian Century* 85 (1968): 191-96.

15. See *The American Family Bible* (Philadelphia: The American Institute for the Study of Racial and Religious Cooperation, 1986).

16. See further Norman A. Beck, *Mature Christianity in the 21st Century: The Recognition and Repudiation of the Anti-Jewish Polemic of the New Testament*, rev. ed. (New York: Crossroad, 1994), esp. 321-28; and my essay, "The Gospel of John and the Jews," *Review and Expositor* 84 (1987): 273-88, subsequently revised and published under the title, "The Gospel of John as a Threat to Jewish-Christian Relations," in *Overcoming Fear Between Jews and Christian*, ed. James H. Charlesworth with Frank X. Blisard and Jerry L. Gorham (New York: Crossroad, 1992), 21-43.

17. Itumeleng J. Mosala, "The Use of the Bible in Black Theology," in *Voices from the Margin: Interpreting the Bible in the Third World*, ed. R. S. Sugirtharajah (Maryknoll, NY: Orbis Books, 1991), 59.

18. Elsa Tamez, "Women's Rereading of the Bible," in *Voices from the Margin*, 65.

19. Gustavo Gutierrez, "Song and Deliverance," in *Voices from the Margin*, 131.

20. Richard J. Cassidy, *John's Gospel in New Perspective: Christology and the Realities of Roman Power* (Maryknoll, NY: Orbis Books, 1992), 1.

21. David Rensberger, *Johannine Faith and Liberating Community* (Philadelphia: Westminster, 1988), 110.

22. Ibid., 111.

23. Ibid., 115, 116.

24. Ibid., see esp. 116-32.

25. Robert J. Karris, *Jesus and the Marginalized in John's Gospel*, Zacchaeus Studies: New Testament (Collegeville, MN: Liturgical Press, 1990).

26. Ibid., 61.

27. This summary of Karris, *Jesus and the Marginalized in John's Gospel*, has been adapted from my review, published in *Critical Review of Books in Religion 1992* (Atlanta: Scholars Press, 1992), 224-25.

28. Dickson Kazuo Yagi, "Christ for Asia: Yellow Theology for the East," *Review and Expositor* 88 (1991): 357-78.

29. Ibid., 358.

30. Ibid.

31. Ibid., 364-65.

32. Ibid., 369.

33. Ibid.

34. See the recent monographs by Michael E. Willett, *Wisdom Christology in the Fourth Gospel* (San Francisco: Mellen Research University Press, 1992); and Martin Scott, *Sophia and the Johannine Jesus*, JSNT Supplement Series 71 (Sheffield: Sheffield Academic Press, 1992).

35. John N. Jonsson, "Wisdom: The Threshold of God in Human Existence" (unpublished ms. to be published in a collection edited by John A. L. Saunders), 3.

36. Ibid., 9. Here Jonsson cites Frederick Cawley, *The Transcendence of Jesus Christ* (Edinburgh: T. & T. Clark, 1936), 101.

37. Hugo H. Culpepper, "Acts 4:12," *Review and Expositor* 89 (1992): 85.

38. Ibid.

39. Ibid., 86-87.

40. Consider the challenges of Itumeleng J. Mosala and Elsa Tamez in the works cited above.

SELECTED BIBLIOGRAPHY

PART ONE: INTRODUCING THE JOHANNINE WRITINGS

A. Introductions

Ashton, John. *Understanding the Fourth Gospel.* Oxford: Clarendon, 1993.
Culpepper, R. Alan. "1-2-3 John." In *The General Letters.* Proclamation Commentaries. Minneapolis: Fortress, 1995.
_____. "John." In *The Books of the Bible, vol. 2: The Apocrypha and the New Testament.* Ed. Bernhard W. Anderson. New York: Charles Scribner's Sons, 1989. Pp. 203-28.
_____. and C. Clifton Black, eds. *Exploring the Gospel of John: In Honor of D. Moody Smith.* Louisville: Westminster/John Knox, 1996.
Sloyan, Gerard S. *What Are They Saying About John?* New York: Paulist, 1991.

B. Authorship, Sources, and Composition

Charlesworth, James H. *The Beloved Disciple: Whose Witness Validates the Gospel of John?* Valley Forge: Trinity Press International, 1995.
Culpepper, R. Alan. *John, the Son of Zebedee: The Life of a Legend.* Columbia: University of South Carolina Press, 1994.
Fortna, Robert T. *The Fourth Gospel and Its Predecessor: From Narrative Source to Present Gospel.* Philadelphia: Fortress, 1988.

_____. *The Gospel of Signs: A Reconstruction of the Narrative Source Underlying the Fourth Gospel*. SNTS Monograph Series, 11. Cambridge: Cambridge University Press, 1970.

Hengel, Martin. *The Johannine Question*. Trans. John Bowden. Philadelphia: Trinity Press International, 1990.

Smith, D. Moody. *The Composition and Order of the Fourth Gospel: Bultmann's Literary Theory*. New Haven: Yale University Press, 1965.

_____. *John Among the Gospels: The Relationship in Twentieth-Century Research*. Minneapolis: Fortress, 1991.

Wahlde, Urban C. von. *The Earliest Version of John's Gospel*. Wilmington, DE: Michael Glazier, 1989.

C. The Historical Setting of the Johannine Writings

Brown, Raymond E. *The Community of the Beloved Disciple*. New York: Paulist, 1979.

Cassidy, Richard J. *John's Gospel in New Perspective: Christology and the Realities of Roman Power*. Maryknoll, NY: Orbis, 1992.

Charlesworth, James H. *John and Qumran*. London: Chapman, 1972.

Cullmann, Oscar. *The Johannine Circle*. Trans. John Bowden. Philadelphia: Westminster, 1976.

Culpepper, R. Alan. *The Johannine School*. SBL Dissertation Series, 26. Missoula: Scholars Press, 1975.

Martyn, J. Louis. *The Gospel of John in Christian History*. New York: Paulist, 1978.

_____. *History and Theology in the Fourth Gospel*. 2nd ed. Nashville: Abingdon, 1979.

Neyrey, Jerome H. *An Ideology of Revolt: John's Christology in Social-Science Perspective*. Philadelphia: Fortress, 1988.

Rensberger, David. *Johannine Faith and Liberating Community*. Philadelphia: Westminster, 1988.

van Tilborg, Sjef. *Reading John in Ephesus*. Supplements to Novum Testamentum. Leiden: E. J. Brill, 1996.

D. The Johannine Writings as Literature

Culpepper, R. Alan. *Anatomy of the Fourth Gospel*. Philadelphia: Fortress, 1983.

_____ and Fernando F. Segovia, eds. *The Fourth Gospel from a*

320

Literary Perspective. Semeia, 53. Atlanta: Scholars Press, 1991.
Duke, Paul D. *Irony in the Fourth Gospel.* Atlanta: John Knox, 1985.
Koester, Craig R. *Symbolism in the Fourth Gospel.* Minneapolis: Augsburg Fortress, 1995.
O'Day, Gail R. *Revelation in the Fourth Gospel: Narrative Mode and Theological Claim.* Philadelphia: Fortress, 1986.
Staley, Jeffrey. *The Print's First Kiss: A Rhetorical Investigation of the Implied Reader in the Fourth Gospel.* SBL Dissertation Series, 82. Missoula: Scholars Press, 1988.
Stibbe, Mark W. G, ed. *The Gospel of John as Literature: An Anthology of Twentieth-Century Perspectives.* New Testament Tools and Studies. Leiden: E. J. Brill, 1993.
_____. *John as Storyteller: Narrative Criticism and the Fourth Gospel.* SNTS Monograph Series, 73. Cambridge: Cambridge University Press, 1992.
_____. *John's Gospel.* New Testament Readings. London and New York: Routledge, 1994.

E. The Theology of the Johannine Writings

Beasley-Murray, George R. *John.* Word Biblical Themes. Dallas: Word, 1989.
Burge, Gary M. *The Anointed Community: The Holy Spirit in the Johannine Tradition.* Grand Rapids: Wm. B. Eerdmans, 1987.
Kysar, Robert. *John: The Maverick Gospel.* 2nd rev. ed. Louisville: Westminster/John Knox, 1994.
Schnelle, Udo. *Antidocetic Christology in the Gospel of John.* Trans. Linda M. Maloney. Minneapolis: Augsburg Fortress, 1992.
Smith, D. Moody. *The Theology of the Gospel of John.* New Testament Theology. Cambridge: Cambridge University Press, 1995.
Thompson, Marianne Meye. *The Humanity of Jesus in the Fourth Gospel.* Philadelphia: Fortress, 1988.

PART TWO: INTERPRETING THE JOHANNINE WRITINGS

Barrett, C. K. *The Gospel According to St. John.* 2nd ed. Philadelphia: Westminster, 1978.
Beasley-Murray, George R. *John.* Word Biblical Commentary, 36. Waco, TX: Word, 1987.

Brodie, Thomas L. *The Gospel According to John: A Literary and Theological Commentary.* New York: Oxford University Press, 1993.

Brown, Raymond E. *The Gospel According to John.* Anchor Bible 29 and 29A. Garden City, NY: Doubleday, 1966-1970.

_____. *The Epistles of John.* Anchor Bible, 30. Garden City, NY: Doubleday, 1982.

Bultmann, Rudolf. *The Gospel of John.* Trans. G. R. Beasley-Murray and ed.R. W. N. Hoare and J. K. Riches. Philadelphia: Westminster, 1971.

Culpepper, R. Alan. *1 John, 2 John, 3 John.* Knox Preaching Guides. Atlanta: John Knox, 1985.

Dodd, C. H. *The Interpretation of the Fourth Gospel.* Cambridge: Cambridge University Press, 1968.

du Rand, Jan. *Johannine Perspectives: Introduction to the Johannine Writings.* N.p.: Orion, 1991.

Howard-Brook, Wes. *Becoming Children of God: John's Gospel and Radical Discipleship.* Maryknoll, NY: Orbis, 1994.

O'Day, Gail R. "The Gospel of John." In *The New Interpreter's Bible, Volume IX.* Nashville: Abingdon, 1995.

Painter, John. *The Quest for the Messiah: The History, Literature, and Theology of the Johannine Community.* 2nd ed. Nashville: Abingdon, 1993.

Schnackenburg, Rudolf. *The Gospel According to St. John.* 3 vols. New York: Herder and Herder, 1968; Seabury, 1980; Crossroad, 1982.

Smalley, Stephen S. *1, 2, 3 John.* Word Biblical Commentary, 51. Waco, TX: Word, 1984.

Stibbe, Mark W. G. *John.* Readings. Sheffield: JSOT, 1993.

Talbert, Charles H. *Reading John: A Literary and Theological Commentary on the Fourth Gospel and the Johannine Epistles.* New York: Crossroad, 1992.

Witherington, III, Ben. *John's Wisdom: A Commentary on the Fourth Gospel.* Louisville: Westminster John Knox, 1995.

PART THREE: RESPONDING TO THE JOHANNINE WRITINGS

Karris, Robert J. *Jesus and the Marginalized in John's Gospel.* Zacchaeus Studies. Collegeville: Liturgical Press, 1990.

Segovia, Fernando F., ed. *"What Is John?" Readers and Readings of the Fourth Gospel.* Symposium Series. Atlanta: Scholars Press, 1996.

Staley, Jeffrey L. *Reading with a Passion: Rhetoric, Autobiography, and the American West in the Gospel of John.* New York: Continuum, 1995.

BIBLIOGRAPHIES

Malatesta, Edward. *St. John's Gospel 1920-1965: A Cumulative and Classified Bibliography of Books and Periodical Literature on the Fourth Gospel.* Analecta Biblica 32. Rome: Pontifical Biblical Institute, 1967.

van Belle, Gilbert. *Johannine Bibliography 1966-1985: Cumulative Bibliography on the Fourth Gospel.* Bibliotheca Ephemeridum Theologicarum Lovaniensium 82. Louvain: Louvain University Press, 1988.

INDEX